SECOND HONEYMOON

Also by Sonya Rhodes

Cold Feet: Why Men Don't Commit (with Marlin S. Potash)

Surviving Family Life (with Josleen Wilson)

The Alpha Woman Meets Her Match:
How Today's Strong Women Can Find Love
and Happiness Without Settling (with Susan Schneider)

SECOND HONEYMOON

A
Pioneering Guide
for Reviving
the Mid-Life Marriage

SONYA RHODES, Ph.D.
with SUSAN SCHNEIDER

WILLIAM MORROW
An Imprint of HarperCollins*Publishers*

The names and identifying details of certain individuals discussed in this book have been changed to protect their privacy.

HarperCollins books may be purchased for educational, business, or sales promotional use. For information please e-mail the Special Markets Department at SPsales@harpercollins.com.

A hardcover edition of this book was published in 1992 by William Morrow and Company, Inc.

FIRST WILLIAM MORROW PAPERBACK EDITION PUBLISHED 2015.

Designed by Ruth Kolbert

Library of Congress Cataloging-in-Publication Data has been applied for.

ISBN 978-0-06-236099-1

15 16 17 18 19   OV/RRD   10 9 8 7 6 5 4 3 2 1

To All Those People
Asking, "What's Next?"

ACKNOWLEDGMENTS

The main ideas for *Second Honeymoon* come from the people with whom I work. Though they remain anonymous, they are my inspiration. Their struggles resonate with me for days, months, and years after I sit with them in my office. I owe all of them a loving acknowledgment as they persevere in my imagination and inspire my inventions. I can only hope that I have given them as much as they have given me.

The second source of inspiration and support for the book came from my most valued friendships. Jean Marzollo, my devoted friend, whose support and criticism I have come to depend on, as well as my other friends, Emily and Michael Abramson, Ellie Amel, Sally Crane, Judy and Tony Evnin, Patricia Holzman, Jane and Bob Keiter, Gail Koff, Suzanne and Jim Pyle, Sara and Tom Silbiger, Susan Strang, Cathy and Alex Traykovski, and Fran Yancovitz, made unique contributions to this project. Special colleagues and friends, Jane Greer, Estelle Rosen, Alan Siskind, Emily Kennedy, Mary Ann Porcher, Marlynn Levin, Claudia Rose, Carol Feit Lane, and Ann Federline, were also critical in formulating ideas and concepts.

I thank my agent, Geri Thoma, for her encouragement in getting me started on another project, for her perceptive comments, which shaped the proposal, and for her steadfast belief in me throughout. My collaborator, Susan Schneider, never had writer's block, and for this and a million other things, including her intelligence, sense of humor, and diligence, I will always be thankful. Our editor, Susan Leon, aided us immeasurably with her thorough and thoughtful editing and her suggestions for a more focused text.

There is no way I can adequately acknowledge the influence of my family on my life. My mother, more than anyone else, shaped my development and gave me confidence in my abilities. My sister, Lynda, has become a main support to me and is someone to whom I turn for her substantial clinical insights as a therapist. My children, Justin and Jennifer, have inspired this project by beginning to take steps toward their own independent lives. I thank my husband, Bob, who, by sharing his life with me for the last twenty-eight years, is the unauthorized collaborator of this book.

—SONYA RHODES

—Contents—

PART

I

VULNERABLE PEOPLE

CHAPTER ONE

Introduction: Necessary Changes

W<small>HEN I FIRST BEGAN WRIT-</small>ing this book, I assumed it would focus on the mid-life couples I have treated in my practice over the last twenty-five years. But as the book evolved, I began noticing similar mid-life issues and themes—and similar turmoil—arising in and disrupting the lives and marriages of my friends (all now in their forties and fifties). It seemed that, both professionally and personally, I was seeing couples in bankrupt marriages divorcing or on the brink of separating; couples whose marriages were thrown awry as children grew up and left home; couples whose marriages were destabilized by career setbacks, financial uncertainties, or serious illness. All around me I saw marriages devastated by affairs, by the partners' changing values, roles and identities, by new sexual needs and anxieties. And I saw joy, as well as devastation, as people set about rebuilding, reworking, and renewing marriages—even, astonishingly, some of those that had come closest to total collapse.

The more deeply involved I became in the work—the research, interviewing, and conceptualizing—the more the book evolved as an expression and synthesis of both my personal and professional lives. And at some point I realized that, without my conscious awareness, my deepening immersion in the people and issues I was writing about had been bringing me closer and closer to "home." My husband and I have been married for twenty-eight years, our children are growing up and preparing to go out on their own, and our marriage is in the kind of creative flux that all the people in this book are experiencing.

To my surprise, this book turned out to be about not only my clients and my friends but myself as well.

In my work as a couples therapist, I have been very moved by the struggles of couples who are reexamining their relationships after being together for ten, twenty, or thirty years. (In this book, the definition of a "mid-life marriage" will hinge on the *longevity* of the marriage, as well as the *age* of the partners.) Both partners know that over the years, they have changed; they know they are not the same as they were when they were first married.

If identity crises strike us at adolescence, they tend to strike our marriages at mid-life. And for good reason: Our "family" focus is shifting back to a "couples" focus, but we're hardly the same couple we were twenty years ago.

For the first time since a couple were newlyweds, they are not defining themselves or their marriages in terms of their responsibilities to others. For the first time since then, husbands and wives are *not* asking, What am I supposed to do or be? but instead, What do I *want* to do or be? Their "mom" and "dad" roles have been stripped away like outdated clothing, and without these timeworn identities, the couple again see each other "naked." In the new, harsh light of mid-life, each partner is asking, Who am I now? Who are you? and finally, Who are we together? Those questions probe into the very heart of marriage.

When couples in their twenties and thirties come to therapy together, women almost always are the initiators. But at the mid-life turning point, men initiate just as often. Now a man may perceive a shift in his life; from a softer, more vulnerable spot in his heart, he is becoming aware of a deep need for love, playfulness, and companionship in his marriage. Now men begin placing a higher priority on relationships.

Important new research reveals that men who manage mid-life well become more receptive to the *affiliative* (the nurturant and sensual) aspects of themselves, while women who thrive in mid-life become more assertive and autonomous. In other words, mid-life is a time for role swapping: as men become more "feminine," women become more "masculine."

Intimacy has also been found to be *less* important to older women than it is to younger women. In one study, women between the ages of forty and fifty-five rated "breadth of interest," "dominance," and "innovation" as more important to them than relationships.[1] This is startling news when so many of us assume that women *always* place a higher value on relationships than on self! Just as strange is the notion that men turn *toward* relationships.

Since these profound changes in identity are accompanied by new sets of needs, values, and priorities, it isn't surprising that so many marriages run into trouble at mid-life. But in my clinical practice as well as in mid-life workshops, I have found that many mid-life women and men need a chance to allow the hidden parts of themselves to blossom. Yet outgrowing old roles doesn't mean outgrowing "old" marriages.

I also have found that marriages stay passionate and vital by following a dynamic cycle of *conflict, repair,* and *renewal.*

Conflict within a marriage results when one of the partners introduces a new element—which could be anything from a new need or wish to a revised self-definition—into the relationship. Any new ingredient added to the makeup of a marriage will most likely make the partners feel at odds with each other, and usually they will argue or withdraw from one another.

Withdrawal is more dangerous; arguing at least allows for the possibility of airing the issues. However, when a couple argues without moving on to the next part of the cycle, it is just as bad for the marriage.

The repair, or healing, phase of the cycle follows when the couple is able to move beyond conflict. Healing does *not* mean smoothing things over or denying the conflict; on the contrary, it means understanding the sources of conflict, becoming more self-aware, and learning empathy for a partner.

It is possible for a couple to *stop* here, *without* going on to the final stage. In this case, however, since the couple has not fully resolved their problems, those problems are recycled, until they are adjusted on a deeper level.

Renewal, the final stage of the cycle, entails the actual reworking of the marriage contract. Now the couple has incorporated new information about each other, changed their mutual expectations, and made new accommodations to each other's needs.

Learning to make use of this cycle, which begins during a period of marital instability and leads to positive change, is critical to the growth of mid-life marriages. I emphasize it in my clinical work with couples, and it will be one of the most important tools that couples will take away from this book.

And finally, I have found that while couples counseling is sometimes the best way to handle a crisis, once couples understand the basic concepts discussed in this book, they can handle crises at home by using the methods and strategies that I will describe. My goal is to help couples use this book as a counselor, adviser, or therapist—a resource to draw upon.

Having treated over two hundred mid-life couples in my practice and interviewed one hundred more specifically for this book, I have concluded that at mid-life *almost every marriage* undergoes a crisis and that most people are looking for a way *through* the crisis—not out of the marriage. And, repeatedly, I have seen that mid-life couples with the determination and staying power to make a marriage work end up happier together and more satisfied than ever before.

Listed below are the basic assumptions and major points—and some of the startling facts about mid-life—that will be developed here:

1. Statistics show three dramatic divorce peaks.[2] The first is at two to four years into a marriage, while the second and third hit at mid-life, at the fifteen–eighteen-year crossroads and again at twenty-five–twenty-eight years. I will show, in the chapter "The High-Risk Marriage," why mid-life marriages are so vulnerable to divorce and identify typical high-risk couples.

2. While men's mid-life "work" is to become more nurturing and affiliative (more eager and available for intimacy), women's "work" focuses on self-fulfillment. Even though mid-life "role swapping" is healthy and necessary, a marriage will become temporarily destabilized. Creating a new kind of relationship, which reflects a high degree of independence while preserving intimacy, will help a couple get their marriage back into sync.

3. When men *avoid* the work of growth and change, they may become seriously depressed or seek a false sense of rejuvenation through extramarital affairs or through questionable and grandiose business ventures. In the chapter "The High-Risk Man," I will describe typical high-risk men, what their more traumatic crises look like, and how a couple can recover and rebuild.

4. At mid-life, the woman who adheres to a traditional "feminine" role risks becoming an Enabler, or co-dependent. I will show how the "High-Risk Woman" can find that her best recourse is self-discovery, self-assertion, and self-fulfillment. A woman may worry that she will lose her femininity if she takes on "masculine" traits, such as assertiveness and autonomy, but in mid-life, "masculinity" and "femininity" are redefined.

5. Men are likelier than women to have mid-life affairs, although the latest statistics show that more women are having affairs than ever before. But men and women have different *kinds* of affairs; while a man's

is more likely to disrupt a marriage, a woman's will probably be *transitional,* an interlude leading her to feel more confident about making changes *within* her marriage. In the chapter "The Mid-life Affair," I will show how these affairs, whether a woman's or a man's, are major turning points that will lead either to positive change or to a more serious stalemate.

6. There is life for a marriage after an affair. But identifiable factors determine which marriages recover, and which don't. Stress disorders are common for mid-life women whose husbands have affairs, and couples who decide to stay together should follow the stages of recovery that I describe in "From Victim to Survivor: After a Husband's Affair," which also include a "payback" period for her as part of the rebuilding process. No matter which partner has the affair, the challenge for both is to avoid making a hasty decision to end the marriage.

7. In their forties and fifties, some women experience sexual awakenings, while many men become more anxious about sexual performance. But a man's greater sense of vulnerability can make him a more tender and sensitive lover. In the chapter "Sexual Renewal," I will discuss the danger that lies in settling for "sexual attrition" at mid-life, which will almost always put a marriage at risk either for an affair or for a divorce.

8. Far too often, couples assume that it is impossible to maintain emotional and sexual chemistry in long-term marriages—that the *longer* the marriage, the *less* likely it is to change for the better. However, I have found that the *longer* the marriage, the *more* likely it is that the partners will find hidden strengths that they may have underplayed or overlooked. Problems that at first may seem dire to these couples often turn out to be reassuringly minor.

9. In the chapter "The Mortal Heart," I will describe how, unexpectedly, the illness of one partner may hit the "well" spouse even harder. The woman who has successfully relinquished her old caretaker identity may find that she is martyring herself to her husband's illness, while another woman may secretly dread that her husband will become dependent on her. Unexpectedly, some mid-life men provide a healthy model for the best and most supportive role a well spouse can play with an ill partner.

10. Divorce in mid-life results from a failure to negotiate new issues, *not* from a sudden, heart-wrenching incompatibility. There are ways to break the stalemate, renegotiate the marriage contract—and survive the mid-life marital crisis.

In a few cameo portraits, I will show couples who are out of sync, out of touch, and in potentially deep trouble. None of them realize that their crises are *typical* for mid-life couples, and that crisis is often—and particularly at mid-life—a vehicle for positive change.

*At the age of forty-eight, Mark decides to scale down his involvement in the small but thriving restaurant he has built from scratch. As well as being just plain tired of the twelve-hour days he has put in for twenty years while building the business, he feels deeply satisfied with his life's work and more than ready to rest on his well-earned laurels for a while. Since the business was his full responsibility, he has always felt too anxious to schedule vacations lasting much longer than ten days (or that were in places not accessible by phone in case of sudden crises at the restaurant). Now he wants to visit the places he has yearned to see ever since he was a young boy dreaming over maps of exotic lands. His first plan is to travel extensively with his wife through the Far East, a place that has always fascinated him. He feels as if he is in a race with time, and that if he isn't careful, he will wake up one day and realize that he has missed out on doing the kinds of things that really make life worth living.

His wife, Nancy, finds the sudden mellowing of Mark a little ironic—and not a little disturbing, if the truth be known. Just when Mark decides he wants to "enrich" his life (after all those years when she had sometimes felt he was married more to his job than to her), Nancy herself is gearing up, putting in long hours and beginning to gain real status and prestige at her job as a marketing representative for the first time. The kids have left home, and she feels relieved, with an almost giddy sense of freedom: At last she can accomplish what *she* wants to! This is supposed to be *her* time to achieve the goals she put aside for so many years as she focused on the family. She feels angry at Mark for not understanding how important it is for her to find fulfillment through work.

How did Mark and Nancy end up so out of sync? Each feels puzzled by and disappointed in the other. Each secretly wonders why the other isn't *happy* about the exciting emotional changes he or she is experiencing, as well as supportive of the actual life changes each wants to make. Meanwhile, Mark resents Nancy because she is not available when he is eager for more togetherness and Nancy resents Mark because he is pressuring her to be more available when she honestly doesn't have the time.

Each is vulnerable, too—Mark because he has given up some of the sense of power that he gained from his work, and Nancy because her hard-won independence is too new to feel unassailable. Nancy and Mark both wonder how they have lost touch, but neither feels ready to define the conflict and address it.

*A sudden financial crisis crushes Neil, and Margaret finds that she is angry all the time. At last she understands that she feels *betrayed* by Neil—the flamboyant, charismatic venture capitalist who was first in his class in business school, who as a Wall Street wizard masterfully rode what seemed to be the endless wave of prosperity in the 1980s. She loved and was seduced by his fabulous energy, his promise, his seeming infallibility.

Now the "endless" wave has broken and the ride is over. At the age of forty, Neil feels humiliated, exposed, and scared. He saw himself as without limits, maybe in some crazy way, as *immortal*. He was soaring; now he is disgraced. There seems to be no end to the psychic battering he is taking.

As well as being angry, Margaret feels disillusioned, and scared. Even though at the age of thirty-nine she is a successful attorney, she always believed that if push came to shove, Neil would take care of her, like a father. The two of them, as a couple, had seemed invulnerable; now they must face a new, harder reality in which she will not be able to depend upon Neil in that way. Now she too must face the fact that Neil is mortal, that he can make mistakes, get burned, come unglued, and even die someday. She must also face the fact that in mid-life, "little girls" must grow up.

Can *he* learn to live with his own limitations? Can *she* accept the fact that her marriage must come of age?

*At the age of forty-seven, Marty, a loyal family man, begins an affair with a woman he met at his health club. While the affair is going on, he feels rejuvenated and sexually alive for the first time since turning forty.

Six months later, he crashes. What has he been doing? he asks himself. Has he lost his mind? He actually feels as if he's been temporarily insane. He loves his wife, Gayle; they have been married for more than twenty years. They have a *life* together. He resolves to end the affair.

At just this time, Gayle discovers a crumpled-up American Express bill in Marty's suit pocket from a hotel in the Virgin Islands she has never heard of on a weekend when he was supposedly attending a business convention in Miami. As she stands there staring at the scrap of paper, she feels as if she has been punched in the stomach.

Later that night, she wordlessly hands him the bill. Staring at it, he confesses that he has had an affair, but that it is over and he has put it behind him and wants only to forget it ever happened. Marty is miserable and contrite; he tells Gayle he loves her and asks her if she can forgive him.

Gayle always thought that she'd walk out if Marty ever had an affair. But her real feelings are far more conflicted, and tormenting. She and Marty share a home, children, a social life, a *history*. Give it all up *now*? The thought of being back at square one, as a single forty-five-year-old woman, is overwhelming. The fact is, she is enraged and hurt, but she can't bring herself to walk out.

So she stays, hoping that eventually she'll forget about it or at least it won't matter so much. But two years later, Gayle still can't forget, and she endures vivid, horrifying flashbacks to that moment of discovery and its aftermath. And she never seems to get a good night's sleep.

Can *he* come to grips with the fear of aging and loss of power that unconsciously fueled his need for an affair? Can *she* forgive him? Should she? How?

No marriage gets out of mid-life alive unless the partners risk making changes. A mid-life marital crisis can be understood either as a mortal threat to the marriage or as an opportunity to renew it. Now the partners will set the course for their marriage for the next twenty years. Will they be loving companions on the same path, or will they go their separate ways?

The first step toward breaking the stalemate is understanding the causes behind the crisis.

GENTLE MEN

A marriage may fail at mid-life because women and men have different kinds of mid-life work to do that is based on new and different sets of needs. As a man faces the first unmistakable signs of physical and sexual decline, he may also begin to feel weak just where he has always felt strongest—in the workplace. A man who has been working in sales for twenty years may feel obsolete when faced with the fact that younger colleagues in his field are schooled in sophisticated computers and data base models. He may sense that before too long, these associates will move in on him, and possibly replace him.

I am always touched by these men when they come to my office because they seem so vulnerable. They feel as if life has played a trick on them. A man may seek to overcome these all too mortal feelings in surprising or even bizarre ways. When a man is floundering among his mid-life terrors, he will probably show one or more of these symptoms: prolonged depression and loss of self-esteem; or else, ironically, an inflated sense of self, a new grandiosity and feelings of omnipotence that may lead him to extravagant spending, risky business ventures, alcoholism, or affairs.

Mid-life is the time when men experience what I call a "softening," or a new sense of vulnerability and neediness. A man's behavior may change in unexpected ways. One woman I interviewed was completely puzzled by the fact that her husband was "not acting like himself." "Suddenly," she told me, "he is questioning me about whether I'm *really* enjoying sex. He seems worried that he's losing his touch as a lover. And he worries about other things that never used to bother him—for example, over the holidays, he was upset that we weren't invited to as many parties as we were last year. What in the world is wrong with him?"

Many women are just as puzzled by a partner's atypical behavior as this woman was. As we dug deeper into what had been going on in her husband's life recently, things became much clearer. First, her husband was worried that a recent downturn in business might force him to take early retirement. Then, to make matters worse, his fiftieth birthday was right around the corner!

As we discussed this, I said, "Your husband may feel that he's losing ground in many parts of his life. He feels weakened. His insecurities are creeping up on him. Now he's anxious about your sexual response because he's sensitive about his sexual performance. Any lessening of desire or capacity will contribute to his fears of decline. He's anxious, too, that he may no longer be considered valuable or important enough by the people in his milieu to be included in social events. At this point in his life, he is sensitive to *all* hints of the diminution of power and standing."

We've known for a while that men between the ages of forty and forty-five are vulnerable to mid-life crises, but toward their late fifties, men hit yet another peak of vulnerability. Because of the slowing of the aging process, mid-life issues may sometimes not surface until later on. In my practice I have seen some men so troubled that it would not be an overstatement to say they are suffering from a form of mid-life crisis extreme enough to be called mid-life *psychosis*. I will talk about a number of those cases later on and show how women can be pulled into the eye of the storm—and what they can do to handle the sometimes shocking changes in their lives.

LEADING LADIES

Because she has already weathered so many transitions—from single woman to wife to mother to working woman—a woman will deal with the emotional changes of mid-life differently than her partner does. She will also deal with the *physical* changes differently than he does because she is accustomed to the effects of the menstrual cycle on her body. Change isn't new for her, so she knows she can survive, and grow.

Still, she feels very vulnerable when she looks in her mirror and sees the unmistakable signs of aging. She is highly sensitive to the fact that our society values the beauty of *young* women. And she can recall that before turning forty, she'd have little trouble shedding those extra five pounds, while after forty, the five pounds stick. She may maintain that she absolutely never thinks about "this middle-age thing," as one woman put it, but ten minutes later say that she is considering collagen injections for her crow's feet. She kids around with her friends about going gray, but she may also be having long, heart-to-heart discussions with them about the pros and cons of cosmetic surgery. In other words, a woman who in her twenties may have told herself that she intended to age gracefully and naturally may now be thinking, Why not do something about my eyelids? Why should I look middle-aged when I feel so young? Today's mid-life woman is interested in transformation—both emotional and physical.

Even though the women's movement in the early 1970s came a little too late for some of today's mid-life women, over the years feminism has filtered into and shaped their consciousness, and they have been preparing, consciously or unconsciously, for a change of focus in their lives. "I always took pride in the fact that I didn't have to work," one woman said. "I married well and felt sorry for women who had jobs. Now, at forty-seven, I have my first real job, and I can tell you that there's nothing like a paycheck to make you feel good about yourself!"

After the kids leave home, many women want to work, although they may find the idea more than a little daunting at first (and jobs not always easy to come by). But usually, they prove to have managerial skills (developed from years of running a home) that younger people can't touch. Professionally, these women are competent, conscientious, and most never look back.

As recently as ten years ago, women's mid-life development either was measured against the male standard that dominated the psychological literature on mid-life, or else was defined entirely in terms of menopause and the empty-nest syndrome. It comes as a shock to delve into mid-life studies and find so little on women—it is almost as if, after a certain age, women become invisible. Even more shocking is to find that most of what has been written is either wrong or seriously outdated.

Writing in 1945, the famous Freudian psychoanalyst Helene Deutsch called menopause "a narcissistic mortification that is difficult to overcome" and went on to say that "the mastering of the physiologic reaction to the organic decline is one of the most difficult tasks of a woman's life."[3] In Deutsch's day, it was believed that a woman's reproductive and child-rearing functions defined her. Naturally, once her reproductive life was over, she would feel unwomanly, worthless, and washed-up.

Today we know that women who define themselves exclusively as mothers are most susceptible to mid-life or empty-nest blues.[4] Also at risk is the woman whose identity depends upon the maintenance of a youthful face and body; for her, menopause will deliver a devastating blow to her sense of self-worth. (In a tabloid newspaper article, the actress Cher is reported to be dreading menopause. The actress's "mid-life crisis" is said to have "hit her like a ton of bricks," and she bemoans the fact that men in their forties and fifties prefer younger women to her.)

But fewer and fewer women are listing "mom" as their one and only occupation or identity. (And fewer still list "sex symbol.") Even so, the myth of women's mid-life depression has a surprisingly tenacious grip on our psyches.

All of the new, groundbreaking studies on menopause and its influence on mood thoroughly debunk the notion that menopause is correlated with depression. As Robert O. Pasnau, M.D., a psychiatrist at the University of California at Los Angeles Medical School, puts it: "Women going through menopause are no more likely to suffer depression than are women of other ages, nor than men, for that matter."[5] The reason is that increasing numbers of women are finding sources of pride and self-esteem beyond their traditional roles as wives and mothers.

Most of these women in their forties and fifties are eager to focus on their own interests, talents, and aspirations—to get on with the second half of their lives. But old roles and assumptions may stand in a woman's way. If she has always looked up to her husband as a pillar of strength, she will find that that view will obstruct her coming of age. And if she has always been a caretaker in her marriage, that role, continued into mid-life, will conflict with her new assertiveness—her desire to focus on her own needs. Her assertiveness is also likely to conflict with her husband's heightened need for intimacy.

Usually, women will find now that *all* men—even those who come to terms with their own softening—will demand more from them than they now expect to give. But if a woman's mid-life work is to develop maximum independence and a man's work is to achieve greater intimacy, the couple's work, which they do together, is to renegotiate their marriage to handle *both* sets of needs. A couple may be skeptical about this, assuming that their needs are mutually exclusive. But paradoxical as it may seem, accommodating a high degree of independence *and* intimacy within a marriage is not impossible. In fact, achieving the right balance is the essential task for *all* mid-life couples.

THE SECOND HALF

Today's mid-life women and men face a new challenge. In the past, mid-life, or "middle age," was considered the beginning of the long, depressing decline into old age. Today, we see it as the second half of our lives, a time for personal change and for a renewal of the marriage that we have nurtured for so long.

I use the term "second honeymoon" to describe the renewal of a marriage. But even if a couple's first honeymoon was idyllic, this one will be different. It will be the couple's reward for the hard work they've put into reinventing their marriage. In my experience with couples, second honeymoons *never* come cheap.

The bad news about change and renewal is that couples have to take risks they've never had to before, at a time when most women and men feel more vulnerable than ever before. The good news is that mid-life is the time when couples get a second chance. By now, we know where our own personal pitfalls and weaknesses lie, which makes us smarter about managing our lives than we were when we were younger. By now, too, along with the sense of satisfaction that comes from accomplishment, we've faced our limitations. We have fewer illusions; we don't live for some shimmering fantasy of "tomorrow"—we understand the urgency (and transience) of the moment.

And for marriages, too, there are no more "tomorrows" and "somedays"; a reality stripped of illusion may seem bleak, but without the buffer of fantasy we are far more likely to act, to make the clear, conscious choices that are necessary if we want to breathe new life into marriages gone stale.

It is a time to renew the marriage vows, to "remarry," or recommit, to the same partner. In mid-life, after so much else has changed—children leaving home, job losses or career changes, parents ill or dying—our marriages clearly are, or must become, the vital heart and soul of our existence. We owe it to ourselves and to our partners to bring to our marriages our best and most loving selves.

As I was discussing the ideas that form the backbone of this book with clients and friends, I found that certain words and terms kept reappearing. I began calling them the "re" words—rebuilding, reworking, renewing, rediscovering, rejuvenating, reinventing, renegotiating, reinvesting, and redefining. All ended up becoming part of the vocabulary of mid-life marriage that I was developing. The "re" words are optimistic, implying that people can change, that stalemates in marriages can be broken.

Since there are a number of concepts that have special significance for mid-life marriages, I have included here a brief list of the words that readers can use to think about and describe the issues they are confronting now.

Stalemate: This is a state of unproductive conflict and/or withdrawal, an erosion of vitality and a deadening of sexual and emotional chemistry that takes place over time, and a resistance to change on the part of one or both partners. In mid-life marriage, a stalemate can develop into an *impasse,* when an event or emotional trauma from a couple's past blocks necessary change and growth.

Collusion: Without even being aware of it, *all* couples make unspoken pacts, or "deals," with each other in order to maintain certain habits or patterns of feeling, thinking, and acting. Their original collusion, from the early part of their marriage, forms the basis of a couple's original *marriage contract,* a conscious or unconscious "agreement" they make to accommodate their tacit assumptions and collusions. At mid-life, however, as the couple faces problems unique to this time of life, they will begin reshaping their marriage to accommodate new sets of needs, desires, and expectations.

Phantom self: Each of us brings into mid-life the husk of a self, or identity, that we are now outgrowing.[6] Rebuilding a marriage depends upon the partners' ability to relinquish those old identities and grow into new ones. A mid-life woman who holds on to a phantom self as caretaker, continuing to put other people's needs first when she needs to be seeking *self*-fulfillment, may end up as an enabler or codependent in her marriage. A man's phantom self will usually be that of the "tough guy," who submerges his feelings in the interest of achievement and places a low priority on relationships. For him, mid-life should mark the beginning of his *softening* process, during which he shifts priorities, reorienting (in the healthiest cases) toward relationships.

Mid-life losses: These losses, which far too often visit us in clusters, have to do with the increased awareness of diminished physical strength and acuity, as well as the necessary surrendering of outmoded dreams and illusions, and outgrown self-images and roles. A career setback, the waxing and waning of sexual passion, the relinquishing of an identity as a parent, all of these also may be experienced as major mid-life losses.

Mid-life terrors: This is the anxiety or even panic a woman or man may feel in the face of the normal and predictable losses of mid-life. In response to the terrors, during which a person may perceive the shadow of decline on his life, he or she may suddenly behave in ways that seem out of character to a partner. The way to recover from the losses, as well as from the terrors, is through *loving grief*,[7] which is a way to compensate for loss through love. Rebuilding marriages is at the vital core of this essential healing process.

In Part One, "Vulnerable People," I will talk about the high-risk roles and patterns of behavior that women and men bring with them into mid-life, as well as the high-risk marriages in which couples collude in resisting the change that is normal and necessary for growth.

Part Two, "Sexual Stalemates," will focus on sex and related issues, including affairs, the postaffair marriage, and sexual stalemates.

In Part Three, "Changing Course," ways to renegotiate the joyless marriage and break some of the most common impasses that block the growth of mid-life marriages will be discussed. I also will talk about the differences between the *destabilized* marriage and the *unrenewable* marriage and show how divorce itself may be used as an opportunity for renewal. Finally, in this section, we will see how illness, the most dramatic crisis of all, may sometimes have unexpectedly positive effects on marriage.

The last chapter of the book, "Portraits of Mid-life Marriages," will describe the turning points of marriage—both positive and negative—and the three levels of marital stress. Since mid-life couples in crisis may experience a sense of urgency, or even panic, about their marriage, accurately evaluating the *degree* of stress is critical in the rebuilding process.

All of the strategies and techniques for reviving mid-life marriages that I will describe in this book, including those in a workbook at the end, have provided the couples I've worked with the tools for making the changes necessary for growth. Now readers can learn to use, adjust, and adapt these same techniques to their own marriages. This book can and should be used, again and again, as a couple's resource in the exciting, ongoing process of renewal.

CHAPTER TWO

The
High-Risk Woman

As WE MOVE INTO MID-LIFE,
we experience the loss of earlier identities. The woman who
tries to hold on to her phantom self is putting herself at risk
for crisis.

In my work with mid-life women, I have found three
types of high-risk women: Little Girls, Enablers, and Eternal
Mothers.

THE LITTLE GIRL

Mid-life is the time for allowing little girls to grow up.
There are two reasons why this is so critical for women: first,
because we cannot fulfill ourselves if we don't grow up; and
second, because men, feeling all too mortal, now step down
from the pedestals women place them on.

On some level, we—all women in our society—are taught
to be little girls. We expect to be cherished and cared for by
men; in exchange, we are expected to honor and look up to
them and build their self-esteem. The woman who carries
with her the wispy, plaintive ghost of a little girl probably

has *always* looked up to her husband, seeing him as brilliant, successful, strong and capable, a leader, provider, and protector. When she suddenly sees his more vulnerable side at mid-life, she may feel an overwhelming sense of insecurity. Women who look up to their husbands the way they once looked up to their fathers must now learn to let go of the fantasy.

At her twentieth wedding anniversary, Sarah Beth, forty-four, prepared a huge, glittering dinner party for herself, her husband, friends, and family. When everyone was seated in front of the gorgeous Limoges china and Baccarat crystal place settings, Sarah Beth stood up and, thanking everyone for coming, smiled at her husband. "And of course I want to thank Charles for everything—for making all this possible," she said. But even as she was saying it, Sarah Beth wondered why she gave herself so little credit for the life they had built together.

Sarah Beth, who had managed a household and raised happy, successful children, was an enormously competent woman. But she felt helpless without her husband around. She didn't believe that she could do a thing without him. At the same time she sensed that she gave Charles an ego boost through her self-putdowns; meanwhile, Charles, needing her support to feel powerful, *colluded* with the role she was playing. By acting helpless, Sarah Beth emphasized *his* superior, take-charge role. Now, just as Sarah Beth was beginning to question the roles and the collusion, her little girl self had piped up at the dinner party, showing her how hard it was to give up this ghost.

When a little girl grows up, or if one partner changes in any way, her partner must be able to accommodate her new set of needs. A woman's *worst* fear may be that if she changes, her marriage will fall apart. Her fears may be realistic; some inflexible marriages don't survive normal mid-life flux.

When Debbie met her husband, Sam, in college, suddenly her life, which had seemed directionless, had a focus. At the age of twenty-six, Sam was launched in his academic career, and Debbie imagined herself the wife of a "brilliant" man. She finished college, married Sam, and had two children soon after. As Sam became increasingly caught up in research, teaching, and fighting for tenure, she raised the children virtually alone. It was a happy time for Debbie; she and a few other faculty wives met for coffee nearly every day, helped each other with baby-sitting and shopping, organized car pools to deliver the children to their activities, and took innumerable chaotic but cheerful expeditions to beaches, parks, and zoos.

When her sons were eleven and thirteen, Debbie started a reading group for her friends that met every month to discuss the classics and contemporary novels. One night, after the group had broken up and gone home, she realized as she was cleaning up that she felt sad. There seemed no reason for it: She had wonderful children and intimate friendships, and now she and Sam were discussing the possibility of a sabbatical in England. Until tonight she had been excited at the prospect, but now Debbie felt uneasy at the thought of drifting through another year.

"It sounds like you're ready for a challenge," her best friend told her, and suggested that she enroll in graduate school in English.

"Do you think I could?" Debbie asked hesitantly.

Her friend laughed. "You could teach most of those classes yourself, Debbie. You're the inspiration of our reading group."

Over the next week, whenever she thought about the stimulation and challenge of being in a classroom again, her heart quickened. But when she mentioned to Sam that she was considering going on for her master's degree and possibly her doctorate in English, he laughed and gave her a quick kiss on the forehead. "Debbie, you don't realize that college students these days, well, they're serious," he said. "They're all on the career track. You'd be way out of your league."

At the age of forty-eight, Debbie still had the round, smooth face and wide eyes of a young girl. "When Sam told me not to bother with school," she said, "I sort of gave up. I saw his world as off limits to me. I saw myself as dumb and inadequate."

Finally, Debbie went ahead and applied to graduate school. Talking to Sam, she made light of it, saying she'd just give it a try. But gradually she increased her course load and became friendly with other students in the department. Sam was miserable. He hated it when she wasn't home to make dinner and listen to his stories about the campus and his problems with his research. Accustomed to having her unconditional support and sympathy, he could not adjust to its absence.

Since Sam continued to want a little girl, adoring and nonthreatening, who would cater to him and look up to him, not an academic colleague or an equal partner, the couple found themselves stalemated. Eventually, they divorced. When one partner lets go of a phantom self, a challenge is presented to the other partner—and to the marriage. In the cycle of conflict, repair, and renewal, the initial disruption of the status quo can lead to rebuilding on a different basis— if *both* partners take on the challenge to accommodate new sets of needs.

A different kind of couple, feeling the urgent necessity of change, will gradually move together in a new direction, even when they have mixed emotions. At first, the partner who initiates the change may actually regret it: She or he will feel as if they have broken into a Pandora's box of problems— then wish they could slam the lid shut and lock it forever. Unfortunately, problems that you try to lock up *always* re-emerge later.

In Doug and Marisa's original, unspoken marriage "contract," Doug had "agreed" to be the provider whom Marisa would depend upon for financial and emotional support; meanwhile, Marisa had "agreed" to be dependent, bolstering Doug's sense of himself as competent, successful, and powerful. As time passed, however, when Doug began comparing Marisa with the wives of his business associates, all of whom had careers, he began to feel unsympathetic to and embarrassed by her lack of ambition. He had been urging Marisa to return to work, but she had resisted, and now he had initiated couples counseling because, as he said, he was "losing patience."

In their first session, I was struck by Marisa's strong, sensual features; vivid, flashing eyes; and a confident, even forceful, way of expressing herself. You would never have known by looking at her that she was a little girl at heart, yet, with two daughters well along in elementary school, she was terrified of taking the first steps toward going back to work in advertising.

Doug took the lead in our session, explaining, "I run interference for Marisa." In other words, he said, he was the guy who ran and blocked—did all the hard, challenging gut work—while Marisa tried haplessly to run with the ball.

I glanced at Marisa. She looked uncomfortable and a little embarrassed. But she nodded slightly, as if ruefully agreeing with Doug's description of their roles. I could see how vulnerable Marisa felt and how Doug, a brash, self-confident businessman, had always sheltered her from the world.

But Marisa had an inner strength that I grew to admire. In the course of treatment, it became clear that Doug was all too comfortable in his fatherly, controlling role. "Marisa just isn't ambitious," he had assured me more than once. "She's sensitive and intuitive. But she's scared of people. At the job she gave up when we started our family, she did okay but she never pushed for raises or promotions. I don't think much has changed since then." The first time he said it, Marisa sat quietly, her hands folded in her lap. A few months later, when he repeated it, she angrily countered him. "I've been sending out résumés and job applications to every advertising firm in town," she told us. "And I've been setting up interviews."

Before this, Doug had offered to help her update her résumé and sit beside her while she made phone calls. "I'm terrific at hand holding," he'd explained cheerfully. Now he was flabbergasted. "Why didn't you tell me?" he asked reproachfully. "I was supposed to look over your résumé before you sent it out!"

"I went to a job counselor," she said matter-of-factly. "I don't want you to help because you always manage to make disparaging comments about me."

"Like?"

"Like saying I'll never get anywhere because I don't have
the drive. You'd say I was shy and scared and didn't have a
tough enough hide. You'd say everything you've always said,
so I just went ahead and did it on my own. Isn't that what
you wanted me to do?"

Quietly and on her own, Marisa had been trying to shake
off her fears and make career moves. For guidance, she'd
consulted a career counselor. But her lack of self-confidence
dovetailed so smoothly with Doug's overprotectiveness that
she still felt very frustrated by her own slowness in getting
results. We kept trying to puzzle out why this talented, resourceful woman was so locked into being her husband's little
girl.

It was time to confront the couple's collusion. Marisa had
married a man who had subtly sabotaged her self-image:
building her up, then pulling her down, keeping her in an
endless girlhood. And now, the more actively Marisa pursued
autonomy, the more we began to see a change in Doug, a
change that made her question the wisdom of her own process of self-discovery. Doug had begun to withdraw from her
and the family, which made Marisa feel so anxious that she
would sometimes defer to his opinions just so that they could
resume their familiar roles for a while. But this pattern of
behavior clearly belonged to a phantom marriage—one that
was fast disappearing.

When one person changes the steps in the familiar dance
of a marriage, the other partner has to adjust to surprising
new rhythms. Marisa, to everyone's surprise, turned out to
be far more open and eager for a change than Doug had
been. Eventually, though, Marisa and Doug broke their stalemate because *both* of them accepted the necessity for change,
even though it was threatening. Marisa hadn't counted on
the fact that giving up the needy, little girl side of herself
would mean that Doug would feel ambivalent and threatened, and the balance of the relationship would be thrown
off. Seeing his weaknesses was painful; she hadn't bargained
for softness when she'd married him for his strength.

By initiating change, Doug ended up getting more than
he'd bargained for: a wife whose strength made his guidance

and protection superfluous. Their mutual dependency was upset, and Doug felt depressed, insecure, and angry. His withdrawal had been an unconscious way to "get back" at Marisa.

Clearly, Doug needed to feel in charge again, but in a less undermining and destructive way. When he complained in one session that the couple's social life had fallen off, we decided that he take over their social calendar instead of leaving it to Marisa. Immediately, he threw himself into planning a big birthday party for her.

When he could assume control in one area, Doug was able to give up control in others. This was a positive sign of his flexibility, and a good sign for the marriage. Marisa was relieved to give this task to Doug; he was far more outgoing than she was. I suggested that this sort of rebalancing of tasks become the model for change in their relationship.

Doug did come to appreciate Marisa the grown-up, whose self-assurance gave her an intriguing, sexy new aura. He planned weekend trips, and even a summer vacation, without the kids. Toward the end of treatment, Doug had an insight that seemed to open his eyes. Speaking about his two daughters, he said that he understood how important it was for them to have a mother who was a strong, independent female role model. "I don't want them to be timid," he said. "Like Marisa. Like Marisa *was*," he corrected himself quickly.

THE ENABLER

In our society, women are trained to nurture and to give to others. These are *valuable* qualities, which are sometimes made to seem unhealthy when they are not. Caretaking becomes *negative* for a woman when she *always* puts other people's needs ahead of her own. In mid-life, that is a particular hazard because this is a time when she should be focusing on self-development instead. If she doesn't refocus, the old role becomes *distorted*, and a woman is at risk of becoming an enabler or a codependent. Mid-life is a time for shedding *layers* of socialization—for giving up much of what we have been taught and rethinking our lives.

A woman who carries the caretaking role into mid-life may practically enable her husband, and her marriage, to death during a crisis by becoming overprotective or controlling in the extreme or even siphoning off her own strength to fuel his flagging energy. The enabler's capacity for self-sacrifice may seem to qualify her for sainthood, but actually, it won't save a soul.

The role of enabler is probably the most familiar, cross-generational woman's role in our society. One fifty-five-year-old friend of mine recalled her graduation ceremony at a prestigious Seven Sisters college. "Adlai Stevenson was the speaker," she said. "He told us not to worry that our wonderful education would be wasted. He said that we would create cultured environments in our homes and be valuable assets to our husbands. We all sat there with our engagement rings on and applauded."

Indeed, for women over fifty, *no other* female role could even be considered, while many younger women grew up struggling with a seemingly opposing desire to be "selfless" in taking care of others and "selfish" in taking care of themselves. The term *"codependent"* has become synonymous with enabler and is a self-description for many women over and under fifty owing to the ways in which women are socialized in our culture: A codependent puts other people's needs ahead of her own or allows other people's needs to become more important than her own. She may allow another person's behavior to rule her life, while trying to control that person's behavior at the same time. As she focuses her time and energy on taking care of another's needs, she perpetuates a cycle of mutual dependency without realizing it.

"Other people's needs always seemed greater than my own," is the way that Marsha put it. When Marsha, who had been a nurse before becoming a wife and mother, became interested in epidemiological nursing at the age of forty-five, she discovered that the only graduate program that suited her needs was in Philadelphia, 150 miles away. She mentioned this to her daugther, Judy, then sixteen, and her husband, Luke. "I guess I'll have to forget about it," she told them.

Much to her surprise, Luke and Judy jumped on the idea. Luke suggested that she take an apartment in Philadelphia and commute home on weekends. Judy chimed in that she would *love* to come visit her mother in the city.

"I told them, whoa, wait a minute," Marsha laughed. "It was all happening too fast. I said, 'Will you two really be okay without me?' When they said yes, I said, 'Don't be silly, it's just out of the question.' I just couldn't accept that they meant it."

In therapy, Marsha discovered why she was balking at making the change. Like many women, she was used to putting other people's needs first; she defined herself in terms of her relationships to others, mainly to her family. Knowing that other people depended upon her made her feel special and important. So now that her family no longer seemed to need her in the same way, she wondered if *she* would be okay without *them*.

Marsha was on the brink of taking a gigantic, unfamiliar step toward a more autonomous future, but she was scared. Admitting that her own needs were as great as anyone else's meant taking unaccustomed risks. But Marsha was ready. Her caretaking role, noble and unselfish as it was, had become a phantom self, as she took the first step of her life that was just for her. After being admitted to the graduate program, she rented an apartment in the city, furnished it, and for the next two years, attended classes all week and commuted home on weekends. "I literally had a 'room of my own,' " she said. "At first I knocked around in it, feeling lonely and disoriented, but as I got into my work, it became a quiet, productive haven for me. I never knew how much satisfaction I could get from having my own life, separate from my family's. I just never thought of it that way before.

"Being committed to and caring for other people was a full-time job for me," Marsha said. "I was proud of it." In fact, she said, she was only ashamed of being a stay-at-home wife and mother when she felt as if society looked down on her. Like so many other women of her generation, Marsha had led a full, rich life devoted to husband, children, relatives, and friends. What she hadn't admitted was the gnawing sense that she was being left behind by her husband. She had begun feeling that he was bored with her and had intuited that the marriage would be in trouble before long.

According to Dr. Carol Feit Lane, a career counselor who specializes in the problems of mid-life women entering the work force, some mid-life women go to work now for external reasons, such as a husband's illness, death, or a divorce, not because they are self-motivated to start careers as Marsha was. The women surveyed by Dr. Lane talked about how they had struggled to "find a balance between . . . commitment to . . . family and [a] need for a work life." Nowadays, says Dr. Lane, even women who are not self-motivated toward careers experience something "comparable to a biological clock—a feeling that women in their 40s have that the time for finding work is running out. If you are over 50 and have never worked, there is a narrowing down of what you can do."

Dr. Lane also found that for some women hit by crisis, the "anticipation of returning to work was accompanied by feelings of desperation and a sense of their own lack of confidence." Typical of women who have focused on family was a woman who said she felt so inadequate that she feared she would not qualify for anything but the most menial job. However, once they were out in the work force, Dr. Lane says, these women experienced a "sense of control over the crises in their lives."[1]

Fifty-two-year-old Barbara was a classic caretaker turned enabler, who was abruptly and unexpectedly propelled into the work force by a traumatic event in her marriage.

When her artist husband, George, decided to give up drinking at the age of fifty-six, Barbara immediately noticed changes in him. For thirty years, he had embodied the popular image of the hard-drinking, hard-living artist. Then, at the very pinnacle of his career, George suddenly began complaining that he felt "pickled" in alcohol and said he wanted to stop drinking. At first, Barbara was relieved.

Actually, there was no relief in sight. Without alcohol, George plummeted into a depression. As a result of alcohol withdrawal, he had panic attacks in which his heart would beat wildly, and he'd clutch his chest saying he was going to die. He couldn't eat, sleep, or paint, but roamed the house all night long like a lost soul. He wore the same stained painter's pants day after day, stopped shaving, and let his hair get dirty and unkempt. He told Barbara that he could barely resist the powerful urge to throw himself out a third-story window or deliberately crack up the car. Barbara hid the car keys from him and hovered by his side twenty-four hours a day to make sure he didn't hurt himself.

Barbara was terrified. She couldn't begin to understand what he was going through; she'd had her own blue periods, but suicide was inconceivable. Finally, George saw a psychiatrist who diagnosed him as a manic-depressive who had been using the bottle to medicate his moods. The psychiatrist then prescribed antidepressant medication, which gradually helped George regain control of his life.

Until George's crisis erupted into their lives, Barbara had played the role of the famous artist's lover/helpmate/muse. At the same time, she had developed a unique personal style of her own: She could throw an expensive designer coat over an offbeat, "artistic" dress, and carry off the quirky combination with style. She was earthy and sexy; and several of George's fellow artists had had crushes on her or had wept drunkenly in her arms. She'd never held a job, but had cultivated patrons for her husband's work and had turned their home into a showcase for modern art. Her parties were famous for her delicious French cooking—the vegetables all from her own garden—and for the prodigious amounts of liquor provided and consumed.

It was only after George began recovering from his depression and attending AA meetings that she saw how lethal their marriage had become to *both* of them. While her husband recovered, Barbara felt increasingly purposeless and empty. She denied it to herself at first, but when she found herself breaking down into tears even while doing household chores, she finally had to admit that her "blue periods" had turned black. Painfully, Barbara looked back on her life and marriage and saw that she had piggybacked

on her husband's sophisticated artistic identity all her life—
which, as she'd been taught, was a wife's proper role. In
return for the identity and purpose she'd absorbed from
him—through the terms of their original marriage "contract"—she had coddled him in his massive hangovers and
drunken temper tantrums and picked up the slack for him
during his frequent lapses in carrying out the responsibilities
of daily life.

I urged Barbara to attend an Al-Anon meeting for the
support that she needed during this transition. Seeing herself
as too special and unique to submit to the structure of a
support group, she at first emphatically refused. But once
she finally went, she began to see her own life through the
lens of other people's lives. She came to understand how she
had protected George's drinking in order to ensure that he'd
always need her. "I'd always thought I was helping George,"
she said sadly. "But I wasn't. I was hurting him. I was keeping
both of us from facing reality."

When a friend who owned a local gallery offered Barbara
a job, she quickly asserted that she had no experience and
was too busy at home anyway. At this point in our therapy,
I challenged Barbara to take the job. She broke down and
cried, saying that she was just too scared.

When I gently asked her to talk about her fears, Barbara
threw up her hands in frustration. "I don't know. I haven't
had a job in twenty-five years! What if I can't do it? What if
I get fired? You ask me what I'm scared of, well, I'll tell you.
I'm scared of everything."

I sensed that if Barbara would take the job, she'd gradually grow into it. Finally, "kicking and screaming," as she
put it, she walked into the store and accepted the position.
"I was shamed into it," she said. "People always told me how
gutsy I was, but it was a big act. My gutsy, wife-of-the-artist
act."

Within a year, Barbara, with her style and flair, as well
as her knowledge of painting, had moved up from assistant
to manager. Soon the gallery was well known for the shows
Barbara put together: New young women artists and indigenous artists of the region were her specialty. Now she and

George attend AA and Al-Anon meetings, and they never serve alcohol at parties. "Our life is quieter, definitely," Barbara said. "But inside, I am excited. I feel full of life, like there's a lot of things I could do if I wanted. When my marriage was my 'job,' it really wasn't enough. Now that I'm putting *less* time into it, we're happier. We're actually closer. Isn't that funny?"

I told Barbara that it wasn't really so funny at all. She and George had made individual choices that had led them away from their poisonous alcoholic environment. In their support groups, each had formed healthy relationships, and Barbara's gallery job had given her a boost toward the personal autonomy that had truly liberated her. And their marriage survived the transition to become *closer* but less *symbiotic* (a term used to describe an unhealthy emotional dependency between partners).

Enablers like Barbara—and almost every woman has at least a little bit of the enabler in her—consider relationships to be their life's work. In a 1980 study, sixty women between the ages of thirty-five and fifty-five were asked if they related to four developmental tasks of early adulthood that were generally accepted as applying to men: Of the four—constructing a dream; forming an occupational aspiration; finding a mentor; and creating a relationship involving love—only the last struck a chord in the women surveyed. Although work was a part of these women's lives, the career-related tasks simply did not resonate in the way that love did.[2]

In the last decade, it has become harder to live for love alone when you also have to bring home a paycheck. Since that 1980 study, women's lives have changed so quickly and dramatically that research is just beginning to catch up. Women who are now approaching forty simply assume they will combine career and family roles. The "crossover theory," developed in the 1980s, reflects the new reality of women's lives in which intervals of work and family life may be interspersed over a lifetime—not in any particular set pattern.[3] More women are now making individual timetables to accommodate periods of work and family, and women seem to adjust more easily than men do to a "crossover" existence that requires the emotional flexibility to have this *combined focus*.

THE ETERNAL MOTHER

A pioneering 1987 study brought to light an important truth for women. Finding that those women who "formulated a new or an importantly revised dream for the second half of life, or who risked making some real changes in their work or daily life" felt happier at mid-life than those who didn't, the study went on to say that the departure of children from the home was critical only for women who previously had been extremely focused on their families.[4]

The eternal mother is the third model to which women in our society are encouraged to adapt. But for women whose primary relationships are with their children, the "forty-something" years may stretch ahead lonely and empty as the children grow up and prepare to leave home. As one woman client said, "My youngest child left for college yesterday. I woke up this morning and asked myself, 'Now what?' "

These days, the woman who wakes up bereft and bewildered the day her last child leaves home seems to belong to a different, long-lost time in our history. But it wasn't really all *that* long ago. And plenty of career women with strong identities of their own feel this same wrenching sadness when their children leave home. "She is my *heart!*" said one woman tax lawyer of her college-bound daughter. "I burst into tears whenever I think of her leaving."

In fact, this is normal sadness for one of mid-life's most significant losses. But what happens to the woman who does not slowly shift her focus away from her children as they grow older?

Jessica is an eternal mother, a woman who is unprepared for and shocked by her mid-life losses. As her children got older, Jessica still lived for and through them, making beautiful clothes by hand and always putting their desires first. She couldn't imagine planning an extended vacation or even a weekend outing without them; at one point, her husband, Don, had suggested that the two of them take a trip together. But Jessica had "ruined the whole idea," he said in a therapy session, by immediately trying to figure out how to arrange the kids' schedules so they could come along.

As she listened to him tell this story, Jessica had looked at him with wondering eyes: What had she done wrong? She hadn't been able to see Don's disappointment that the "coupleness" of their marriage didn't exist. Nor had she understood that he felt rejected: Why didn't Jessica *want* to be alone with him?

Every marriage has two aspects: the partners as a couple and the partners as parents. Until mid-life, the soul and strength of a marriage may have been located within the family. Even in some of the worst marriages I've seen, a couple's belief that they were good parents often formed a solid core for their relationship. But once the children are gone, this couple may find their marriage depleted of life and energy. And even in the *best* marriages, each partner secretly wonders, What do we have without the children?

Jessica had no idea how to fill the void. The more she thought about the past, when she and Don were first married and the children were small, the more perfect it seemed. And the more she tried to think about the future, the bleaker it looked. When her children went to college, she called them every day and lived for the holidays when they came home. As she struggled to avoid facing this inevitable—and healthy—separation from her children, Jessica lived more and more deeply within a phantom self.

Since women are almost always the primary caretakers of a couple's children, separation from the kids is usually, although not always, more wrenching for women than it is for men. All women, even those who have healthy, separate identities, must mourn their losses when their children leave home. Jessica needed to confront her children's empty bedrooms and allow herself to grieve; after that, she needed to redefine her focus.

If a woman anticipates a large hole in her life when her children grow up, it is unrealistic to think that it won't ache.

Jessica was a wonderful mother, but she denied that her reality had changed. Burdened by a phantom self, she resisted beginning the second half of her life.

All of the research points to the fact that it is normal for mid-life women to focus on themselves, and that the key to a good adjustment is a "sex role reversal."[5] (In fact, we now know that women's mid-life depression is directly related to the *degree of acceptance* of the traditional feminine role.[6]) Sometimes researchers refer to a woman's urge to become more self-determining as an assertion of her more *masculine* traits, while a man who becomes more affiliative is said to be discovering the more *feminine* side of his nature. But at midlife, terms like masculine and feminine lose their meaning. Women and men alike simply become more *human* by unearthing their buried selves.

A woman may feel as if her buried self has been waiting eagerly for a chance to emerge. Or she may still secretly feel that the love of her husband and children is central to her identity. This woman should take an inventory: How much of her day is spent on family-oriented activities? How much time does she devote to activities that are self-fulfilling? Gradually, every woman needs to start shifting her focus so that she is prepared for the natural changes in her life that will occur as her children grow older.

This is by far the best antidote to feeling empty inside when children leave. Unfortunately, it is not only the more traditional wife and mother who may be caught in the eternal mother trap. Even women with active, involving careers may leave their hearts at home, only to be shocked to discover that they are hurting the families they love so much.

THE ETERNAL MOTHER IN DISGUISE

The woman who has an active, involving career may never suspect that she is an eternal mother in disguise. Feeling *guilty* about working puts a woman at risk because she may end up becoming too proprietary of her children. If she spends a lot of time away from her child, she may focus on her too much when they're together, or she may create an overly intense, exclusive relationship with the child. In some cases, working mothers actually seem to "divorce" their husbands and "marry" their children.

This was the case for Maureen, forty-four, a costume designer for theater productions. Maureen had been married to her husband, Ian, for fourteen years when she first consulted with me. She had red hair and blue eyes and a lively smile that lighted up her face. When she wasn't smiling, a shadow of unhappiness lingered around her mouth and eyes; sometimes she'd speak with unexpected sharpness, and I could feel a tiny knife-blade of anger. Maureen came to therapy because she was upset about her ten-year-old daughter, Sharon, who was disruptive at school. She and Ian couldn't seem to agree on what to do.

"Basically," Maureen said, "I just can't understand why Sharon is acting this way. She's always been a great kid. We have a wonderful family life." She sounded almost annoyed. "Even though I work long hours sometimes, I always make sure Sharon has my full attention when I'm at home. Ian's very involved with Sharon, too. We feel great that we've really worked it all out." Maureen went on to describe how different her own family of origin had been. From a poor background, Maureen's own mother had worked out of necessity. "She was old-fashioned; she wanted to stay home with her children," Maureen said. "I'm different. I love my work, and I want my daughter to grow up to have work *and* a family just as I do."

Her mother had always demeaned Maureen's father in her children's eyes. "Be sure to say hello to your father when he comes in," she'd whisper to Maureen as her father opened the door, implying that Maureen couldn't possibly *want* to greet her father and would only do it as a favor to her mother. She'd also point out to Maureen how unreliable her father was about coming home on time and remembering to do errands. In subtle and less subtle ways, her mother made Maureen's father seem incompetent and pathetic, the odd man out. Maureen remembered an overwhelming sense of hopelessness and depression pervading her childhood.

But her own marriage to Ian was a different story, she asserted. More than a decade after they'd met and married, they were still deeply in love.

However, by Maureen's third month of treatment, hints of trouble began to seep out. Returning from a shopping trip one Saturday, she and Sharon had been giggling together like teenage girlfriends as they came in the door. When Ian saw them, he had turned without a word and gone into his study, slamming the door behind him. On another night, he had slipped on some of Sharon's clothes on the floor and kicked them away, then stormed off. He wouldn't tell Maureen why he was so angry. "Ian has no right acting this way toward his own child," Maureen told me firmly.

When I then suggested that she bring Ian in for a couples session, Maureen suddenly broke down. "Look," she said, "I can't kid myself. I know there's trouble. I'm so depressed, and I feel guilty all the time."

When Ian finally came in for a session, a true picture of the marriage finally began to emerge.

Ian, an environmental lawyer, was very likable. He had a tangle of dark, curly hair, and was dressed casually in jeans and sneakers; his handshake was warm and friendly, and he seemed very much at ease in his long, loose-limbed body. After greeting me, he sat down next to Maureen on the couch and immediately put his arm around her shoulders. She stiffened and even moved slightly away from him.

Earnestly, Ian leaned forward as he began to talk. "I want you to know that I love Maureen," he said, as if everything depended on my believing him. "I know there are problems with Sharon, but..." He turned to look at Maureen, then continued. "Before Sharon was born, we had what you could call an ideal relationship. It was romantic. It was sexy." His eyes shone while he was talking, but Maureen looked embarrassed by the memory.

"And what happened after Sharon was born?" I asked.

"Everything changed," Ian said at once.

"Yes, I'll never forget how it was," Maureen said in a rush. "When she was less than a week old, I had to take her back to the hospital because she woke up from a nap and she was orange with jaundice. It was *serious*. Ian was supposed to attend a college reunion, but instead of doing what any normal person would do—cancel his plans—he went anyway. While I was in the hospital with our child!" To this day, Maureen was clearly appalled by this memory.

"I guess I shouldn't have gone," Ian said wearily. "But I knew the baby was going to be fine, and what could I do anyway? Even so, that was ten years ago, Maureen. I can't believe you're still holding a grudge about it."

"It wasn't just that," she said furiously. "I knew right then and there that you wouldn't be responsible. I knew it would have to be me and Sharon from then on. You don't love your own child, admit it!"

Ian looked devastated. "I do love her," he said. "But I haven't got much going with her," he admitted sadly. "And I feel just awful about that."

He spoke, too, about his "library" at home, where he loved to sit and read after work. "I value books and reading," he said. "When I was a child, my father and I would read together and listen to music." He hesitated, then went on. "My dream was always that Sharon and I could share that, too. Instead, when I come home from work, I find that Maureen's let her play in there and she's thrown everything all over the place. Neither of them has any respect for anything that I value."

I turned to Maureen. "Can you see that when you let Sharon do this it makes Ian feel violated?"

"No," she said angrily. "That's really ridiculous. When I was a child, I wasn't allowed to do *anything*. *My* child has the freedom to express herself. *I* give her the chance to be creative. All Ian thinks about is himself."

"No," Ian insisted. "That just isn't true. But it seems like Sharon was always Maureen's child. There's a distance between Sharon and me."

Suddenly Maureen blurted out, "Of *course* there's a distance. Sharon is *my* daughter—I've felt that ever since she was born."

I saw Ian wince. The unhealthy core of the family had suddenly been revealed, and it was unsettling. Disturbing as it was, though, it was clearly a turning point that could lead to a break in their stalemated patterns. But first we would all have to understand how these patterns were shaped. I finally broke into the prolonged silence, saying, "Seeing that there's such a painful split in your family, I think it might be helpful to figure out what each of you has brought to your marriage from the families you grew up in." Then I suggested that we do genograms for each of their families.

Genograms are collections of information about people's families of origin. I call genograms "family trees with all the dirt"—"dirt" because as we trace three generations of a family, we unearth the buried patterns, myths, and behaviors that are unconsciously transmitted from parents to children. The best moment to undertake a couple's individual genograms is when they have pinpointed the source of their stalemate. With the problem as the first clue, people often discover that, without being aware of it, they have been repeating destructive family themes.

Tracing out genograms for Maureen and Ian, which I did separately with each of them, helped us begin to unravel a very tangled collusion. Maureen discovered that even though she'd thought she'd made choices that had taken her worlds away from her childhood, she'd actually brought her past with her. Over time, and without her realizing it, it had become an inextricable part of her present.

"I can see that I'm doing what my mother did," she said slowly and painfully. "I'm having a relationship with Sharon and cutting Ian out of it. The truth of it is," she added, "that I've put my relationship with Ian on the back burner, while I've been totally preoccupied with Sharon. And Ian knows it. I can see that I've cut him off at the knees about her at every opportunity."

Maureen was unusual in the rapidity and intensity of her insights during her genogram session. When she began speaking about her father and how her mother had prevented her from having a relationship with him, she began to cry. "I feel so much loss about my own father," she said. "Is that what I'm doing to Sharon? Will she grow up feeling as though *she* never had a father?"

She looked devastated. I assured her that these new revelations, painful as they might be, were the first step toward making some basic changes in her way of relating to her family. Because Maureen was so intelligent and perceptive, it made sense to speak to her frankly. "Every mother knows how easy it is to form an exclusive relationship with a child," I told her. "But a parent should never make the sort of cross-generational alliance that counts out the other parent. Whenever you hear yourself making a coalition with Sharon that excludes Ian, all of your red flags should fly." I suggested that as a start, she keep a list of all the times during the day that she found herself usurping Ian's authority or criticizing his parenting.

"But I don't even know when I'm doing it half the time," she said in despair. I assured her that once she started paying close attention, she'd develop special antennae for detecting the nuances of things she said.

Sure enough, when Maureen brought her list to her next session, she said that all week, she'd constantly heard "alarms going off" and was shocked at the number of times each day that she was critical of Ian. "I just can't believe it," she said sadly. "I don't want it to go on like this."

For most people, the process of change is slow and laborious. Maureen was a glowing exception to the rule. When she uncovered the poisoned fruit on her family tree, she was able to stop the poisoning of her own family. Because she had suffered so much pain and bitterness herself, she was acutely aware of how Sharon would later experience the absence of her father from her life. And she also became aware of Ian's pain.

In truth, Maureen had never had a chance to learn how to be a wife *and* a mother. She couldn't share her child with her husband. In the guise of being a wonderful mother, she became just as smothering and constricting as her own mother had been, and excluded Ian just the way her mother had excluded her father from Maureen's life. The extra ingredient was Maureen's work life: Her own mother had felt guilty about working and had been overinvolved in her children's lives. Maureen had denied feeling guilty, while in fact her own guilt had played a destructive role in her marriage—driven to overcompensate for the time and energy spent away from her child, she had put her marriage on hold, with devastating results.

Ian's genogram turned out to be just as revelatory as Maureen's had. As he and I discussed the patterns of relationships on his family tree, we discovered that when Ian was a child, his father had become depressed and withdrawn from the family after an accident at work had left him partially crippled. Unconsciously identifying with his father's passive role in the family, Ian was now repeating that pattern in his own marriage.

Instead of challenging Maureen's domestic hegemony, he either withdrew or resorted to childish temper tantrums that played into the family pattern by alienating him still further from Maureen and Sharon. Over the years a sense of hopelessness had set in. Beneath Ian's warm, friendly exterior, there lingered a genuine despair, which he now had to confront as he never had before.

Our culture is just beginning to accept that women can have both work and family lives, but couples need to be aware that inner conflicts over this issue can have a surprisingly powerful effect on a marriage. Many marriage "contracts" contain a collusive "provision" allowing for women to develop stronger bonds with their children than with their husbands—the heritage of a culture in which women are close to children, while men keep their emotional distance. But as their children prepare to leave home, these couples in collusion are left gazing blankly at one another across a chasm, with no bridges connecting them and no way to rebuild their marriage.

The case of Maureen and Ian is a good example of a very *avoidable* mid-life crisis. After Maureen had taken steps to change the terms of their marriage contract, it wasn't long before Ian and Sharon began spending time together, discovering a mutual love of music. By the time Ian and Maureen left therapy, Ian and his daughter had signed up to attend a concert series together.

"I've never seen the *two* of them looking so happy," Maureen reported, looking genuinely happy herself.

CHAPTER THREE

The
High-Risk Man

WRITING IN *THE NEW YORK Times* about the experience of turning fifty, Tom Brokaw, the anchor for the *NBC Nightly News,* said: "A profound change [occurred] when I crested 49: I had the uneasy feeling I was now looking down a long trail, no longer up." Wryly, he added, "My life is full.... In fact, life has been so rewarding I may have been lulled into believing ... the aging process would be slowed on my behalf. Obviously, it has not."[1]

Even for the man who copes well with mid-life change, the slow awakening to the inevitable loss of power and status is painful. But all the evidence points to the fact that men who learn to define themselves in ways beyond their work identities[2] (through other interests and hobbies as well as relationships with wives, children, and friends[3]) move on to develop far richer and more rewarding lives than men who don't.

THE TOUGH GUY

While I have seen three typical phantom selves in women, I have found that men generally bring *one* phantom self—

the tough guy—with them into mid-life. Unfortunately, it often turns out to be just as difficult to relinquish as any of the phantoms that haunt women.

The tough guy is the man who expects to conquer the world and be a sexual superman and a warrior in the workplace. A rational, goal-oriented problem solver, he prides himself on being strong, firm, and in control at all times. He can fix the toaster and knows what that clunk in the engine means. He seems immune to adversity and may consider that someone else's hardships stem from what he thinks of as an innate "weakness." He has been taught from the time he was a child to hide his feelings from himself and from others and to value achievement over intimacy.

The typical tough guy comes into mid-life with his identity firmly grounded in his work. For the most part, this man has not been introspective; his career trajectory has left him with little time or inclination to question who he is or what he wants from his life.

However, by his mid-forties, he may suddenly become aware of subtle changes in his mind and body. He may not have the same sexual stamina he once had: "My wife wants to have sex more often than I do," said one man in his late forties. "But I remember when it was the other way around." Another man talked about losing a squash game to a younger colleague and realizing with a pang that this will happen again and again. A man may experience a moral or spiritual crisis in which he questions the choices he has made. His life's work may seem finished or suddenly unfulfilling, or he may lose his job or his career direction.

Unlike the woman who enters mid-life poised to explore her personal and professional potential, a man at mid-life, who has run the race and taken the hurdles, may suddenly find himself at a dead end. He has a case of the mid-life terrors, a sense of anticlimax and foreboding, a poignant awareness that he has come this far only to face the reality of decline and death. He is asking, Is this all there is? *Now what?*

THE DELAYED MID-LIFE REACTION

At one time forty-five was considered prime time for a man's mid-life crisis. But recently, some psychologists of middle age have come to believe that men's inner struggles occur with renewed intensity in the mid-fifties—a decade of the life cycle that has been ignored and avoided. "There may be more taboos about looking at your life during the 50s than any other decade," said Daniel Levinson, Ph.D., an expert on male mid-life development. "For many there is a silent despair, a pressing fear of becoming irrelevant in work or marriage, with no real alternatives in sight. And for others who are able to make vital choices during their 50s, there is a hard time of personal struggle early in the decade. The struggle centers on questions like the value of a marriage or career, or what changes will allow a more meaningful life."[4]

As the population ages, we realize that the decade of the fifties is a critical juncture in the life cycle. In my own experience I have seen the delayed mid-life reaction occur in two different sets of circumstances. First, there is the man whose prime seems nearly endless (he is the 'real-life' version of the tough guy who never softens). He peaks in his career at fifty and his eminence extends over the years that follow. He adds luster and dominance as he ages: This might be the novelist whose writing reflects a deepening wisdom and power, the doctor whose humanity and expertise are unsurpassed, the CEO who is riding the crest of a successful business empire he built from scratch. The man who is reveling in a sense of personal power at the age of fifty may mock the very idea of self-doubt or physical or sexual decline, not believing any of it will ever apply to him. But it almost certainly will later.

In the other set of circumstances, a man may have put off marriage and children until he is in his forties. He and his active wife are so busy working and raising small children they barely notice the passage of time. Before he knows it, the first of his children will turn eighteen, as he turns fifty-eight.

Just as he finds that he is no longer able to push as hard at work, a man may begin to notice that his son's backhand out on the tennis court is more powerful than his. According to Dr. David Karp, a sociologist at Boston College, "The psychological crises that typify the 50s are triggered by the quickened pace of reminders of aging. Physical disabilities— even slight changes like less endurance or physical agility during sports—are usually the first undeniable harbinger of old age."[5]

But whether a crisis strikes a man at forty-six or fifty-six, he is experiencing the same sense of decline and loss of power, a sense of mortality that is shocking and frightening.

It isn't always easy to know what a man is really feeling when he hits this stage in his life cycle. Since our society has not encouraged men to reflect on and express their feelings, it isn't surprising when a man is unable to find the words he needs. But since mid-life is a time when men *do* become more receptive to their feelings, it can also be a time for him to learn to talk about them. A woman can encourage him to do so, while keeping in mind that the most revealing signals of his feelings will lie in his *behavior*. I will describe here three possible behavioral routes that a man may take.

THE EX-TOUGH GUY

If women find it hard to give up being little girls, enablers, and eternal mothers, it may be even harder for men to give up being tough guys. But the man who does end up coping well with the unsettling questions of mid-life is tough enough, in a deeper sense, to lay aside his old tough guy identity.

We now know more than we ever have about this time in a man's life, and this knowledge can be used as a guide toward understanding mid-life marriages. As men grow older, they naturally become more *affiliative* than aggressive, more tuned in to love than power, and more appreciative of the value of human relationships.[6] For many mid-life men, marriage becomes a major source of well-being and happiness.

But first, a man must take a journey through his own soul and discover the softer side of his nature. That journey has its terrors, but the man who can face them and grieve for his losses is the man who will change in surprising ways.

Bart, a forty-two-year-old investment banker, had denied for nearly a decade that anything was wrong in his life. But now his career—always the most important part of his life—had reached a plateau. When Bart came to my office for the first time, he seemed almost painfully vulnerable.

As soon as the session started, Bart began chain-smoking and pacing back and forth from his chair to the windows. As he paced, he told me that he had been married for ten years to Fran, a lovely, successful lawyer, and that they had two happy, well-adjusted children, eight and five, who were enrolled at one of the best private schools in the city.

He stopped and stood by the window, staring out at the windy fall day. Then he told me how over the last few months, he'd had trouble eating, sleeping, and focusing on his work. Sometimes, he'd found himself feeling dizzy and nauseous; occasionally, he'd felt his heart speed up, then seem to leap into his throat. He'd gone to a cardiologist for tests, but nothing had shown up. At that point his doctor had recommended therapy.

"I never thought I'd need a therapist," Bart told me. "I still can't believe I do."

As gently as possible, I asked him if anything had happened lately that might be causing unusual stress.

"The only thing is," he said hesitantly, "that a month ago, a neighbor's child died of leukemia. Suddenly, I began to think about what had happened to *us*. I just didn't expect to feel like this."

With his voice shaking and tears running down his face, Bart said that there had been another child, born before the other two, who had died from sudden infant death syndrome. Struggling to regain control, he said, "I've always been able just to shrug things off. Nothing could touch me.

I knew Fran was devastated, but I told her there was no use crying about something she couldn't help. For me, it just meant putting it behind me, going back to work, business as usual. Until now."

From the raw pain that Bart was experiencing, I knew this must be his first full-blown emotional crisis. After a while, I said, "You seem so troubled by this loss, Bart. It seems as if you're doing some genuine soul-searching."

At first he just shrugged and said, "If it is, it's too little too late." Then, almost in despair, he added, "I don't want to be the same callous thirty-two-year-old man I was back then. I feel as if I've been insensitive and unfeeling my whole life. I didn't support Fran. I didn't grieve for the death of my own child. . . . I don't want to be that kind of man anymore."

Bart is not unique. Men in their forties today grew up in an era of intense questioning of social roles. For the first time, men were encouraged to be more open and aware of their feelings. At mid-life, these men may be especially ripe for experiencing a profound inner shift of identity. Instead of focusing exclusively on work and achievement, men like Bart may learn about the implications of love and loss and the impact of their behavior on the people they love. They learn to look inside themselves and feel shame, remorse, and empathy for others. For Bart, the worst part was the thought that it might be too late to make things right.

Fortunately, it was not. After several weeks, Bart brought Fran to a session. Fran, a large-boned, athletic-looking woman, sat quietly while he talked about his grief over the baby and his pain over not being emotionally present when she had needed him. When he finished and waited anxiously for her reaction, she said, "At the time I was so angry because you weren't there. If only we could have dealt with it together back then. And I'm angry now, too, because I hate to go through all this again, just because you're finally ready."

I said, "Do you think you could discuss it here? Not discuss it at home but use these sessions as a way to deal with a painful episode from the past?"

Over the next several sessions, Fran spoke about how,

over the years, the distance between them had grown. Both of them had retreated into a cocoon of work and responsibility at the expense of the marriage. "When Bart started getting so upset lately, I had a strange reaction," Fran admitted. "I resented it. I wanted him to keep up appearances. I hated seeing him looking weak."

In speaking about their marriage contract, I said, "It seems to me that yours was based on preserving appearances and getting ahead. The two of you seem to have agreed to maintain silences so that you could focus on outside achievements."

"That's true," Fran said thoughtfully. "I can see that I contributed to the silence over the years. I think that both Bart and I have been overly focused on our careers and on making it. Neither one of us has wanted to deal with the distance between us."

Because Fran had been able to put aside her anger and discuss the past, she and Bart were able to understand how they had colluded over the years in denying their painful feelings, and how they had allowed the bonds of attachment to erode. Bart's personal crisis disrupted the status quo and ultimately allowed the couple to begin the work of repair and renewal.

The first step was for them to mourn their loss together. I explained to them the concept of loving grief through which sharing the pain can offset a loss and deepen a relationship. Moving on toward renewal involved a reordering of values, in which they agreed that time spent together as a family and as a couple would now assume far more importance than it ever had before.

ON THE EDGE:
THE QUEST FOR SENSATION, POWER,
AND SEXUAL ECSTASY

Unlike Bart, who came to terms with a new stage of life, another kind of man may experience mid-life as an agonizing period in which he takes a *detour* around the transition he needs to make. A man may be terrorized by signs of decline and vulnerability, and desperately try to avoid facing them.

In the throes of mid-life terrors, he may experience a need for *sensation* in order to console himself or else ward off a numbing reality. He has fantasies of great pleasures, passions, and triumphs. He may involve himself in a self-destructive, grandiose business scheme, or in a wild, lustful affair. A man either may despair or undergo a reinforcing of what psychoanalyst and mid-life authority Elliot Jaques calls "manic defenses" in the form of "unconscious fantasies of omnipotence and magic immortality."[7] A woman may think her husband isn't the "type," but one of the main characteristics of this kind of behavior is that it seems wildly *out of character*.

I have found that some men—about 10 percent of those interviewed—react so extremely to mid-life terrors that they actually seem to undergo a *transient psychotic episode* that may last up to two or three years.

Two or three years is a long time. Knowing that it's temporary isn't enough to get a woman through it. She also needs to know how to handle her own ups and downs, how to stay sane when she's living with a sickening sense of danger and imperilment and how to make the best possible choices for herself and her marriage.

I always emphasize the importance of not denying a reality, even when—particularly when—it is a disturbing one. If she notices that a man is "not himself," a woman should not look the other way. She should acknowledge that it's quite likely that he's undergoing a serious mid-life crisis that will have serious consequences for both of them.

When fifty-six-year-old Janet, a former dancer who runs her own ballet studio, came to see me, she had just finished selling off the entire contents of the home where her family had lived since her children were small. The first thing she did was show me the ad she'd placed in a New Jersey newspaper. It was heartbreaking: From linens to cutlery and pots and pans to furniture, oriental rugs, clothing, and jewelry, everything was up for grabs. For Janet, those possessions represented an entire lifetime. Why in the world was this elegantly dressed woman who moved with a dancer's flexible grace selling everything that was dear to her?

The answer was chillingly simple. Her fifty-seven-year-old husband, Victor, a research scientist in product development at a pharmaceutical firm, had been approached by an acquaintance with a product to market. This man had told Victor that with his expertise behind them—and his seed money—they would be able to attract investors and the thousands of dollars they needed. Victor, who had worked unnoticed and unheralded on staff for his entire career, without ever gaining royalties for any of his products, suddenly threw that familiar, behind-the-scenes role aside and went into business.

He'd applied for a patent and hired an investment banking company to help their fledgling operation get off the ground, all the while assuring Janet that they couldn't miss. Early on, Janet had felt uneasy; she had never seen Victor working so feverishly as he prepared the proposal he'd use to lure investors. It just wasn't *like* him.

But Janet had wanted to believe that Victor knew what he was doing, and she hadn't wanted to involve herself in their finances. That had always been his province, and he was so conscientious about it that she'd never worried for a moment. Of the two of them, she was the creative one who couldn't really be bothered to balance the checkbook or make decisions about investments. Willingly, she had handed this responsibility over to Victor. In this sense, Janet had played the little girl to Victor's father/protector. It had given her a secure feeling to know that he was the grown-up when it came to the finances.

On the night that changed the course of their lives, Victor had come into the kitchen while she was making dinner and told her that he had a confession to make; wildly, she'd thought, Oh my god, he's having an affair. But what he'd gone on to tell her seemed, if anything, worse.

It turned out that over the course of the preceding year, while Janet had assumed that Victor was signing up investors and accruing capital, he actually had been unable to raise more than a few thousand dollars. Instead, without telling her, he had borrowed against their savings and, later, had put up their home as collateral for a loan. The deeper in he had gotten, the more desperate he had become until he had thrown in everything they had—including her valuable collection of ballet memorabilia, which included letters written by well-known dancers and choreographers.

She'd been in a state of shock for days and weeks. All she remembered from that night was the sight of Victor's gray, drained face and the way he'd sat hunched over at the table, his hands folded uselessly in front of him. By the end of the next week, she found out that Victor had been forced to initiate bankruptcy proceedings.

When she told an old friend that she could think of no solution other than divorce, he advised her to "pull together" with Victor to get through the crisis. Janet had always believed in pulling together. Throughout their married life, she had supported Victor in career decisions and unfailingly consulted with him before making any major decisions of her own. Fourteen years ago, when she'd set up her dance studio (with her own savings), she'd made sure that her schedule coincided with Victor's so that they could be together as much as possible, and she'd put all the money she made into their joint savings account. Now her work was ruined, her home was ruined. She was shattered—and people were telling her that she and Victor must keep on trying to save the marriage.

Were her friends right? Wearily, Janet thought maybe so. Shouldn't she share in the blame? Why hadn't she stayed on top of their financial affairs? Hadn't she seen him huddled over the phone in his den late at night and overheard snatches of conversation punctuated by numbers? Hadn't she found scraps of paper scribbled over with figures? She had, and once, she had even asked him if everything was all right. Victor had said, Yes, yes, everything was fine. And she had believed him.

Janet was vacillating—it was more like *careening*—between disbelief and rage at Victor, and then pity for him. While she felt victimized and betrayed, she continued to be-rate herself for not stepping in. At all times, she was in a sinking mire of conflicting emotions.

"I can hardly understand my own feelings," Janet told me. "One part of me is suffering because *he* feels so bad and he needs me so much. Another part of me is so angry, I can't bear to look at him."

"Shifting between those feelings must be painful and confusing," I said. "You're angry, yet you want to comfort him."

"He's so much a part of my life," she said. "And I know how terrible he feels."

She hit bottom the day that the bank auctioned their home and belongings. She'd known it was coming, of course, but when bank officials showed up and started tagging her silver and her furniture, she plunged into the darkest moment of her life. "If you don't get me out of here right now," she told Victor, "I will lose my mind!" They spent the day of the auction aimlessly driving, but when they returned, strangers were still carting the final bits and pieces of their life out of the house. Janet sat paralyzed in the front seat of the car. "I couldn't even cry," she said. Victor's solution was to turn the car around and go out to dinner, but Janet knew she couldn't eat. So she told him, "If you want to go out to dinner, go. I have to stay here and deal with this."

On the day that Janet first brought Victor with her to a session, she began asking him the painful questions she needed to know the answers to. "How can this have happened?" she asked. "One thing I always loved and admired was your integrity. What's so terrible now is I feel I don't even know you. You lied to me and ruined everything that was precious to me. Why?"

Victor lifted his glasses by their frame and rubbed the bridge of his nose. His dark hair was sprinkled with gray, and he had a quiet, unassuming, almost scholarly look about him. "I felt a sort of hunger for excitement," he began. "It's as if I needed to take some sort of risk that I'd never dared to before."

"Was this the sort of risk and excitement you hadn't found in your work?" I asked.

When he nodded, I asked him if he'd been feeling restless and unchallenged at work. "I was on a treadmill," he said. "Research and development money for new projects wasn't coming in. I was at loose ends. I felt as if this might be my one big, last chance to *do* something. At the beginning, it felt great. I felt more alive than I had in years."

I could see that Janet was listening closely, trying to fit in this new image of her husband with the man she'd lived with for so many years. It struck me that Janet wasn't here solely to express her own rage and hurt (although it certainly would have been understandable if she had); more than that, she truly wanted to understand this man who was her husband.

"I want to tell you," I said to Victor, "that you're not alone. There are lots of men who go through a stage of life when they feel stale and in need of a surge of excitement. What seems to have happened is that you lost your perspective and your judgment."

"You have to understand," he said, speaking more quickly, as if he were once again affected by excitement, "how *up* I was. I imagined myself marketing this new invention and setting up a company for a breakthrough product. If we'd had the money..."

"So you'd always been a behind-the-scenes man before, but this time that would be different."

He nodded vigorously. "Exactly. I was taken over by a fantasy. I was a wheeler-dealer, a big player. I didn't think anything could go wrong."

"What made you believe you could pull this off?" I asked him. "You didn't have business experience before, did you?"

Victor shook his head and leaned forward. "No, of course not. But I always had this secret feeling that I could really make a killing if only I got the chance. I believed it. I still do."

"But," Janet put in, "what about when things started going wrong?"

"I didn't think anything was going wrong," he told her. "Until it was too late. Before then, I just kept thinking I'd get loans."

"It sounds as if your confidence in yourself got a little out of hand," I told him, "even a little inflated."

He looked taken aback and said firmly, "I didn't use sound judgment."

"Did you ever think of the effect this might have on Janet?" I asked this question not to make Victor feel guilty but to try to put together for all of us a truthful picture of his psyche. When he told me that he hadn't considered the possible fallout on his wife, I began to see Victor's narcissism as a part of his mid-life crisis.

Narcissism is a central contributor to the inability to make a good adjustment in mid-life. Its earmarks are a lack of empathy, a sense of entitlement, a need for constant approval and grandiosity. Janet had described Victor to me as gentle and sweet-natured, which hadn't jibed easily with her story of his recent actions. Now I could see that this *was* a part of Victor, but that it coexisted with another side: In his most secret heart, Victor had an image of himself as invincible, a guy who could pull off a risky but wildly innovative business venture that would put him in the forefront of the field. He had felt *entitled* to carry out this scheme, regardless of the effect on Janet. Even now, after his ignominious failure, it seemed that Victor did not entirely regret what he had done: If nothing else, it had been a thrill; for a few moments, he had been a player on a bigger stage. And throughout he hadn't considered the risk to Janet, until now, when he saw her anguish and confronted the major marital crisis his actions had precipitated.

This crisis became a turning point in their lives and in their marriage. Since Janet needed some time for personal recovery, I supported and encouraged her in her decision to rent a cottage for a few months in upstate New York. Leading to her decision was something that I said to her during a session: that Victor had been victimized by his need for power and excitement, and by his denial to himself that anything could possibly go wrong. Janet then had realized that she, too, had been a victim of denial; she had questioned Victor but had been too easily reassured. "I see that we were both

victims," she said, "but I don't want to be a victim anymore.
I'm taking my life into my own hands."

Explaining to Victor her decision to take some time away
from him, she said, "I'm not giving up on the marriage, but
I need to be alone and think things through." Victor said
that he understood, although he told her he would be lonely
and unhappy without her.

Even so, Janet was not conflicted about carrying out
the temporary separation. I encouraged her to stick to her
plans. "You aren't waiting for it to be okay for him," I
said.

"No, I have to do this, and he has to adjust," she said
firmly. And she spoke about her sense of herself as an *emotionally* battered woman determined to make a recovery. "I
have no intention of taking on 'battered woman' as a badge
of identity," she said. And we spoke about her idea of starting
a group with other traumatized women, who could share
their experiences and help each other.

Janet and Victor continued to see me through the spring
before the summer that Janet moved upstate. There was a
sweetness between them before the parting, a strong sense
of a loving bond that made me understand that this marriage,
in spite of the severity of the trauma, would in all likelihood
survive.

When I saw her a few months later, it seemed that the
tide within her was turning toward forgiveness. "I love him,"
she told me. "We have a history together. We have children.
All of this will get us through. I also feel that this crisis has
helped me grow."

There are no easy solutions for the woman who is married
to a man who goes over the edge in mid-life. (As I'll discuss
later, "going over the edge" also applies to the man who has
a mid-life affair.) But if it happens, a woman will need to
undergo an assessment of what the couple has shared and
what their life together means for both of them. At first, she
can realistically expect to feel a deep sense of betrayal and a
period of disillusionment. Most likely, she will be torn among
anger, guilt, and compassion. She will want to blame someone—herself or him.

It is likely and appropriate that she will also experience a period of mourning for all that she has lost—not just material possessions, if that is the case, but a loss of trust, shared dreams, and shared assumptions. But it is critical for her to keep in mind that even if she decides to leave a marriage after a devastating crisis, she will need to go with a sense of acceptance and forgiveness, not anger.

No one can tell a woman in Janet's position whether or not to stay in a marriage. A woman might feel too violated and betrayed by a man ever to feel comfortable with him again. (The worst part for Janet, which Victor eventually did come to understand, was not the bad investment but his *deceit*, the fact that he never *told* her about borrowing against their savings and taking a loan against their house.) Still, she must acknowledge and accept her own part in the crisis before she decides to divorce.

Janet made decisions that were right for her, such as moving away from her husband for a time, even when Victor didn't like it. Nonetheless, she never lost her compassion for him. It is fine to stand by a man, as long as a woman doesn't fall into the enabler trap. Even when his crisis pulls her in and brings her down, she must guard against taking the victim's role. For instance, the woman who sees herself as a victim may try to *punish* her husband. I warned Janet just as I've warned other women: beware of a power reversal in the marriage. "You now are in the position to accept Victor or condemn him, and he knows it," I told her. "He relies on your good graces. In the past Victor had more power in your relationship because you depended on him and accommodated him. Now he's so contrite that he's willing to defer."

"I've appreciated his being contrite," Janet replied. "But you're saying now that there's a negative side to that."

"Right," I said. "There are two things to keep in mind— don't be a victim, and don't use power to control and punish."

"I've always believed that you have a choice in life between power or love," she said thoughtfully. "I've always chosen love."

"If you confront your anger and find a way to come to terms with it," I told her, "then your decision to stay in the marriage is based on love. If you spend the next twenty years getting back at him for what he did, you've chosen retaliation, which is a kind of power. There's a danger that if you were the little girl and he was the grown-up before now, he'll be the little boy and you'll be the grown-up from now on—unless both of you want to change the underlying dynamic of your marriage. At this point, you feel a lot of justifiable rage. That isn't going to magically vanish. He did some terrible things that hurt both of you. He may not have meant to hurt you, but he did. You may have an unconscious wish to make him pay for what he did. But this isn't a solution."

Janet and Victor ultimately were able to make the kinds of changes necessary to the growth of their marriage. The *repair* part of the cycle, during which they talked through the crisis and its consequences, also included Janet taking some personal space in order to reevaluate the marriage. It is common for women in situations similar to hers to need to pull back, at least psychologically, in order to develop a clearer perspective on the situation. Once she knew she *could* survive without Victor, she made the decision to stay in the marriage.

This period led to *renewal*. Now the couple made a conscious choice not only to stay married but to rebuild their marriage on different terms: They would lead more independent lives—both would work—while at the same time *sharing* decision making, particularly on financial matters. With Janet more independent and less accommodating, and Victor more realistic about his limitations and aware of how much Janet means to him, they have begun again on a new basis.

As Janet put it, their survival of the crisis and their personal growth was a "testimony to our resiliency as a couple." It seems likely that while the blow they suffered will always cast a shadow on their lives, the effects eventually will fade.

THE MASK OF ANGER

When women ask why so many mid-life men become depressed or angry or out of control at this point in their lives, I point out that our society *teaches* men to construct their sense of self-worth on a foundation of earning power and status. No one bothers to tell men how dangerous it is to build one's identity solely on an *external* factor.

At mid-life, a man who loses a job or is demoted or who simply loses interest in his chosen work may be left with an aching void where his self-esteem has been. What is a man to do when the supports of his life collapse? The men I've worked with and interviewed initially responded with despair as well as unanticipated explosions of rage against fate, bosses, and, most unfortunately, wives.

Frank, at the age of fifty-eight, had opted for early retirement from the insurance company where he'd worked for twenty-five years. However, he told me, he hadn't really *chosen* to retire. He'd left because he'd no longer felt valued at the office and his pension plan did not reward further work.

Frank's situation is not unusual. More and more people are retiring from the work force at increasingly younger ages. Nowadays, the majority of American men leave the working world before the age of sixty-three. And the Bureau of Labor Statistics projects that by the year 2000, only one in four men over sixty will be working. Retirement appears to be expanding into a substantial portion of our lives, but a large number of early retirees are leaving their jobs before they really want to or before they are ready to face the emotional consequences and adjustments.[8]

"I loved my job," Frank said wistfully. "And I resented feeling forced out." Once at home, left to his own devices, Frank could never find enough to do. He had no hobbies, no interests outside of the work he'd done. (Even men who

have had outside interests tend to devalue them after retirement. "Oh, I just putter around with this carpentry," a man
might say. "It isn't real *work*.") When his wife, Bette, suggested
that he find some part-time work at the local library, Frank
felt degraded: He, a former insurance executive, shelving
books! "What a stupid suggestion!" he told Bette furiously.

He and Bette then went shopping for furniture to dec-
orate the new apartment they were moving into. When Bette
suggested mixing some interesting Early American pieces
with the basic modern decor, Frank told her this was stupid,
too, and insisted on having it all modern. When they were
choosing a carpet for the living room, he bristled angrily
when Bette, who knew quite a bit about decorating, disagreed
with his selection. "Why are you always so competitive with
me?" he asked.

Bette began to notice that whenever she was on the telephone for longer than ten minutes, Frank would start "cleaning up" in the kitchen, with as much banging and crashing
and swearing as possible, and would usually end up marching
in and telling her that *he* had to make an important call, so
please get off the phone. He would object to the clothes she
wore, the friends she saw, and even the way she held her
knife and fork. That time, Bette got up from the table and
walked away without a word.

When Bette, who is eight years younger than her husband, came to consult with me, I asked her if she could
pinpoint exactly when Frank had become what she called a
"bully." She thought it over and said, finally, "He's always
had a tendency to be critical. But I suppose it's worse now
since he retired."

When she'd walked into my office, I was struck by her
air of self-confidence, and when she told me she managed a
large real estate firm, I could easily imagine her coordinating
projects and handling people. It was not so easy to imagine
Bette's role in her marriage: that of target for her husband's
anger.

"It seems to me," I said, "that Frank is trying to control
you because he's lost control in other areas of his life."

It is very common for women in Bette's situation to feel torn between: bewilderment, anger, and love. Professionally, Bette felt secure and competent—while at home her self-esteem was taking a daily beating. She understood and empathized with Frank's anger and frustration, but she didn't know how to help him. Instead, she had become his scapegoat.

I told Bette that before she despairs, we should devise a plan. I suggested that instead of arguing with Frank, she should tell him when he was being critical and make it clear that she didn't like it. This works for some women, but Bette found it too difficult to stay detached enough from the substance of Frank's attacks. Instead we decided that since their new apartment had an extra room, she'd make it into her "sanctuary." Whenever Frank bullied her, she'd walk quietly to her room and close the door behind her.

Since she usually argued back when Frank attacked her, Bette had to make a major change in her own behavior. But she saw the logic of it: Once she stopped following his lead, he'd be left with no partner, and their unpleasant dance would come to a blessed end.

I find that when women walk away from arguments with critical, nitpicking mates, they are giving these men a valuable opportunity to reflect on their own behavior. If a woman's husband takes out his frustrations on her, she should create a room—or even a corner—of her own, where she can go when he picks a fight. She should make it clear that this room, corner, or perhaps the garden is *her* sanctuary. (When a woman says she doesn't have enough room in her house or apartment to get away, I suggest that she take a walk or a drive.) Even if she is in the middle of cooking a soufflé, she shouldn't hesitate to walk away from a deenergizing argument so that she can regroup and feel more relaxed.

Anger and hypercriticalness form a *typical mask of depression* for men. Since that is the way in which a man acts out his unacknowledged feelings, the worst thing a woman can do is get sucked into a constant round of bickering and blaming. Saying something like "I think that you may be depressed," "It hurts me when I see you like this," or "This is hard for me to live with" may help. It is better for a woman to tell her husband how his behavior affects *her* than to try to tell him what *he* is feeling. It's also useful to suggest seeing a therapist together.

Generally, my advice to "understanding" women who are tired of being their husbands' targets is to step out of the line of fire. If he takes out his feelings on her, a woman should not make excuses for him or minimize his effect on her (these attacks are real and they hurt); nor should she take the bait and argue back. When he criticizes her, she should point it out to him and tell him she doesn't like it; also, she should feel free to just walk away.

A FAMILY CONFRONTATION

One night, at a family dinner, Frank and Bette's grown sons, Ed and Tom, got up and walked away from the table after Frank had called Bette "dumb" following her expression of an opinion about upcoming local elections. Later, the sons told their father that they were tired of hearing him criticize and attack their mother.

At first, Bette was horrified by what the boys had done. A few weeks before, Ed had told her that he and Tom were upset by how their father was treating her. He had been angry, and she had soothed him, telling him that Dad was just upset because things weren't going so well since he had retired. Then she'd put it all out of her mind. But obviously, her kids hadn't stopped worrying, and they'd decided that things had gone too far.

After that fateful dinner, Bette felt fiercely protective of Frank, whom she saw as sad and frail compared to their sons. A small part of her even felt guilty; in the past, she'd always been able to make Frank happy. Why couldn't she do it now?

By now Bette had been in therapy for a few months and had become adept at sidestepping fights with Frank. But she was depressed because the problem obviously wasn't "solved."

"Think of your ability to walk away as step one in the process of changing the marriage," I said. "Now that your sons have gotten in on the act, use them to help."

Bette reluctantly agreed. After the incident at the dinner table, she was beginning to understand that she had a tendency to submerge her own feelings in her concerns about Frank. She also saw that she had been actively colluding with Frank in denying that he had a problem and that she and Frank had always colluded in his blaming stance toward her. The problem, and the collusion, had never been as extreme and obvious as they were now.

When walking away doesn't work, I sometimes suggest using a more extreme technique called *intervention*, which was originally devised for alcoholics and their families, and which I usually only advise as a last resort because it must be handled extremely tactfully. During an intervention, the family is advised to confront the alcoholic with the terrible ways in which he is destroying himself as well as the people close to him. The goal is to get the alcoholic to take responsibility for his problem and make necessary changes.

I've broadened this technique as a way for handling other situations in which a family member is denying that he has a problem while acting in a way that is hurting the people around him. If a man is depressed or hostile and attacking, or if he is behaving destructively by making bad financial decisions, for example, and a woman feels that she can't handle it alone, she should consider bringing in her family for advice, support, and help in confronting him. Using this technique can be risky if it is not handled with sensitivity and consideration, but I have found that enlisting the help of family or close, trusted friends can be an amazingly effective alternative to couples therapy.

A woman's initial problem may be admitting to *herself* that her husband needs help. Once she does confront it, she should talk to family and friends about what is going on and ask for their advice and help. This means going public, but in a dire situation, her actions may be justifiably extreme. She is trying to help him and save their marriage. The important thing for a man who is in the midst of a mid-life crisis is that he face his problem and, like the alcoholic, admit that he has been overpowered by it and needs help.

Once she understood her own collusion in Frank's behavior, Bette decided to involve two couples she and Frank knew in an intervention. (This was a good choice: The three couples had been a support network for years, helping each other out with baby-sitting and errands as well as celebrating Christmases and birthdays together.) All of these people, including Jake, Frank's oldest friend, had witnessed Frank's attacks on her. She called each person, explained what she wanted them to do, then met with them as a group to plan what they would say to Frank. They decided that each of them would speak for five minutes, and that all would cooperate in creating a loving rather than accusatory atmosphere. Then they set a time when they knew Frank would be home.

Jake led off by saying, "We care about you, Frank, that's why we're here. But we feel that we can't just stand by and watch you destroy your relationship with Bette. We've heard you criticize her and humiliate her publicly, and we are hurting for her."

"You have to realize that you are putting your marriage at risk," Donna put in. "I feel that Bette is being hurt, and that the marriage has become abusive. Bette will ultimately be forced to leave you."

Hearing these taboo truths spoken for the first time, Bette felt pain washed over by relief. Yes, Frank's verbal attacks were painful; yes, she would be forced to leave the marriage if they continued. But she was touched by the love and support that their friends were showing not only for her but for Frank. The group effort made her feel strong and hopeful that things could and would change.

Alan then voiced everyone's concern about Frank. "We feel that you have lost your direction," he said. "We don't blame you for your behavior. We see the pain behind it. If there is anything that any of us can do, or if you just feel like talking, you can call on us. We are your friends, Frank."

Frank was furious. He sat silently, then ordered everyone to leave. Bette's heart sank—had it all been for nothing?

For a few days, he barely said a word to her and when friends called, he wouldn't speak to them. But the fact is that gradually, Frank *did* change. After a few weeks, he volunteered, at Jake's suggestion, to work for a local politician he'd known for years, soon catching the infectious energy and excitement of a campaign. Before long, he'd made himself an indispensable member of the team, and Bette saw his self-esteem soar. His attacks on her came less and less frequently, and he even started catching himself when he was being a bully.

In our culture, people often feel isolated from other people, and interventions can be a way of setting up personal helping communities, networks of people who care about each other. Also, don't be afraid to suggest that your husband see his minister, priest, or rabbi for counseling or get professional help. Even if you think all of these methods will hurt his pride at first, you should know that the results are usually positive.

If a woman is an enabler, she may have a tendency to act as her husband's therapist. But she will need to control her helping impulses and to keep her good advice to herself. He must go through his own suffering in his own way, and she must *resist the temptation to try to make it all better*. She should share with him her thoughts and feelings about his depression and attacks on her, but suggest that he talk with other caring people for advice and support. Solutions can be found through medication, career counseling, or short-term therapy. Cognitive therapy, which helps depression by altering the thinking process, has been shown to be helpful, as has short-term couples therapy around the issue of a spouse's angry attacks.

If trying to solve his problems for him won't help, staying detached, waiting out his depression with love, will. He needs to undergo a period of self-evaluation and reflection so that he can experience his pain, learn how to grieve and how to accept his losses, and finally, how to find new goals and move on. This is his task.

Frank and Bette's story has a happy ending, but not an uncomplicated one. Once a woman succeeds in helping her

husband out of his depression and back into a healthy, productive life, she may suddenly find herself feeling deflated
and let down. "Am I crazy?" Bette asked. "Sometimes I think
that I actually *miss* the problem."

Bette isn't crazy. It is very common for enabling women
to feel a sense of loss when a marital problem is solved. A
man may be hounding her and carping at her, but at least
he's *involved.* When he stops, she feels a pang of sadness.
Suddenly he doesn't need her anymore. And she needs to
be needed.

If you feel this way, don't deny it or think you've gone
mad. But needing to be needed in an unhealthy way will
make your marriage sick and unhealthy, too. As Bette saw
so plainly and shockingly during the intervention, she was
being abused. And no one needs that.

CHAPTER FOUR

The
High-Risk Marriage

So FAR, I'VE TALKED ABOUT the kinds of behavior that make women and men vulnerable at mid-life. Now I will show the *impact* of high-risk behavior on *marriages* by developing profiles of marriages that are at particular risk for crisis at mid-life.

On their wedding anniversary, Vicky and Dan celebrated by going out to their favorite restaurant. After they'd ordered dinner, Dan smiled at Vicky, put his hand lightly over hers, and raised his glass of champagne. "To us," he said, just the way he always had on their anniversaries. Vicky nodded, and started to raise her own glass. The next thing she knew, she was fighting back tears. This anniversary, not so different from the others, seemed to have opened the floodgates to sadness, anger, frustration, impatience, and a strange excitement, too.... Time was flying by, and suddenly she and Dan were in their mid-forties—middle-aged! How had it happened so fast?

And what about their marriage? Somewhere along the way, it had become stale and routine. In the early years, there had been finances to worry about and children to raise; they had been terrific parents and good problem-solvers. Now, when they were alone, they had so little to talk about. Sexually, they were just going through the motions, and they never talked about that, either. Actually, Vicky felt far more involved with her work than she did with her husband. Somewhere along the line, the marriage had begun to feel like a warmed-over anniversary dinner in an all too familiar restaurant.

Who was this man she had married, and once loved so much? Who was *she*? What did she want from her marriage now?

Vicky put down her glass. Quietly, she removed from the fourth finger of her left hand the thick, burnished gold wedding band that she'd always felt naked without. She slid the ring toward the center of the table, near the vase of perfect pink roses.

Dan never took his eyes off her. "Vicky..." he said. "What are you doing?"

"I think," Vicky said slowly, "that we need to ask ourselves what we really want from our marriage." Looking into his eyes, she was touched. She'd caught him off guard, and he looked anxious.

"What do you mean?" he asked. "Are you saying you don't want to be married anymore?"

"It isn't that I don't want to be married," Vicky said. "It's just that things have changed. I want to look again at our marriage. I want to look at us. And I want us both to do it."

Both Vicky and Dan turned their eyes to the wedding ring gleaming on the table. Uncertainly, Dan rubbed the bridge of his nose, then looked at her. Vicky drew a deep, shaky breath. The future was uncertain, but now change was in the air. She looked back at her husband with fear, relief, and exhilaration mingling on her face...

At mid-life, things catch up with us. It's as simple as that. Suddenly, the familiar patterns of a marriage, a couple's most basic habits of being together, which we may have assumed would last forever, no longer work. Like Vicky, a woman (or a man) may realize it at an anniversary dinner, or while she's making a shopping list or driving to the store, or maybe on the day a child goes to college. It may hit her when she least expects it, but suddenly she realizes she feels bored and empty and purposeless. That moment of clarity is the culmination of a slow and gathering awareness that her marriage has lost its life. That is the turning point, and the choices a couple make now will determine the future of their marriage.

Clients sometimes ask me about the *particular* risk factors for mid-life marriages.[1] In my practice I see three common ways in which couples relate that will nearly always derail a long-term marriage, sometimes permanently. Knowing what these patterns are and facing them straightforwardly—before the crisis hits—is the best and in fact the only way to lower the risks.

THE DENIERS

A client who had just faced the bitter truth that her husband was having an affair showed me a cartoon drawing of an ostrich with its head buried in the sand. "That's me," she said. "Hiding from the truth."

Denial is the psychological equivalent of burying our heads in the sand. Couples often practice elaborate forms of mutual denial in order to avoid facing unpleasant realities. A woman, such as my client, may discover that over the years her husband has had a series of affairs. Sometime after that painful discovery, she may also realize that she colluded with him in his behavior by *avoiding* marital sex and not insisting that they address their sexual problems together. Instead, they had created the facade of a happy couple; their friends had believed it—and so had the couple themselves.

Because our self-images are often based on not seeing certain things, people sometimes agree not to see. Both partners *want* to think of themselves as happily married and well-adjusted. Mutual denial then gives rise to family myths, which are shared beliefs between partners that support the denial. Facing something—anything—which is at odds with their

self-images, or the images they have of their marriage, is
jarring. Suddenly, they are questioning things they don't
want to question.

Looking frankly at the myths of a marriage may be
disruptive to the relationship, there's no denying *that*. But
it's the first step toward restructuring a marriage that has
gone stale or become destructive to the partners. When a
couple decides *not* to look at their problems head-on, they'll
run a good chance of being hit by a crisis while they're not
looking.

That's exactly what happened to Rick and Lynda. Rick,
a magazine editor in his late forties, commanded respect and
even deference at the office. By paying top-notch authors
high fees to produce innovative work for the magazine, he
had brought style and wit to its pages, with acclaim and
awards following. He also enjoyed the perks of the job: the
wining and dining and traveling. Over the years, he had
become accustomed to spending a great deal of money at
work; after a while, the habit of extravagant spending spilled
over into his personal life.

Lynda, at forty, was the administrative assistant to the
publisher of a children's magazine, an interesting but low-
paying job. But, as she put it, "I never considered it a 'real
job.' I do it more because I love it than for the income. My
family was always comfortable financially, and I was encouraged to pursue work that was satisfying to me. I always relied
on Rick to actually maintain our life-style." Clearly, Lynda
perceived Rick as the breadwinner and intellectual and herself as a little girl depending on him for guidance and protection.

I waited for one of them to start talking about what had
brought them to my office. Finally, Lynda hesitantly admitted
that they'd recently suffered a financial crisis that was threatening to destroy their marriage.

"Over the past couple of years, Rick's spending habits
have been so ... extravagant," she said. "Things like a ten-
thousand-dollar stereo system. . . . I'd actually clutch my stomach thinking about it. I *knew* all along this spending was crazy,
but then I'd tell myself, Stop worrying, it's fine. Rick knows

what he's doing. To make it worse, I was running up bills on credit cards, too. And all along, we kept taking trips to Europe, we bought our country house and then we bought a new co-op. A year or so ago, I began to notice that Rick was upset when he was paying bills, but I kept pretending that everything was okay."

I watched Rick while Lynda was talking. Even in a carefully pressed gray wool suit, he looked depressed and defeated. When I asked him if he'd like to continue the story, he straightened up with an effort. In the set of his shoulders, I could see the ghost of the confident, powerful man he had been until recently.

"I guess you could say I'm in a state of shock," he said slowly. "I told Lynda I didn't think I'd be able to talk about it here. All I can say is I'm humiliated. I can't keep up with the payments we owe. I was counting on a big raise this year, but revenues at the magazine aren't what they used to be. We've been scaling down."

"And you blamed me for your overspending," Lynda blurted out. Her voice was hurt and angry, and from the quick way the tears filled her eyes I sensed she'd been doing a great deal of crying during the last crisis-filled months.

Rick didn't look at her, just took a deep breath. "I know I blamed Lynda. I always felt that she expected a lot, that I'd keep more and more money rolling in. Well, I always paid the bills because I was the one with the money, up until now anyway. But now I resent that she always made *me* pay the bills. We both should have been doing it and trying to keep tabs on our spending. I feel guilty for letting her down, but angry at her, too. . . . I just can't keep up the pretense any longer that there'll always be more money just down the road."

"I don't know who's to blame," Lynda interrupted despairingly. "I just know I feel betrayed. I feel as if I trusted Rick, and he let us all down. We don't even know if we can send the kids to college." Now the tears were streaming down her face. "I think I may want a divorce."

Rick and Lynda looked away from each other.

* * *

Deniers are people who live in a world of fantasy in which problems magically disappear or correct themselves. For years, Rick and Lynda were pleasantly distracted from reality; Lynda had ignored the uneasy flutterings in her stomach, even though that message from her guts had been telling her something important: that she was living in a world supported by credit and expense accounts and dreams.

In their original marriage contract, Rick and Lynda had agreed that Rick would be the indulgent Daddy who would maintain the family in a comfortable life-style, while Lynda would be the pampered little girl who would work simply for her "personal satisfaction." But, like so many baby boomers entering mid-life, Rick and Lynda were forced to confront an era of diminished expectations in which their old collusion disintegrated, much to their pain and confusion.

Unfortunately for Lynda and Rick—and for all Deniers— it took a crisis to shock them into a consciousness of their imperiled reality. Because Deniers don't face the problems born from their collusion, those problems can feed and flourish underground and finally overwhelm a marriage.

When Deniers are hit by a crisis, I explain the cycle of conflict, repair, and renewal. In order to begin the work of repair, which may last for months, it is important for the couple to take a one-day-at-a-time approach and deal only with *immediate* feelings without making any big, impulsive decisions about the marriage; next, they move into the renewal state of the cycle by taking the time to reevaluate and rebuild the marriage in terms of both partners' needs.

I make a point of telling couples in long-term marriages that they should not throw away their marriages before they're sure the relationship isn't salvageable. It is *very* worthwhile to invest the *time* to find out if a marriage of twenty or thirty years can be rebuilt. Almost always, I will sense a couple's relief at hearing me say this.

Along these lines, I suggested to Rick and Lynda that they consult a financial adviser on how to conserve their assets while they pay their debts. I also suggested that before they made a decision either to separate or divorce, they take six months of marital therapy to figure out how and why this financial crisis had developed.

They agreed to those measures, but I had the distinct feeling that Rick was keeping some of the bad news secret, and in fact, during one session, Lynda discovered that Rick had taken a bank loan for ten thousand dollars. I saw the blood drain from her face, and then she said quietly, "You never told me this, Rick."

"You never really asked me . . . "

"Okay. Tell me everything."

At that point, Rick revealed some other, smaller loans he'd taken and told her exactly how much they owed. For these Deniers, it was the moment of truth in which they faced just how bad things really were. There was little anger in this session, just sadness and the beginnings of acceptance. To build upon and reinforce this new, more honest way of relating to one another, I suggested some "homework" as a way to extend our sessions from one week to the next: Every week, Rick was to pick a moment when he felt close to Lynda, and tell her something that he had been afraid to tell her. I asked Lynda *not* to react, just to listen, and then to wait for our sessions to discuss these disclosures and her feelings about them.

In those six months of therapy, as they moved away from denial and myth toward reality, Lynda and Rick went through four stages: first, her disappointment, his humiliation, and mutual blaming; second, the realization that they had colluded and that neither was more to blame than the other; third, acceptance of the situation and an objective evaluation of whether they could rebuild their relationship on a new basis; and fourth, a sense of commitment to the work of rebuilding.

By the time Rick and Lynda reached the second stage, they had begun to take action. They sold their co-op and their country house, figured out how to finance their children's education, cut back to a more modest life-style, and spent quiet weekends together at a friend's house in the country far from the usual round of restaurants and parties. One night, several months later, as Lynda was lying awake in the country, she had a wild idea: There was a plain but nice old farmhouse for rent down the road...why didn't they rent it, pack up, and move there for a while?

She woke up Rick, and they spent the rest of the night talking. Both kids were in private high schools, and they would certainly resist changing to a regional public school and leaving their friends. But Lynda felt that it was time for the kids to face up to the family's new austerity budget. No sense in denying to *them* the changes in the family life-style they'd have to cope with.

Rick admitted he had been tiring of his fast-paced job, and it seemed perfectly plausible that he could set up an office in the house and work for the magazine as a contributing editor. And since the house was located near a university, Lynda thought she might be able to find work on campus using her editorial or administrative skills. They looked at each other and realized it would be nice to spend more time together, just the two of them, without so many outside pressures. From that night on, they began looking forward to and planning for a simpler, easier life.

They joked about becoming middle-aged hippies and "going back to the land," spending their time gardening and putting up preserves. But the truth was that Rick and Lynda weren't dropping out; minus the material clutter of their lives, they were able to assess their values with open minds and ask themselves and each other what was really important to them now.

Why were Rick and Lynda able to break their stalemate? For one thing, their marriage was not dependent upon the luxurious trappings they'd cushioned it with. Both were flexible enough to imagine a different kind of shared future. They could laugh about becoming latter-day hippies while genuinely enjoying the idea of moving off the fast track and starting fresh. Plus, neither was so dependent upon the collusive roles they'd played until now that they could not imagine giving them up and evolving new roles.

For example, since they accomplished their emotional and physical relocation, they deal with the bills together. Little girl Lynda takes just as much responsibility for balancing the checkbook and understanding their investments as her husband does. "I always assumed that Rick would take care of money matters," she said. "I wanted to believe I could count on him to take care of me." Now her fantasy of her husband as an endlessly indulgent parent has gone the way of all fairy tales. "I see that he's only human, and so am I. When everything blew up in our faces, at first I wasn't sure whether I loved a life-style or a person. Fortunately it turned out to be the person. We're in this thing together," she added. "I couldn't have accepted mutual responsibility a year ago, but I accept it now."

As Lynda faced her own part in the collusion with Rick to deny their financial reality, her sense of disappointment and betrayal waned. This is an important step: All collusions take at least two people. But the tricky part for women is a tendency toward taking *too much blame* for a bad situation. There is a critical difference between *acknowledging* a collusion and taking on the *burden* of blame. Later, I will describe how some women mistakenly blame themselves during a marital crisis in order to protect their husbands and their marriages. A woman's self-blame will always be bad for her *and* for her marriage.

For his part Rick found that he was resourceful enough to withstand a vast change and to flourish in a different setting. ("I love gardening," he says. "I must have been a farmer in a past life.") He was also tremendously relieved to give up trying to sustain an unconvincing financial fiction. He realized that he had always secretly depended upon Lynda to hold things together at home and take care of *him* emotionally. We spoke about how each of them had unconsciously wanted parenting from the other, and that in the crisis they'd discovered they had to function *together* as responsible, equal grown-ups.

A marriage based on denial is usually the most vulnerable to a very serious mid-life crisis because the crisis seems to come out of nowhere. Of course, that isn't true—the crisis is the legitimate child of the relationship and is born with all of its earmarks.

THE STALLERS

While Deniers are in the worst trouble—they don't see the problem until the crisis actually erupts—Stallers allow a bad situation to worsen because they fear confrontation, often assuming that acknowledging one problem will open the field to a swarm of problems that will be too threatening, confusing, and overwhelming to deal with. Stalling is a close relative of denial: Both arise from the fear of, and resistance to, change. Both come from a belief in magic: that avoiding a problem will make it go away or fix itself.

Roberta, forty-three, was a resourceful woman who tried to solve her husband's problems *indirectly* but eventually came to see the value of what I call "loving confrontation."

When Roberta's husband, forty-five-year-old Mike, lost his job as a mid-level manager at a New Jersey manufacturing company that was phasing out its operations, he was told there was a possibility that he would be rehired within a year. An active man who had many hobbies and who had worked all his life, Mike uncharacteristically decided to wait it out. Soon he seemed to lose interest in everything. Roberta, who had worked for several years as a special programs coordinator in a neighborhood nursing home, was shaken, too. She had a special sympathy for very vulnerable people, and every sympathetic chord in her body was now tuned in to her husband. When she saw that he was losing weight, she ran herself ragged fixing his favorite dinners even though he still didn't seem to have much of an appetite. For a while, he talked about returning to school to finish up an engineering degree he'd started years ago, but he never got around to making a move. Roberta said nothing to him, thinking she'd figure out *something* to help him.

The harder it became to solve Mike's problem, the harder Roberta worked to find the answer. For Roberta, there were no hopeless cases, only people who didn't get enough help. Everyone always said she had a magic touch with people; she could get anyone to talk and confide and feel better for it. But she found she couldn't help Mike.

As the months dragged by, she began to dread seeing Mike at night. She'd walk in, only to be greeted by Mike's bleak face and the endless drone of the television. By now, she felt in her bones that his company would not rehire him and that he needed to start looking for another job. She knew she had to confront Mike, but she feared it. She wanted to solve problems by nurturing, not by confrontation.

Sitting in my office, Roberta looked listless and depressed. She tugged at her skirt and crossed and recrossed her legs. "I don't want to live this way," she said flatly. "You know, sometimes I feel like taking the next train out of here."

I could tell that she had never put it to herself that bluntly before. We sat silently for a moment, then I said, "It sounds like you're awfully worried about your husband."

She nodded vigorously. "I am. I'm tired all the time, and I see Mike just letting himself go . . . "

"Have you talked with Mike about how concerned you are?" I asked.

"Oh, I couldn't," she said quickly. "He's so sad, I just hate to make him feel worse."

"It sounds like the two of you need to talk."

"I know," she said. "But he's not a talker."

I tried to reassure her. "In my experience," I told her, "a man like Mike might actually be relieved by getting it out into the open. You and I can start by discussing it here, and Mike can join us for the next session."

To Roberta's surprise, Mike agreed to come to the next session, and to her further surprise, a direct confrontation produced much-needed changes in their lives.

Until then, however, Roberta and Mike had colluded in allowing Roberta, a caretaker, to slide into becoming an enabler. Trained to help and to give to others, Roberta had taken an old role to an unhealthy extreme, overprotecting her husband until *she* had been debilitated by self-sacrifice and *he* had lost all motivation to change. It is possible for a woman to be *too* sympathetic to her husband. Tender loving concern, carried to an extreme, can be crippling, and in fact, it was only when Roberta became a little *less* sympathetic that she became *more* objective.

When Mike came to therapy with her, she told him that she loved him very much and was terribly worried about him but that she couldn't live with a man who had given up on himself.

Mike was stunned. Finally, he said, "I've never thought of myself as a quitter."

"You're not," she agreed.

"But I feel as if I've let you down."

"You haven't," she replied. "It's just that you need a job, not only for the money but to feel better about yourself." She hesitated, then added, "*I* need you to feel better, too."

Mike had always prided himself on being strong and dependable, and he genuinely hated thinking that Roberta couldn't count on him for financial and emotional support. In his mind, it just wasn't manly.

I suggested to them that they sit down together and come up with a list of people who might be helpful in finding Mike another job. When he said he couldn't see going back into management, we talked about his finding an interim job while he finished up his engineering degree. For the first time, I saw a spark of excitement in Mike's eyes.

Stallers who finally instigate crises keep some control over the situation and are not as vulnerable as Deniers to a truly shattering crisis arising out of the blue. (In the case of Mike and Roberta, a far worse crisis eventually would have evolved: exhaustion for her, despair for him, and an overall deadening of their lives.) A woman should not be afraid to be a troublemaker—by unbalancing and disrupting a marital collusion she is pushing her marriage out of its stalemate.

A collusion may make the couple feel safe for a while. But at this stage of the life cycle, this same collusion may confine both partners to worn-out roles and prevent them from solving a problem or exploring other aspects of themselves.

Couples should not expect to be exactly in sync when it comes to making mid-life changes. What I see among my clients is a more jagged pattern: As soon as *one* partner stops colluding in old roles and patterns, the collusion no longer works. But for the marriage to change and grow, *both* partners must acknowledge the end of the old collusion and start rebuilding on another basis. That is hard work and doesn't happen overnight. It is a *process* of change that unfolds over months and years.

Rocking the boat may be the best thing for a marriage if it pushes one or both partners toward self-realization. In the two couples I've talked about so far in this chapter, changes in one of the partners touched off changes in the other. Lynda shed her little girl role as Rick gave up being the all-powerful protector; when Roberta stopped enabling, Mike began defining new goals for himself.

Even though their marriages were at high risk, both of these couples broke their stalemates. But what if one or both partners refuse to change even when a crisis is at hand? While not many of us really *like* the idea of changing our basic habits and patterns, some people can't even imagine it. Here is what happened to a couple who dug in their heels until they had dug their marriage into a hole.

THE RESISTERS

It was their first couples session. Charlotte, an almost too thin blond woman in her early forties, graceful and feminine in a simple linen dress, sat stiffly in her chair, looking upset and confused. I felt that she was the sort of person who ordinarily would pride herself on impeccable grooming, but her hair was a little disheveled, and there was a flush rising on her thin cheeks.

"I don't know why we're here," she said so softly that I had to lean forward to hear her. "We have a wonderful marriage. We have lovely children. I just don't understand this at all."

Her husband, Will, didn't look at her. He looked at the floor, out the window—anywhere except at me or at his wife. "We're here," he said in the tone of a man who feels that explanations are futile, "because I want more from my marriage. From my *life*. It just isn't enough..."

I asked him if he could be specific about what he wished were different in his marriage.

"One thing I'd really like is if Charlotte and I could go away together sometimes. I like the idea of being more adventurous and doing things spontaneously. Just the two of us," he added. "But she doesn't see the need. She keeps planning family outings, the kind we've taken since the kids were small."

"But why *not?*" Charlotte asked immediately. "Why can't we do things with the kids the way we always have? As it is, you spend so much time at the office that you hardly see them. You should be spending more time with *them*, with *all* of us together."

Not noticing how frustrated Will looked, she went on to emphasize to him how important family life was. When he said nothing in reply, her voice trailed off, and she sat watching him, intent on his seeing things as she saw them.

At the beginning of couples treatment, I usually will see a couple together, then individually, then together again for however long the therapy takes. In his first individual session after our initial couples meeting, it became clear that Will had initiated therapy because he was thinking about leaving Charlotte. For a few years, he told me in an individual session, he hadn't been conscious of the problems; all he had known was that he was dissatisfied. When I asked him what sorts of things had bothered him, he thought for a moment, then said, "This might sound stupid, but last year I suggested that we go to southern France for our summer vacation while she insisted on Maine as usual. We've gone to Maine for eighteen years."

"So you found that Charlotte didn't want to make any changes in your way of life as a couple."

"She wouldn't consider it."

"Did you ever tell her how you felt when she wouldn't make changes in old routines?"

Will shook his head. "What was the use?" he said. "She wouldn't have listened."

I then asked Will a question that I always ask clients whose marriages are in trouble: Was he seeing another woman?

Looking me straight in the eye, he said, "Why no, of course not!" Because he seemed so genuinely shocked and offended, I was afraid that I was way off base with Will, especially when he went on to say, "You don't know me well, but you have to understand that I have traditional values and beliefs. I would never have an affair." Then suddenly protective of his wife, he added, "And I hope you don't ask Charlotte if she's seeing someone. She would be offended."

But the marriage continued to deteriorate. Will spent late nights in the city, never bothering to tell her what was keeping him out so late, while in therapy, he was increasingly evasive, distant, and preoccupied. Charlotte was confused and upset, but she still didn't believe that anything could be seriously wrong with her marriage and resisted any suggestion that it might need updating and renegotiating.

Then in one session, she mentioned the fact that Will had recently started working out at a health club. With a slight quaver in her voice, she asked him if he were "interested in anyone else."

Will sat straight up in his chair. "Absolutely not," he said indignantly. "Here's my datebook. See for yourself." And he actually thrust the book at his wife. Charlotte held it uncertainly in her hands for a moment, then passed it back. The long, intent look that she gave him said it all: Please, let me trust you. Please let my suspicions about you prove to be wrong!

One morning, before our next session, she called me. There had been unexplained hang-up phone calls at home. Did I think Will was having an affair? Without waiting for my answer, she asked, "Should I hire a private detective?"

I told her I thought she should tell him about the phone calls, ask him directly if he was seeing someone else and get her own answers. But it was clear that Charlotte had to do this her own way, so she went ahead and hired a detective. Then she called me and said that she didn't have all the evidence yet, but she had enough to confront Will. During the next session, she asked him flat out if he was seeing

another woman. And finally, Will, with tears in his eyes, admitted that he was.

"I'm not proud of myself," he said then. "I'm ashamed.
I can't believe our marriage has come down to this decep-
tion."

When she saw the tears in his eyes, Charlotte covered her
face with her hands. I thought for a moment that their mutual
sadness might unite them. But a few minutes later, Will drew
himself up and said that he wanted to move out.

Looking sad but relieved that the charade was over at
last, he quickly added that he would make arrangements to
move at once so that they could "get it over with." Charlotte
just looked at him wordlessly.

I suggested to them that they continue with therapy even
though they were temporarily separating. It seemed to me,
I told them, that they needed to give themselves the chance
to evaluate the marriage objectively so they could decide
whether to end it or rebuild it.

But the rupture between them had been sudden and
shocking, and both said it would be too painful for them to
face each other in this room again.

Throughout the sessions that we had together, Will had
spoken repeatedly about his need for excitement and companionship, for a shift away from a family-oriented marriage
toward a couple-oriented partnership, as well as his need for
a partner who understood the work he did and with whom
he could talk on an equal basis. *All* of these needs are a normal
part of a man's mid-life development. But Charlotte had dug
in, insisting on a continuation of the family focus, exaggerating her old caretaking role by trying to be an even "better"
wife, shopping for just the "right" ties, socks, and shirts for
a man in his position, and having new pictures of herself and
the children framed to display on his desk—outdated solutions for new problems.

Will knew there were problems in the marriage long before Charlotte did but hadn't been motivated to take action
until he felt stressed to the breaking point. The web of de-
ception and self-deception about his affair was falling apart.
But guilt and fear had kept him from confronting his un-

happiness, until it was too late for the marriage.

And even then, when he'd first initiated therapy, it seemed as if he were just going through the motions. In his heart, Will felt that the marriage was over, but he honestly believed that the right, moral thing to do was to give it his best shot. It was important to him to do the right thing. Since he was obviously a decent man, I was puzzled for a while about why he had lied to me about the affair. Why had he so blatantly made the *wrong*, immoral choice there?

Simply, Will did not see himself as the kind of dishonest fellow who would cheat on his wife. Coming as he did from a deeply religious background, he was ashamed that he had broken his marriage vows. But so much was changing—from being a man who had assumed he would stay married forever to a traditional woman, he had become a man who required a woman who was an equal companion. His lover was a woman in her late thirties who worked in his office; he was *excited* by her in a way that he was not excited by Charlotte.

Some studies show that at mid-life, men turn toward their wives for companionship, but Will couldn't imagine his marriage evolving toward a new level of intimacy. By keeping his dissatisfactions to himself for so long, only airing them in therapy, when he was already on the verge of leaving the marriage, Will had continued to collude with Charlotte in a shared fantasy of a happy family life.

After the separation, Charlotte came to see me one more time. Just after he'd moved out, she told me, Will had suggested taking both of their extended families to a restaurant for Christmas dinner. Interpreting this as a sign of his attachment to her, Charlotte offered to cook Christmas dinner at home for their families. Reluctantly, Will had agreed.

Charlotte then had spent days cooking and baking and fixing up the house into a greeting-card-perfect version of a family Christmas. She started to cry as she described to me the hope and anticipation she'd felt: Once Will had eaten the special traditional meal she'd always prepared at Christmas and reimmersed himself in the warmth and beauty of the home she'd made for their family (she'd built a fire in the fireplace and set up and trimmed an enormous tree with all of the homemade decorations), she believed, he'd realize his mistake and come back. And she'd forgive him and take him back and, together, they'd blot out the memory of this terrible time.

Beside this rosy picture, the reality was grim indeed. After the family left, Will put on his coat, gave Charlotte a quick kiss on the cheek, said good-bye to the kids, and went home to his new apartment.

Charlotte looked at me with tears shining in her eyes. "I've never felt so alone and abandoned," she said. "He's really gone. God help me, I thought all I had to do was show him what he was giving up, and he'd come back."

Will, of course, knew very well what he was giving up. Charlotte's problem was not being able to see that all of her loving would not be enough to save the marriage. She didn't understand what had gone wrong, and she still hopes that her husband will come back. I felt when she came to see me that last time that she would be too proud to provide another Christmas party like that one. Nonetheless, she's kept his den exactly as it was, not even moving the clothes he left behind out of the bedroom closet. Part of Charlotte is still hoping.

She told me she's spending a lot of time crying on friends' shoulders. She asks them over and over, "Why did he leave me?" No one can tell her.

Any high-risk marriage is vulnerable to one or both partners having affairs. In the next part of the book, I'll talk about the root causes of affairs, which are different for men and women. For a man, there are two possible reasons, or a combination of both, that will lead him to relationships with other women. The first is that the marriage has gone stale, as was the case with Will and Charlotte, whose marriage badly needed updating but stayed stuck in the status quo instead. Other men have affairs in direct response to their mid-life terrors; in those cases, a man will be fighting the softening process, instead of easing into it. Affairs, for many men, function as consolations for getting older.

SEXUAL
STALEMATES

CHAPTER FIVE

The Mid-life Affair

THE LARGEST NUMBER OF marriages that fail at mid-life do so because of a partner's affair. However, an affair does not necessarily signal the end of a long-term marriage. Certainly, it is a devastating event in a marriage, but many couples, often to their own surprise, find that they have the resources to rebuild. The cycle of conflict, repair, and renewal now can play a particularly critical role.

Men are still likelier to have mid-life affairs than women are. In fact, a very bad case of the mid-life terrors may compel even a man who has always been faithful to go to the edge sexually.

A man may feel a need to live dangerously, to push against the limits of experience. In Sue Miller's novel *Family Pictures,* the middle-aged husband recalls a sexual experience he'd had with a younger woman that had brought him to the brink of loss of control.

> He hadn't even liked her much, but he'd felt nearly out of control with an almost self-willed passion for her.... He had smoked dope with her, he had eaten peyote. He had danced wildly and without self-consciousness. He

had fucked her in ways he had never even wanted to fuck anyone. And while he was living through all of it, he felt utterly free, in a mean, desperate way. He felt it was the only reality—or at least the only life he could learn anything from.[1]

And indeed, all of the men interviewed for this book indicated that their mid-life affairs were motivated by an urge for *sensation,* a desire to experience life deeply and intensely.

It may appear that a man has everything: roots in the community, financial and emotional security, a loving wife. But suddenly, "everything" is not nearly enough. Now, without passion, excitement, and drama, he feels he has nothing. His wife may ask herself, her friends, her therapist, How can this man, whom she thought she knew so well, be willing to throw away the life they've made together? For a woman whose husband may seem to be the *least likely* man to have an affair, his betrayal is all the more shocking because it seems so out of character.

But the man who has everything has a mid-life affair because he is desperately trying to ward off a sense of numbness and staleness, as well as a sense of his own mortality and the fear that life is passing him by. He senses the shadow of decline on his youth; a voice inside him cries, "I'm not old yet!" For him, an affair acts as a *consolation* for the waning and loss of his young manhood.[2]

An affair with another woman can also rekindle a man's sexuality during a time when married sex seems to have lost its luster and settled into a dull routine. He remembers what it had been like to be a tireless and dynamic lover. In his mind and in his senses he can still vividly experience the erotic glow of those days when he could make love anytime and anywhere he wanted: the shower, the beach, the bed, or the backseat of the car. In those days he had assumed he would always feel strong and sensual and potent, but he had been wrong.

Now he feels that his sexuality is going to waste, and he resents it. At the same time that he feels cheated of the chance to allow his true sexual nature to blossom, he believes himself *entitled* to fulfillment. His wife may become the target of his dissatisfactions as he becomes convinced that she no longer appreciates his sexuality. He blames her for having this blind spot in her perception of him, and at the same time, absolutely believes that another woman will elicit from him the sexual response that his wife cannot or will not. His need for sexual redemption is so profound that his judgment becomes skewed; he may choose to have an affair with a woman who seems wildly inappropriate. Seeing her as his last chance, the final vehicle for the fulfillment of his dreams, wishes, and illusions, he will pin all of his hopes on her.

A wife who is becoming tougher and more achievement-oriented may make her husband even more uncomfortably aware of his softer, more vulnerable side. It is not uncommon for a man to reject his newly assertive wife for a younger, more passive woman whose worshipful attention makes him feel strong again. He basks in her admiration for his status and authority rather than confronting the blurring and softening of his familiar tough guy image. One reason that men in their forties and fifties are often attracted to women in their twenties and thirties is that they fear their own "passivity" and "tenderness."[3]

There is no better illustration for this dynamic than Donald Trump, who acted out every man's fantasy of what it means to be powerful and successful in our society. His story is a mid-life parable, with all the classic ingredients—only in a larger-than-life version. When Trump lost key aides in a helicopter crash in 1989, he may have felt his first intimations of mortality. Meanwhile, in a soft economy, we can speculate that Trump faced his own psychic softening as he saw his tremendous business empire begin to decline. It is intriguing to speculate still further and suggest that as Trump softened, Ivana toughened, shedding her role of dutiful wife and starting to demonstrate that she could become an empire builder herself. When Trump began having an affair with a younger woman he acted out yet another familiar fantasy when he fell on hard times: He found a dream girl, young, soft, and deferential.

There's nothing new about mid-life affairs; what *is* new is our understanding of how complicated mid-life issues are for men and how affairs are just one of several ways in which a man may try to deflect his mid-life losses and terrors. But while an affair may make a man *feel* as if he's recapturing his youthful virility, he is actually taking a costly detour around the important developmental issues of mid-life. Instead of doing his mid-life work, which means relinquishing the phantom tough guy side of himself, he plays with fire, in the form of having an affair, as a way to escape facing his softer side and undergoing the process of loving grief for the loss of his former self, which leads to healing and growth.

Some affairs break marriages; others strengthen them. For the therapist working with couples, the challenge is to distinguish between the marriages that will be ruined and those that will be renewed. For *both* partners in the midst of the crisis, the challenge is to avoid making any hasty decisions to leave the marriage while the affair is still going on.

THE AFFAIR THAT CHANGED
A MARRIAGE

Since an affair is a symptom of marital distress, as well as of a man's personal disturbance of the heart, it may provoke a much needed crisis that results in renewal of the marriage. A couple that ends up taking stock may breathe new life into a marriage contract that has gone stale. Jason's affair is typical of the affair that is a catalyst for the *rebuilding* of a marriage.

Jason felt that his marriage had reached a dead end. He had been married to Valerie for fifteen years; they had an eleven-year-old son. At forty-nine, Jason felt that he had "plateaued." From the high of landing a job as curator of a small museum eight years ago, he had sunk to a bored, restless low. And he and Valerie had reached a sexual low, a stage of sexual atrophy. As each joyless encounter built his resentment, Jason began to avoid her in bed. Alone on her side of the king-sized mattress, Valerie felt as if Jason was punishing her for something, but she had no idea for what.

One day, Jason noticed that Monica, a new assistant administrator in the office, was very attractive. She was in her late twenties, dark, petite, and demure-looking—very different from his tall, blond wife. And, while Valerie was elegant and sophisticated, Monica seemed naive and touchingly vulnerable. As his office subordinate, she looked up to him and drank in his every word. He reveled in being perceived as wise, strong, and capable and realized how much he missed this in his marriage. He became convinced that going to bed with Monica would make him feel like himself again.

He made up excuses to visit Monica in her office and go out for coffee with her. When it turned out that Monica lived only a few blocks from the museum, Jason suggested they go to her apartment for lunch. Soon, they were spending several lunchtimes every week in Monica's apartment, in her bed. He was thrilled by the secrecy, the complicitous looks during the day, the elaborate plans to leave and return to the office separately. In Monica's small apartment, with the curtains discreetly closed, Jason felt daring and young and vigorous. He felt defiant, flying in the face of all the rules of his, until now, strictly monogamous marriage.

On the weekend of the annual backyard picnic Valerie and Jason held for the museum staff, Monica and Jason stole moments together in the kitchen. For Jason, the thrill was in the illicit outrageousness of having his lover in his own home, helping his wife set out the hors d'oeuvres.

When Valerie caught them whispering in the kitchen, she ignored the jolt in her heart and filled the ice cube bucket. She didn't consider that he might be having an affair, but from then on, she began tuning in more carefully to Jason's moods, quickly picking up on his air of distraction and boredom.

At times in the past, when they had become distant from each other, she had responded by provoking marital minicrises, or, as Jason put it, by "picking a fight." Her technique was simple and energetic: Out of the blue, she would remark that they had been fighting a lot or that they seemed to be taking each other for granted. Then she would spring the question, "Should we split up? What do *you* think?" Always, Jason would say no, of course not, whatever did she mean? Then they'd air some of their complaints, which were always fairly petty, and for a time after the "crisis" was over, they would feel closer. But it never lasted.

Now Valerie tried her time-tested formula again. Facing Jason across the dinner table after their son had gone to his room, she asked him the usual question and waited for his predictable answer.

But Jason dropped a bombshell. Well, as a matter of fact, he said, he had been very dissatisfied with the marriage. He then admitted that he was having an affair with Monica, adding that he thought he might be falling in love with her.

Valerie listened in absolute shock. How could he betray her like this? And with *Monica*. Valerie flashed to the scene in the kitchen, and it hit her that she was probably the only person at the picnic who hadn't known what was going on. She wondered if her guests had been laughing at her behind her back.

Valerie was in a quandary. It wasn't clear to her whether or not Jason intended to continue his affair, and she didn't feel confident enough to demand that he stop seeing this woman, or move out of their home. The only solution she could think of was going to couples therapy together to save their marriage.

But when she suggested it, Jason hedged. He knew he wasn't quite ready to make a permanent break with his family; on the other hand, he and Monica shared the kind of passion that he couldn't imagine giving up. He also couldn't imagine telling Valerie that he had been sexually bored in the marriage for years; they never talked about sex, not even during those times of "crisis" when they were supposedly being open and honest with each other.

But Valerie insisted that they try therapy before giving up on their marriage. She sensed that family ties meant more to Jason than he might think, and this made her feel that the marriage was worth fighting for. And, if it wasn't, then she wanted to find out sooner rather than later. Finally, Jason agreed to go to one session.

In my office on that first day, Valerie was all business; clearly, she knew the stakes were high. Meanwhile, Jason was nervous, chain-smoking, and occasionally pacing to the window and back. I asked him to recall and talk about the best times in their marriage—a suggestion that sometimes helps people in troubled marriages focus on the positive experiences they have shared. Unhesitatingly, Jason replied that he had been happiest when they were first married and struggling to make ends meet. He had felt passionate and *alive.* "Over time," he said, "we've become more comfortable financially, but we've lost touch with each other. We hardly ever talk."

Valerie leaned forward in her chair. "Why didn't you *tell* me how you felt?" she finally burst out. "All I want is for you to be open with me."

"You say that's what you want," he said, "but when I tell you what I'm really feeling, you get angry or you start crying. And then," he finished in an exasperated tone, "I end up apologizing for upsetting you."

Like so many couples, Jason and Valerie were "conflict avoiders," which means they were threatened by all conflicts, from trivial tiffs to major fights, as well as by anything that might lead to conflict, such as differences in personalities, feelings, or points of view. For conflict avoiders, the problem, whatever it is, is never resolved because the partners' priority is to *reconnect* instead of actually confronting the issue. Usually, one partner—in most cases, the woman—will play the role of peacemaker; in this instance, Jason was the reluctant bearer of the marital olive branch.

"Looking the other way," "making do," "solving" problems without really solving them—we're all familiar with these patterns of denial, practicing them often without realizing that when we do, we are shortchanging our marriages *and* helping to ease a man over that dangerous edge. By provoking minicrises at intervals, Valerie had fooled herself into thinking that she was "solving" her marital problems, while, like many women, she was completely unprepared to hear her husband's true feelings about their marriage.

Over time, this conflict-avoiding pattern becomes ever more damaging to the marriage. Soon, the couple are colluding in looking the other way *whenever* there are problems in order to avoid the discomfort of conflict altogether and to maintain the illusion of a happy marriage. But when problems are denied and conflict avoided at all costs, a marriage inevitably will pay the price in staleness and boredom.

Because it was so important for Jason and Valerie to learn how to deal with conflict, I decided during their third session to provoke a "real" crisis. When Valerie got up in the middle of the session to make a phone call to the sitter who was to pick up their son after school, I asked Jason about their sex life. Was that one of the good things they shared?

Without a moment's hesitation, he shook his head and said, "It's just routine."

"Let's discuss this with Valerie," I suggested.

When Valerie returned, I asked her the same question about their sex life. "It's pretty good," she replied confidently.

When Jason said nothing, I turned to him. "Jason, do you agree?"

He grimaced guiltily, then told her the truth about his feelings.

Like many women of her generation, Valerie had never made love with anyone except her husband. Having no basis for comparison, she had assumed their sex life was all that it could be. Jason, meanwhile, had been disappointed for years but had kept silent, assuming that if he voiced his dissatisfactions, Valerie would be embarrassed and upset. Although this couple had trouble talking about all serious issues, sex was an especially sensitive area. (Jason and Valerie are typical; sex is still the most common taboo topic for couples because it concerns our most basic, primitive needs and is the most intimate part of a relationship. It is very common for couples to say they can't discuss sex because they don't want to hurt each other's feelings.)

By mid-life, when there is a *history* of not talking about sex, it is even harder to begin. But difficult as it is for conflict avoiders, breaking the silence is the only way to break the stalemate.

Even though Valerie was stunned to hear Jason's truthful opinions of their sex life, she recouped and started "fixing" things with her usual energy. She stocked up on expensive new lingerie and how-to sex books. When she wasn't seducing him, she was "hounding" him—as Jason put it—to talk about their marriage. "She thinks we can solve our problems in one weekend and tie everything up with a bow," he complained in my office. He said that her "fix-it" approach made him feel too pressured, and that he needed some space so that he could think things over. For this reason he wanted a temporary separation.

Hard as it was to absorb yet another shock, Valerie began to understand that any fix-it plan, no matter how clever or appealing, would have to fail unless Jason was as committed to the marriage as she was. She saw that now was the time to find that out.

Once Jason had moved into a friend's apartment, I saw Jason and Valerie in individual sessions. During one, Jason complained bitterly about what had gone wrong with the marriage. "Our relationship was fragile," he said. "It eroded when things weren't taken care of."

"Who was supposed to be taking care of things?" I asked, but he just shrugged.

"You aren't a passive person," I said. "You're successful at handling problems at work. But it doesn't sound like you've taken on responsibility for problems at home."

"I guess I really haven't," he said slowly. "I don't like to admit it, but I think I actually expected Valerie to take care of things. Maybe that was unfair."

Although she had been devastated by his announcement that he wanted to move out, Valerie actually felt an exhilarating sense of freedom once he was gone; finally, she had the energy and opportunity to explore her feelings. "I realize I've been most happy as a mother," she said, "not as Jason's wife. He always expected me to accommodate his needs and wishes, and I tried to do what he wanted." In a complete reversal of her role as victim in our first couples session,

Valerie now became adventurous. She went out to parties and away for weekends with friends; she felt so much more alive, she told me.

Jason, on the other hand, became morose and depressed. The thrill of the illicit affair with Monica was wearing off, now that he was free to see her any time. And his wife—now that *she* was less available, as well as obviously happy and carefree—was beginning to seem far more desirable. The major turning point for Jason was his realization that he was lonely without his family.

At this point, though, the consequences of his actions were a bit more far-reaching than he had imagined. It was clear that if Jason wanted Valerie back, he would have to work very hard to win her. He would have to *make* it happen. But it took Jason awhile to understand that even if it is possible to go home again, it isn't always so easy.

First, he told Valerie he wanted to come back, while admitting to her that he was still occasionally seeing Monica. "But it doesn't mean anything," he hastened to assure her.

Valerie wasn't buying it. ("If it doesn't mean anything, give it up!" she told him.) No longer so "accommodating," as she put it, she also told Jason that if he wanted to come back, they would have to make many changes. She laid out her terms: First of all, of course, he had to break up with Monica; second, he must agree now that if he ever cheated on her again, the marriage would be over. She went on to warn him that in a divorce she would demand their house and custody of their son. There would be no further negotiations or reconciliations.

Valerie acknowledged that, at least partly, she wanted to punish Jason. More important, though, she knew how easy it would be just to slip back into their old patterns if Jason moved back in. "We can't afford to take the easy way," she said. "I want a deep, thorough analysis of our problems."

I agreed with Valerie that this crisis in their marriage was an opportunity to look closely at what they had and at what they wanted from it. This marks the *repair* stage in the cycle that begins with conflict and concludes with renewal. At that point, the couple may find that the pieces of a marriage actually can be reassembled in a stronger and more cohesive pattern, although it may seem hard to believe at first that the *destabilization* of a marriage may be necessary before rebuilding can begin.

Now I could see that Jason was coming to understand how Valerie was becoming tougher and more articulate, determined either to improve the marriage or walk out.

As often happens, the affair had turned the tables of the marriage, and the "victim" was now in the one-up position. After Jason moved back in with his family, Valerie shocked him by refusing to hold their annual picnic for his business friends since all of these people had been in the know about Jason's affair with Monica. In the old, preaffair days, despite her humiliation, she would still have gone along with Jason's wishes; now she was asking herself what *she* wanted. It was clear to her that before she would "accommodate" Jason again by having his colleagues in their home, their marriage would have to be redefined.

"Can't we put this behind us?" he pleaded.

"I will *never* put this behind us," she told him emphatically.

Even though he insisted that *he* would be more magnanimous than she if the situations were reversed, Valerie stuck to her guns, and Jason eventually had to accept her terms. He also had to accept the fact that Valerie would be calling the shots far more often than ever before. Having initially sought consolation for his mid-life terrors through an affair, Jason finally chose to reinvest in his marriage.

If Valerie's big breakthrough after the separation was to learn that she could be independent and self-confident, Jason's was to see that it was his job as well as hers to revitalize the marriage. Women are almost always the emotional caretakers of marriages in their earlier stages, but at mid-life, this *can* change. At that time in their lives, men place more value on relationships, are less willing to make do, and are likelier than ever before to take responsibility for a marriage's emotional maintenance.

Like many men, Jason had reached a point where he simply *couldn't* live with the marital status quo any longer. His immediate "solution" to the problem was to go outside the marriage; however, a woman should be aware that if she can get past a crisis like this one, a man may end up ready and willing to share the work of rebuilding. Shocking as it may be for a woman, as it was for Valerie, this may be the most important mid-life turning point in the marriage. If a couple has been glossing over the real problems and issues in their marriage until now, a crisis of renewal will help prepare them for dealing with other serious crises down the road around the difficult issues of aging.

The Affair That Ended a Marriage

The case of Dennis and Cynthia has many of the same elements as Jason and Valerie's, but with some crucial differences. Both Dennis and Jason were overwhelmed by mid-life changes and acted impulsively. Jason, however, reinvested in his marriage, while Dennis made an overall decision to turn *away* from long-term relationships and initiated a pattern of continuous, short-term relationships. His experience exemplifies the affair that *ends* a marriage. (The marriage that is ended by an affair is one that does not have the resources to use conflict to make changes that can lead to repair and renewal.)

Dennis, a software analyst for a large corporation, volunteered to be interviewed for this project because, as he said, the emotional content of his life had undergone so many changes that he now needed to get a handle on it. At the age of fifty-five, he had admitted to himself that he had been depressed for several years. He had always been a good provider and an involved father, but once his son had left home and started his own family, Dennis had begun to feel the emptiness of his marriage. He and his wife, Cynthia, had routine, perfunctory sex once every few weeks that always left him feeling more disappointed than ever. Even when Cynthia complained to him that he always turned away afterward, leaving her feeling alone and abandoned, he still could not bring himself to hold her lovingly and fall asleep in her arms. He felt too resentful to be loving. Convinced that she lacked the sensuality he craved, he could not make the effort to tell her how he felt.

Both at home and at work, Dennis felt as if life was passing him by. He felt "enslaved" by conventions that dictated his behavior as a husband and father. One night he dreamed he was listening to other people talking and laughing and making love behind a closed door. He woke up feeling an almost unbearable sadness.

If not now, *when?* he asked himself.

As it happened, *when* was *now.* A while ago, Dennis had noticed an attractive dark-haired woman jogging past his house in the early morning. Suddenly, Dennis, who had never jogged, felt a surge of power, energy, and desire. Something about this woman made him want to get into shape.

He set out jogging every morning, just after she passed his house. One day she fell into step with him, and they had a promising conversation. Her name was Katherine and she and her husband had just bought a house down the next street. Her husband traveled a great deal on business, and Katherine, who did not work, was lonely and bored.

That was the beginning of the best—and the worst—two years of Dennis's life. He and Katherine soon began making love in Katherine's house, just a block away from his own home. At first, Dennis invented errands to run when in fact, he was going to see Katherine; then he didn't bother to create pretexts. Soon, they started being seen in public together; then, Dennis knew it was only a matter of time before Cynthia found out. But it was just this danger, this tempting of fate, that was so thrilling and addictive.

Soon, Dennis realized he was in love with Katherine; she made him feel strong and lighthearted and handsome and desirable. He felt godlike, as if nothing could ever go wrong again. This was the way life *should* be. This was probably his last chance for happiness. The next step was obvious. Katherine agreed that the two of them must divorce their spouses and get married.

Telling Cynthia was awful. She was devastated, and as she dissolved into tears, he was stricken by guilt. He realized that he loved Cynthia, but she didn't make him happy. Even when they were with other people, or on vacations together, she never seemed able to let go and enjoy herself. She was a good woman, but not an *exciting* woman. It was sad, but he was compelled to follow his instincts, which were urging him to marry Katherine.

Typical of women in her situation, Cynthia grieved and felt victimized. Then she realized that what she had valued in marriage—companionship and security—was at odds with Dennis's dream of excitement. Not seeing any way that they could reconcile, she soon sold the house and moved across town.

The first six months of Dennis's new marriage seemed like an extended honeymoon. Then Dennis heard that Katherine was having an affair. Having believed without a doubt that Katherine loved him as he loved her, Dennis was crushed. He had thrown away his whole life for her, and now she had thrown *him* away. He moved out of their home and for a few months withdrew into a self-protective emotional shell.

Unlike Jason, Dennis did not relinquish his phantom self and become more available for intimacy; on the contrary, he became less capable of forming deep attachments. Five years after breaking up with Katherine, Dennis never has a relationship that lasts longer than a few months—nor does he want one. When women realize that Dennis is not interested in commitment, they leave him. But for Dennis, the gratification of these sexual encounters with women whom he finds attractive and interesting has turned out to be far more important than the stability of a committed relationship. (His no-strings affairs also have the virtue of not interfering with the long hours he now puts in at work after a big promotion and salary raise.) After a lifetime spent in a passionless marriage, Dennis has had a breakthrough, a mid-life sexual awakening.

At the same time, Dennis, who was always a good father, has become very involved with his two-year-old grandson. "There are *many* satisfactions in my life," he said. "I have freedom and the kinds of relationships I want."

Looking at Jason's and Dennis's backgrounds helps to explain the striking differences between the choices they made: While Jason had absorbed the values of his traditional, close-knit family, Dennis had identified closely with his father, a charming but unstable man whose extramarital affairs were well known in the neighborhood where the family lived.

Ultimately, Jason valued his wife and family more than anything else while Dennis's priority was the reclaiming of his sexuality, the symbol of his vitality. Once out of his marriage, he felt "alive" again, both personally and professionally.

WHEN WOMEN HAVE AFFAIRS

It isn't only men who sometimes feel that mid-life is their "last chance" for passion. A woman may have been a good wife and mother, even as she felt as though life was passing her by. Like the man who goes too far, she may surprise everyone who knows her, particularly her husband, by heading straight for the sexual precipice, throwing all other considerations aside. Like Dennis, Judith found her marriage dull and passionless, lacking the capacity for satisfying deep needs that began surfacing with increasing intensity during mid-life. Like Dennis, she felt bound by convention and yearned for the personal freedom to explore her own potential.

Judith and Chuck, in their mid-forties and married for nineteen years, were well-respected members of the community, with a college-age daughter. While her child was growing up, Judith had volunteered her time as a tutor for disadvantaged children and organized summer programs for them in the schools. She gained a reputation as a tireless and resourceful worker as she continued over the years to organize community programs for children.

But when Judith became involved in the election campaign of a local congresswoman, she met Lou, the campaign manager, a big, hearty guy known for his passion for politics and women. A "good girl" all her life, Judith, who had married when she was twenty-four, would never have considered having an extramarital affair while her daughter was still living at home. But now she was intrigued: Lou was the opposite of Chuck, who was quiet and steady (and who had never shared her interest in politics and community organizing).

For the first few years of their marriage, Judith had thought that she might someday discover untapped sexual passion lying buried within her husband. But that had never happened, and she had resigned herself to a sexual relationship that was affectionate but hardly the passionate experience that she had dreamed of when she was in college.

College had been an exciting but somewhat daunting time for Judith. While her friends were joining women's consciousness-raising groups and talking about finding their identities outside of relationships with men, Judith had hovered on the sidelines. When friends had affairs, she had shied away from having her own. She had been intrigued, wondering if she were missing out, wishing she felt free to experiment. At the same time, though, she felt put off. Too much of what she had seen and heard about went against her own upbringing, with its emphasis on sexual fidelity and its strong disapproval of both premarital and extramarital relations.

Now, years later, after an evening spent working on a campaign leaflet, Judith and Lou went out to dinner. They talked for hours about the people they knew and the work they were doing, and Judith felt as if Lou could read her mind. At some point, a thrill, edged with a sense of danger, swept over her, and Judith began an affair with Lou that night.

The news seemed to get faxed along the office grapevine, and since many of Judith's coworkers knew Chuck, it wasn't long before he found out about the affair and confronted her. Humiliated, angry, but willing to work on the marriage, Chuck persuaded a reluctant Judith to come to my office for a consultation.

In that first session, Chuck told her he loved her and
that he would do anything to save the marriage. Looking
touched, Judith responded that she loved him, too. But
when Chuck told her bluntly that he wanted her to give
up her lover, she balked. "I can't give up something that
is giving me so much," she said. In a private session, she
said, about herself and Lou, "We're mates on every level,
sexually, emotionally, and in our perspective on the world."
She added that even though she and Lou had not spoken
about marriage or even living together, she thought she
should move out of the house she shared with Chuck and
find her own apartment. She felt, she said, that she'd never
been truly independent in her entire life, and that it was
time for her to establish herself.

Unfortunately, women often suffer for "pushing the
limits" of sexual behavior. Judith soon found out that her
affair with Lou had caused her to lose her credibility with
coworkers at the campaign office. Eventually, she dropped
out of the campaign and saw Lou only occasionally as he
became more politically involved once their candidate had
taken office.

Then, in an attempt to salvage the marriage, Chuck
contacted her, asking her to return to therapy with him.
He told her that he didn't see her affair as an obstacle to
working together on their marriage. Judith hesitated,
thought about it overnight, but finally felt that returning
to her marriage was not an option. She knew she could
never feel as stimulated by or attracted to Chuck as she
had been to Lou. The idea of the *stability* of marriage was
tempting, but not that tempting. Judith wanted to be on
her own, free to explore her sexuality in a way she never
had been before.

If most women reorient toward self-actualization and independence at mid-life, Judith went one step further. I believed that she was experiencing a profound, long-overdue
revolt against her conventional upbringing. Finally, at mid-
life, all of the desires and yearnings that had been suppressed
her whole life suddenly erupted, and her marriage was a
casualty of the explosion.

Like Dennis, Judith feels comfortable with the choice she made, even though so many of her friends and colleagues judged her behavior as "outrageous." Resourceful as ever, she found a job in public school administration and feels that she's finally gained the independence that she never had.

Women like Judith are unusual. Since our society does not celebrate the desirability of women over forty (despite the lip service now being given to attractive older women in the media), women tend to be less confident about their bodies than men are. Historically, men have asserted maleness through their sexuality while women have asserted femaleness through nurturance and caretaking. Most women in long-term marriages have been trained to preserve marriage, so having an affair means that a woman is sacrificing her wifely identity for a purely sexual identity. Unlike the man who is having an affair, the woman who does so is breaking a lingering and still powerful taboo.

The Transitional Affair

Even while the taboos linger, increasing numbers of mid-life women are becoming more independent in the working world, with more *opportunities* to have affairs than ever before. I have found that one difference between women and men who have these options is that while a woman may be *tempted,* she is less likely than a man to act on impulse, and, even if she does, she probably will not allow her affair to break up her marriage. When she sees that an affair is endangering her marriage, a woman will usually choose to end the affair and preserve the marriage.

Leslie, typical of many mid-life women who have affairs, had what I call a *transitional* affair. By making her feel vital and attractive, it helped to build her self-confidence. Armed with these strong, healthy feelings, she then had the impetus she needed to *go back to* her marriage and work toward its renewal. (As we'll see later, women also use transitional affairs to help them feel prepared to *leave* a marriage.)

When she was a young wife, Leslie, who has been married for twenty-two years, could never have imagined straying from her husband, Dave, whom she had considered her "romantic ideal." He had wooed her with flowers and dinners and gifts, proposing to her beneath a flowering cherry tree in Riverside Park. In the first few years of their marriage, he had taken her on surprise vacations, and after a while, as his income continued to increase, bought a beautiful home in the suburbs of New York City for them, which Leslie had furnished with antiques.

But when she was forty-six and Dave was fifty-five, Leslie began feeling restless. In contrast with the romantic high of their early years, she and Dave now rarely had sex, and she felt, too, as if Dave had stopped appreciating her. Even when she dressed up on the few occasions that they went out, he never commented on her appearance. She was afraid she'd become too old to be attractive.

Other things had changed, too: Dave was slowing down at work and making fewer commissions, while Leslie felt her own career clock ticking away; if she was going to find work she liked, it was now or never.

Leslie decided to start her own catering business. She took out a bank loan and, after she'd begun to get her business off the ground, joined a health club. She had never felt—or looked—better in her life. Then, when a man for whom she had catered a business luncheon asked her out for dinner, she accepted. Dave was out of town at a sales meeting, and there seemed to be no reason not to go.

Leslie and Robert struck an immediate rapport. When they saw each other again, the attraction deepened, and they began having an affair. It lasted a little less than a month. Leslie felt that her newfound independence and business ventures were already taxing her marriage, and the bottom line was, she didn't see the sense of putting any further strain on it.

At the same time, she said, "The affair gave me the confidence to stand up for what I wanted in the marriage. We've started discussing our sex life, what we both want and need from each other. I wanted some of the old romance, and I wanted Dave to appreciate me. I love hearing that I look sexy and attractive."

Leslie also found out that Dave needed reassurance; he needed her to initiate sex more often so that he felt desirable, too. "I know I wouldn't have another affair," Leslie said, "because I'd be evading intimacy. Working it out with Dave may be harder in some ways, but I don't want to start pulling the threads out of our marriage now. I think the marriage can become far more satisfying for me than having encounters with men I don't really know."

THE MIDDLE GROUND

If a couple chooses to stay and rebuild their marriage after an affair (as well as other crises), they will both need the patience, understanding, and determination first to identify the issues that have stalemated them and then to find what I call the middle ground, the right balance between closeness and autonomy for them.

Some couples, such as Jason and Valerie, do find a middle ground after an affair. The middle ground in a mid-life marriage is different than it is for younger marriages in that it must be able to accommodate a greater degree of independence for women. Valerie realized, after Jason moved out, how hard she had been working to keep the marriage together. Once on her own, she gained a new perspective: In the past, she'd always felt she *had* to be married; now she saw that she had a terrific support network of friends and that she would do quite well on her own if she had to. When she and Jason decided to move beyond his affair and rebuild their marriage on a new basis, she knew that she wanted a greater degree of autonomy for herself, and at the same that she wanted to share the work of the marriage with Jason. When Jason seemed ready to accommodate those changes, she felt confident that re-building could take place.

For Judith and Dennis, however, there was no middle ground between total enslavement—which was how they experienced their marriages—and total freedom, which meant answering to no one and discarding the conventions they had always felt bound by.

Even though some studies suggest that as many as 37 percent of married men and 29 percent of married women have had at least one extramarital affair,[4] other studies have shown a surprisingly high level of faithfulness among married couples.[5] The statistics are confusing, but fidelity may be the choice for more of today's couples who have a heightened awareness of the potentially damaging physical and emotional consequences of affairs. One long-married, faithful husband laughingly reported that he thought about having affairs "maybe five or six times a day, particularly if I'm in a cranky mood. Sometimes when I'm on a business trip, I see a woman and think, 'Gee, wouldn't it be great.' It's a general sexual excitement. But I can't imagine actually breaking the contract of fidelity between myself and my wife. It would hurt us in too many ways."

These days, many couples are placing a high premium on sexual monogamy, creating a foundation of trust that allows for more independence for each partner. A friend of mine named Laura has always enjoyed an independent life, traveling on business all over the world, and having her own set of friends and interests apart from those she shares with her husband, Joe. "Even though we spend a lot of time apart, faithfulness is a requirement for us," she said. "In return for that, what we get from and give each other is very special." Laura and Joe have found their middle ground in which their various needs for intimacy and independence can be met.

At mid-life, along with a career time clock, many people experience a monogamy "clock." One couple in their mid-forties, who had colluded in "looking the other way" from each other's affairs, finally made a conscious decision to reinvest exclusively in each other. "I sensed that the marriage could no longer tolerate the strain of our relationships with other people," the wife said. "I felt that we had never given each other the chance to become intimate, and that if we didn't commit to each other now, we never would."

Now that "older" women are getting "younger" every day, women are more likely to look for romance and sexual satisfaction outside of marriages that have gone stale. The impulse is understandable, but the risk is great. Even those happily married women who have managed ongoing affairs for years are playing with fire because, now more than ever, couples need to reshape their marriages to accommodate new needs and priorities. It can be far more daring and exciting to work out a new marriage contract than it is to plunge into an affair that is likely to end in its own kind of stalemate.

THE SEXUAL BAROMETER

It is critically important for a couple to "take a reading" of their sex life. "Our sex life has fallen way off," a client named Larry told me. "When I approach Ginny, she usually says she doesn't feel like it. We've become very distant."

When a couple does not pay attention to their sex life, they will almost always end up paying a price. It came as a shock to Ginny to learn that Larry felt not only rejected but unattractive and undesirable, too. Since men become sensitive about sexual potency at mid-life, a marriage is at risk if a couple's sex life has atrophied. Taking a reading of their sexual barometer means that a couple puts aside the time to ask themselves and each other (and they can do this at home just as easily as in a therapist's office) such questions as: Do we have sex regularly? Does one of us initiate most of the time? Does one of us say no more often than the other? Do we have sexual variety? Are we spontaneous?

Jason, Dennis, and Judith, as well as having the urge to live dangerously, were in marriages that were not meeting their sexual needs. But if each partner instead chooses to take active responsibility for reinvigorating the marriage, most mid-life affairs can be turning points, not endings.

CHAPTER SIX

From Victim to Survivor

AFTER A HUSBAND'S AFFAIR

IN THE 1987 FILM *MOONSTRUCK*, an older married woman knows that her husband is having an affair. She puzzles over why he is doing it and asks people for their opinions, to no avail. But she wants to understand, she is searching for wisdom, so she keeps asking. Finally, a middle-aged man tells her that her husband is being driven by his own fear of death. Aha! Now she understands.

In truth, the underlying motivation for most mid-life affairs does stem from a sense of mortality and vulnerability and can lead both women and men to seek feelings and experiences far beyond the parameters of everyday reality. But, since it is usually a husband's affair that will end a marriage (for, as we've seen, a woman's is more likely to be transitional), I will focus here on women who go on, after their husbands' affairs, to rebuild their marriages and their lives.

AFFAIR AFTERSHOCK

For a number of reasons, a sexual betrayal at mid-life may be more wounding to a woman's sense of self than anything she has experienced before. First, she may be dealing with her own mid-life losses. Maybe she has started exercising to compensate for the physical changes in her face and body, but still, a sexual rejection seems to confirm all her worst fears that she is no longer "womanly" enough to hold on to her man.

Second, a betrayal at mid-life comes just as a woman is starting to create a new identity and self-image. As she shifts her attention and energy away from family toward self-fulfillment, she is not always sure of her direction. She may feel a bit uncertain and vulnerable as she gropes her way toward a new focus in her life.

If she *is* becoming more autonomous, she may feel that her husband is punishing her through his affair. On an unconscious level, she may believe that because she is no longer the loving caretaker she once was, she has gone astray and deserves to pay a price for her hard-won autonomy. On the other hand, if she is a traditional woman who has not shifted her focus away from her family, she may feel she is being punished for *that*.

In either case, she feels mistreated and abused. She feels like a victim.

THE MID-LIFE AFFAIR AND POSTTRAUMATIC STRESS DISORDER

This disorder was first identified as a diagnostic category to describe the devastating emotional aftermath for soldiers who had survived the Vietnam War. By now the definition has been broadened to include the reaction of survivors to any event that is *unusually* traumatic—beyond the effects of normal bereavement, illness, business losses, or routine marital conflict. Sadly, I have found in my clinical practice that the responses of mid-life women to their husbands' affairs often bear many of the distressing earmarks of the posttraumatic stress disorder.

A woman is experiencing this disorder after a husband's mid-life infidelity when she endlessly relives the event and the sense of betrayal and humiliation she has suffered. She may startle easily, have trouble sleeping and experience recurring nightmares, as well as experience a persistent sense of numbness and detachment from other people. And all of those symptoms may intensify if she is directly reminded of the event. Sometimes a woman continues over time to feel like a victim, incapable of regaining control of her life.

Eventually, a woman either will accept an identity as a victim or evolve as a healthy survivor. The victim will continue to identify with the sensibility of the abused woman who feels helpless and powerless. She doesn't understand the reasons behind her husband's affair, and her low self-esteem leads her to blame herself.

Feeling victimized is normal and understandable at first. But assuming the victim's role as a badge of identity will keep a woman from resolving the crisis in her marriage. A client of mine named Rachel knew that her husband had a mistress, but felt she had to make do with a bad situation, choosing not to rock the boat.

Rachel felt as if the affair was her fault to begin with: "I know I'm not as pretty as I used to be," she said. "I've gained weight." She also feared that if she confronted him with what she knew, he'd leave her for the other woman, so instead she colluded with him in maintaining silence about the affair. Once, she complained to him that he was never at home and the kids missed him, but afterward, she was afraid that she'd said too much, even though she hadn't even hinted at the affair.

In the hope that he'd voluntarily give up his other life Rachel turned her attention toward making her husband happy at home. She cooked elaborate dinners and threw herself into entertaining her husband's business associates. She organized family outings so that he would appreciate the closeness and inviolability of family ties, and she bought an exercise bicycle and tried to lose weight. Meanwhile, she had her fingers crossed, wishing and hoping he'd come back to her.

Wishing and hoping won't make him come back or break a stalemate. Nor will suffering and self-blame. Figuring out how to be a survivor, not a victim, will.

A man's mid-life affair is usually a time-limited crisis, and there are ways a woman can survive without compromising herself. In previous chapters we've seen how a devastating event in a marriage can become a crisis of renewal, an opportunity to relinquish phantom selves and outmoded patterns of relating to each other. Now I will show the ways in which a couple can rebuild their marriage once an affair is over.

There is no right or wrong way for surviving and thriving during and after an affair. In my office, I've seen two kinds of survivors—those who wait out the crisis and those who confront it—but how any woman chooses to act will depend on her individual style.

WOMEN WHO WAIT

At first glance it seemed that Emily, like Rachel, had chosen the victim's role. However, unlike the *victim*, who tries to wish the situation away, the *survivor* will face reality and take steps to reinforce her own strengths and, eventually, to rebuild her marriage on a different basis.

Over a period of months, several nights every week, Emily's fifty-one-year-old husband, Paul, had been coming home very late and going to the office most weekends, claiming that the case he was working on would either make or break his career. Emily had uneasily accepted this story, until a friend of hers who worked in the same law firm as Paul told Emily that he was having an affair with Rita, an up-and-coming young associate in the firm.

A few days later, Emily quietly told Paul that she suspected he was having an affair.

"You're imagining things," Paul told her abruptly. "I'm working. Do you think I *want* to spend my whole life working? This is my *career*, this is *important*. I need your support, Emily, and instead I feel like you're cutting me down."

Emily said, "Paul, you know I've always supported your career."

But Paul ended the discussion by telling her he had to get to work, he was late already, making her feel even guiltier.

Unlike Jason, who "confessed" his affair with Monica and brought the marital crisis to a head, Paul denied *his* affair and defended himself by taking the offensive. Like many women in this situation, Emily then began to doubt herself and backed down. She reminded herself that Paul had never had affairs before now, nor had he ever given her cause to distrust him, so maybe she was being paranoid. It actually seemed preferable to think she was imagining things than to think he might be betraying her *and* lying about it. And it stung to hear him say she wasn't being supportive; she'd stood behind him through many career ups and downs. By saying this, Paul had attacked her at her most sensitive point. Since Emily defined herself in terms of her nurturing qualities, she now had to wonder if in fact she had failed.

Uncertainly, Emily called her friend at the law firm: Was she *sure* that Paul was having an affair? Her friend told her that everyone knew about Paul and Rita. The next day, desperate to save the marriage, she told Paul she was willing to see a couples therapist to discuss their problems. They didn't seem to be communicating very well, and maybe a therapist could help them get in touch with each other again.

"You have no idea how busy I am," Paul snapped at her. "I don't have a minute free in my schedule to see a therapist." He then upped the ante still further by informing her coldly that he was going away for the weekend.

Stung, Emily pulled back again and decided to come into therapy on her own. On her first day in my office, she said, "Paul attacks me whenever I suggest there's anything wrong in our marriage. But I'm a very patient person. I feel that I can wait out the affair because I believe that Paul will eventually realize that our marriage is the priority." She sensed, she said, that Paul "just wasn't himself," but that he would "get over it."

For Emily, the bottom line was that she was simply not prepared to rebuild her life as a single woman at the age of forty-eight. So, thinking of the affair as a temporary aberration made her daily life tolerable, although just barely. She told me that she was trying to focus on memories of the good things they'd shared—their children, their home, the wonderful vacation they'd taken the year before.

Since her children were getting older, involved with their teenage friends and rarely at home, one of the first things I suggested to Emily was that she make plans for herself in the evenings so that she wasn't sitting by the window waiting for Paul to come home. A look of dismay crossed her face: Who in the world would she see in the evenings? she asked me. All of her married friends would be at home with their families.

Emily's initial panicked reaction to the idea of making her own plans in the evenings is typical for the woman who is *overidentified with* and *overdependent upon* her marriage. Valerie initially had felt the same panic when Jason had moved out, but had soon found out just how rewarding it was to develop a life independent of her marriage. When I told Emily about the experiences of other women in her situation, she looked reassured and said that in fact she did have single women friends as well as married friends who would certainly be available for dinner without their spouses once in a while. Emily began setting up dates.

Unlike Rachel, who devoted herself to making her husband as comfortable as possible at home in the hope that he would end his affair and come back to the marriage, Emily focused on *herself*, on her own needs. She began to consider returning to school for her master's degree in genetic counseling. Taking the kinds of steps that helped to build her personal autonomy served as a hedge against the possibility of her marriage collapsing; it also strengthened her to make further changes at home.

Now Emily decided to move out of the master bedroom into the spare bedroom. When a startled Paul asked her why, she told him, "Since we aren't living like married people anymore, I don't feel comfortable sleeping in bed with you." She told me that Paul hated this new arrangement, and we discussed the fact that he seemed to want it both ways: to have a wife *and* the freedom to do as he pleased.

One weekend, while Paul was out of town for another business meeting, Emily called his hotel room on a hunch. When a woman answered, she hung up, knowing that the situation finally had come to a head. When Paul came home, she told him, bluntly, "I know you're having an affair with Rita, Paul. Stop lying to me about it." At that moment, Paul caved in and confessed.

Not surprisingly, it wasn't long before Paul's affair with Rita burned out. At first, Emily was awash with relief. Paul was being attentive to her again, wooing her with flowers and gifts, and on their anniversary, he took her to the Rainbow Room in Manhattan for dinner and dancing; when they went to bed together that night, for the first time in months, she reveled in their emotional and sexual reunion. But suddenly, while they were making love, she thought, "But this is just what he was doing with Rita!" Without warning, tears and anger surfaced.

After that, Emily became conscious of the need to make Paul pay for what he had put her through. She was gratified by his apologies and thoughtfulness, and she was aware that she loved being courted by her own husband, but often she was either angry or depressed. If she happened to see lovers clinging to each other on the street, she would flash to Paul and his pretty young lover and experience a sharp, stabbing pain in her heart. She had trouble sleeping and found herself reliving in the darkest hours of the night the hurt and humiliation she'd experienced. Often, she wanted to punish Paul, and she would be cold and withdrawn.

She forced herself to sign up for courses at the university, but her self-esteem was so low that she couldn't imagine ever succeeding at anything. Deep down, she believed that if she had been a good enough wife, Paul would never have left her, even temporarily, for someone else. On the other hand, she was furious at him for devaluing her and their marriage.

Finally, a year after the affair ended, Emily broke the stalemate by suggesting that they attend marriage-enrichment workshops at the local YWCA, and when Paul went with her on the first night, she felt hopeful for the first time in months. They heard from other people in the group that many men go to extremes when confronted with the aging process. Listening to those stories, Emily saw clearly that Paul's affair had been a reflection of his distress over getting older and his insecurity about his place in a law firm in which most of the other partners were younger. Winning the case he had been working on had rewarded him with the respect he'd felt had been lacking before. Rita's understanding of his work situation, as well as her admiration for his expertise, had bolstered his ego and provided him with a source of energy.

Emily also came to see that while the aftereffects of the affair might reverberate for years to come, her symptoms were normal and natural for a person who has suffered an unusual trauma. A woman's decision to wait it out is usually a positive sign for the marriage; by doing so, she demonstrates the strength of their bond. However, if a couple is to go on from there, the husband's appreciation for the pain his wife has endured must equal the patience and understanding she showed while the affair was still going on.

Emily and Paul started out as Resisters, a couple refusing to give up outmoded phantom selves and a phantom marriage. But Paul went on to learn about the work he had to do if he wanted to feel better about himself and his marriage: "I really didn't know what I was doing when I had the affair," he said, "and I don't feel good about it. I just knew I felt dissatisfied with my life, but I couldn't talk about it. We had gotten out of the habit of talking. Now I know we have to."

Emily had already begun her self-fulfillment work when she decided to pursue new friendships and graduate studies. By going *outside* her marriage, she became stronger *inside* herself and better able to deal with the potential loss—or renewal—of her marriage. (I always present the cases of Emily and Rachel to women clients who are in similar situations: Emily builds her resources and is able to deal with *any* outcome, while Rachel hides her head in the sand and hopes for the best. The wiser choice is clear!)

Also, from the beginning Emily had shown the wisdom of the survivor who knows that her patience and determination will outlast a time-limited event, no matter how traumatic it may be. She came away from the experience saying, "This crisis provided us with a real opportunity to grow and change in a deeper way."

This positive outcome can be true for *all* mid-life crises— whether it is an affair, a business deal gone bad, or a debilitating depression—depending upon whether both partners are willing to find the middle ground by evaluating and sharing with each other their new feelings and needs.

Indeed, four years later, Emily wrote to me: "Paul has become the most sensitive and devoted husband. In fact, he acts as if the affair and that whole time in our lives was a bad dream."

This sort of turnaround in a man who has had an affair is surprisingly common, while Emily's reaction is typical, too: On the one hand, she is genuinely thrilled by the changes in their marriage; on the other hand, there *is* a part of her that stays conscious of the painful episode in their past. She can't blot it out and doubts if she ever will. This consciousness creates a tiny but very real wedge of separateness between her and Paul, which has turned out to be healthy for Emily. While the affair was going on, she developed an independent life, which has become richer and more rewarding. For this reason, Emily can't imagine going back to a time when her life was fully joined and enmeshed with her husband's.

At the same time that she feels more separate from Paul, she also feels *closer* to him. "It sounds like a paradox," she said. "But it just means that we each have our own lives that we share with each other. We've finally learned to turn to each other for the support and companionship we need."

WOMEN WHO CONFRONT

Another kind of survivor is the woman who provokes a direct confrontation over her husband's affair. Shortly after Heather's husband, Tim, made a big killing in the stock market, he began having an affair with a thirty-five-year-old mutual acquaintance.

It is not unusual for the man who attains professional success at mid-life to feel "entitled" to have an affair. This sense of entitlement, along with grandiosity and lack of empathy, are the earmarks of narcissism (as I discussed earlier) and may lead a man to make choices that endanger himself and his marriage.

Heather, who was forty-eight at the time, was unprepared for Tim's "out of character" response to his success. "I had blinders on," she said. "We had a happy marriage, as far as I was concerned, and I wanted it to stay that way." But when a friend told her that she'd seen Tim in a restaurant with a woman they all knew, Heather felt as if she'd been punched in the stomach. Pretty soon, the first report of Tim's extramarital "dates" was confirmed by several other people.

She asked herself, "Do I want this marriage?" Then something inside her clicked, and she thought, "*Yes,* I do want it. But if this is the case, I have to change some things *now.*"

A few days later, Heather taxied downtown to the woman's office, walked in unannounced and confronted her. "Stay away from my husband," she said. "I won't let you ruin our lives." That night, she told Tim what had happened, and that she wanted him to end the affair and work with her to find solutions to their problems.

This incident proved to be a critical turning point in their marriage. Always shy and timid (for which Tim had often criticized her), Heather proved both to him and to herself that she could take off the gloves and fight for her marriage. Now he saw another side of his "passive" wife, he said during a counseling session, and he respected her "spunk." To him her actions meant that she was motivated to make changes in the marriage, which in turn motivated *him.*

At that point I presented him with a choice: If he and Heather were to use therapy to evaluate and rebuild their marriage, he would have to end the affair. Within a month he *had* ended it. For Tim, the choice became clear: At the same time that he could see problems developing with the woman he was seeing—she now wanted him to leave his marriage and commit himself to building a life with her— he was beginning to value the history that he shared with Heather and to appreciate the merits of staying married to her.

Over the course of a year in couples therapy, I saw changes in both Heather and Tim, but particularly in Heather. As a sign of her inner transformation, she shopped for a new, more becoming wardrobe and colored her graying hair its original deep reddish-brown. At work, she fought for—and won—a promotion she'd assumed would go to someone else.

Like Emily, however, Heather would sometimes find herself flashing back to the trauma, while tears streamed down her face. But much of the time, she said, she felt numb, as if her emotions had been anesthetized. She stated honestly that she didn't know if she could ever trust or feel close to Tim again, but that the only way to find out was to see if they could learn to be more open with each other.

Women often ask me the pros and cons of "waiting it out" and "confronting." On the negative side of waiting it out, a woman may enter a state of *denial* that the affair is going on; if she does, she becomes complicitous with her husband in *allowing* the affair to continue. For some women, too, the humiliation of the situation leads to an intolerable loss of self-esteem. The *advantages* of waiting it out depend upon a woman making a *conscious* choice to do so, in which case she will be using her patience and determination as a strategy. She views the affair as a phase in her husband's life, meanwhile strengthening herself by developing her own independent network of friends and interests.

The negative side of confrontation is the risk a woman takes that her husband will not only admit to the affair but tell her that he wants out of the marriage. Before confronting him with her knowledge of his affair, a woman first must ask herself if she is prepared for this response. If she *is* prepared, and she *does* confront, then at least she knows where she stands, which is a definite advantage. Once the affair has been acknowledged by both partners, the couple has the option of choosing a *temporary* separation, which may work for the couple who want the time and space to evaluate the situation privately.

POSTAFFAIR RECOVERY

Many women who are accustomed to being understanding and sympathetic toward their husbands have asked me if, once a husband's affair is over, they shouldn't just forgive and forget.

Trying to create the illusion that the affair never happened, or that an affair was merely a blip on the big screen of a marriage, means that a woman is backtracking into an unhealthy state of denial. "Forgetting" may smooth things over temporarily, but the end result will be a reinstatement of the stale routine that contributed to the affair in the first place, instead of a more dynamic and involved marriage.

Even when rebuilding the marriage is a priority, a woman should not expect it to happen overnight. In my experience, women often want to start couples therapy prematurely; usually, I will suggest to a woman that she allow six to eight weeks for individual therapy *before* bringing her husband in for sessions. Any woman whose husband has had an affair must have the chance to evaluate the impact the affair has had on *her*. Whether or not a woman is in therapy, she first must build a strong sense of self—a process that will help her move beyond her feelings of victimization. Before she can move on to rebuilding her marriage, she must expect to experience uncomfortable feelings that lead, in stages, toward her own *personal* recovery. Such feelings will include the following:

1. *Shock and despair:* She will first experience an enormous sense of *betrayal*. She will feel abused and powerless; her trust and belief in her husband will be shattered; physically, she may feel nauseous and

dizzy and have trouble eating and sleeping. She will feel like a victim.

2. *Resentment* and *guilt:* She may decide that the affair is all his fault; then she will decide it is all *her* fault: If she had been a better wife, he would never have turned to another woman. If, at this stage, guilty feelings predominate, she is likely to become depressed.

3. *Anger:* She will have fantasies of *revenge* and want to hurt him back; she will want to hurt the Other Woman; she will want them to hurt each other; she will want him to beg her for her forgiveness—which she will withhold. These fantasies may be obsessive, and she may find herself dreaming of retaliation at home, at work, day or night.

4. *Reflectiveness:* Her emotions will become less intense; now she will be able to honestly evaluate the factors that led to the affair, including his mid-life terrors and the status of their marriage; she will accept the fact that eventually she must let go of her hurt and anger if she is going to work on the marriage. She will reject, with finality, the label of victim.

5. *Forgiveness:* No longer envisioning a return to the preaffair marriage, she accepts the challenge of reinventing the relationship with her partner. She accepts, too, that both partners must work *together*, honestly evaluating their individual contributions to the crisis.

Throughout these stages, as she has grown away from the victim's role, she has taken steps toward becoming more independent and self-fulfilling—and she has developed personally as she has survived the crisis. When she envisions her postaffair marriage, she sees herself as *less* focused on her husband and *more* focused on her own needs. She has come to see that they can turn his affair into an opportunity to build a better, more dynamic marriage.

The Stages of Rebuilding

As a woman strengthens herself, she is preparing to work toward changing the outdated terms of her marriage, rebuilding it on a basis that is better suited to the evolving needs of *both* partners. Marital recovery and rebuilding after a midlife affair is a three-stage process that a couple must commit to and work on *together*.

1. The first stage is a vital part of a marriage's recovery— a retaliatory, or "payback," period in which a woman *acknowledges* and *vents* her anger, while her husband learns to tolerate it. This may be daunting to him at first, but couples should try to see it as a necessary *ritual* through which feelings can be disclosed and discussed. In order to cleanse and heal the wound, a woman needs to *feel* and express her hurt and rage—to her husband.

It is now absolutely appropriate for a woman to be angry and want to punish her husband. Expecting her just to turn a corner and forgive him is asking her to forgo her personal recovery and, by doing so, to stunt the growth of the marriage.

For this *time-limited* period, the first critical stage of rebuilding, I recommend a technique called "acting in." Instead of acting out her anger by lashing out at him, crying, or withdrawing, a woman takes opportunities to talk *directly* to her husband about how his affair affected her. The couple sets a time to sit down together, without distractions, while she expresses her feelings, and he listens and empathizes. The eventual goal is for her husband to *appreciate* her feelings and take responsibility for his behavior. Before they move on to the next stage, both partners must feel ready.

The reasons for a time limitation are very important. If a couple agrees to see the need to retaliate as temporary, they can avoid a postaffair marriage that becomes an ongoing nightmare of revenge. One woman I know never lost an opportunity to make her husband pay for his sins; in the middle of an outing to the store or during a phone conversation about something inconsequential, she would suddenly sigh and start sounding depressed. Her husband would then question her anxiously about what was wrong. She'd drop hints until he realized with a sinking heart that once again she was referring to the affair he'd had six years before. He would feel a familiar wave of guilt and promise to take her out to dinner or buy her a special gift. This kind of behavior will soon make him resentful, no matter how contrite he may actually be.

2. Now the wife acknowledges the part *she* played in the stalemate that led to the affair. Remember: Taking *responsibility* for a situation is quite different from *self-blame*. While her husband examines his own mid-life issues and motives for starting the affair, she takes an honest look at the marriage, without blaming anyone. She may look back and realize now, for example, that she made do with a sex life that had become dull and routine; if so, her collusive denial of that problem was *her* contribution to his affair.

3. Finally, the couple is ready to make a dramatic new start. They should acknowledge to each other that this really *is* a new beginning, that they aren't just trying to turn back the clock, and, for example, do something together that they've always wanted to do but never had the time for. (One couple took tennis lessons; another began to explore starting a small business.) Things are different now—the partners are talking, listening, and empathizing with each other. The stalemate is over.

By this stage, the couple will begin to see the affair as what I've been calling a crisis of renewal: a chance for a man to become more introspective about himself and for the couple to become closer. At this point I often suggest that couples use an "active, nondefensive listening" exercise at home whenever they feel that stress or anger is accumulating.

Active, Nondefensive Listening

When a couple is communicating very poorly, the therapist's office can function as a controlled environment in which they learn *how* to communicate. The point is to learn to tolerate what may be initially hurtful or angering. Most of us like to think we are open to constructive criticism from our partners, but even in good marriages, it is very common to react too quickly with anger or tears, effectively shutting down a discussion.

Active, nondefensive listening is the best solution to this problem. When a couple is ready to do the exercise at home, the partner who wants to talk establishes a time frame. He might say, for example, "I would like to take two minutes to tell you what I'm feeling. Is this a good time for you?" If his partner isn't ready, they should negotiate a time that suits both of them. Then they should sit down together with their knees touching and make eye contact. He should then tell his partner what he is feeling. It is her task *not* to respond; she should simply repeat back to him what he has told her, convey sympathy for his point of view and *not* take a position on what he says. Then both should take some time out to think it over.

The goal of this exercise is to avoid the major negative responses—combativeness, accusation, withdrawal, and defensiveness. The purpose of taking time out to think over what has been said is to ensure that negative responses are not brought into a positive discussion. When both partners feel ready for the next step, she now should tell *him* how she felt about what he said; and this time *his* task is not to respond.

This exercise has helped numerous couples I've worked with to learn to *understand* each other's points of view, articulate their feelings, and *empathize* with a partner's feelings. Couples tend to get locked into opposing positions; learning how to listen nondefensively breaks down the barriers.

One thing that is very important: A couple should never try to do this exercise in the heat of the moment; they should wait until they've cooled off. The point is to make a loving, not an angry, communication.

Active listening does *not* have to be used only when partners are fighting or withdrawn from each other. Some couples find that using it every day helps them foster and maintain intimacy. In this case, determine together a time that is mutually suitable, then take turns talking and listening.

One partner may use the time to ask how the other's day went, not in terms of the details of a business deal, but in terms of his or her feelings. At other times, one partner may convey how he or she felt about something the other said the night before (it can be something that upset her *or* something that made him feel loved and understood). Once again, the goal is to empathize with each other. When couples listen actively on a routine basis, they are establishing a consistent way to touch base with each other. When Heather and Tim did the exercise at home, she said, "It's surprising how just fifteen minutes a day can make a difference. I feel closer to Tim, and we're speaking more openly than we ever have."

The Healthy Survivor

One evening, at a fund-raiser for an environmental group Heather had started working with, she eagerly joined a circle of people she knew the moment she walked in. Tim drifted off, getting himself a glass of wine and some canapés from the buffet table, and circled the room. Because he knew so few people, he felt awkward and, after half an hour, he signaled to Heather that he was ready to leave. She waved to him and went on talking.

Tim felt irritated but shrugged it off and finally began talking to an acquaintance. After another half hour, he caught Heather's eye again, pointed at his watch, and signaled that he'd meet her at the door. Again, she waved and smiled, and ignored his request.

When they finally left an hour later, Tim was furious. "Why didn't you leave when I asked you to?" he asked.

"Oh, I'm sorry," Heather said. "I guess I just wasn't ready."

"Well, I wanted to go. Did it occur to you that I don't know anyone here? You weren't thinking about me at all."

"I really wasn't thinking about you," Heather admitted. "You know, working with this group means a lot to me. There were people here I really wanted to talk to. But you're right, of course. I guess I was inconsiderate. I'm sorry."

Tim is experiencing a changing reality: He is no longer the center of his wife's world. Meanwhile, as is normal for mid-life men, he is feeling needier and more vulnerable. He's truly repentant about having had an affair and he wants her forgiveness; at the same time, he wants Heather to be as attentive and focused on him as ever.

In our society, men learn to expect sympathy from women, and women learn to give it. But after Tim's affair, Heather, a survivor, is tougher. She loves him and cares about him, but her sympathy for his feelings has healthy limits; she doesn't sacrifice important needs of her own in order to focus on him. As an unexpected and positive consequence of Tim's affair, Heather is less other-oriented and more self-fulfilling. It is an exhilarating time for her.

This small incident clearly shows the profound changes in one postaffair marriage in which the affair was transformed into an opportunity for renewal, for each of the partners as individuals and for the two of them as a couple.

POSTAFFAIR PITFALLS

To maintain a good balance in a postaffair marriage, a woman should take regular "readings" of her position: To what extent is she compromising her marriage? How much is she compromising herself? Her goal is to maintain the bonds of marriage, while carving out as much room for personal fulfillment *within* the marriage as she can. Keeping a marriage growing means guarding against these three extremes:

1. Becoming too strictly focused on her own needs, to the exclusion of her husband's.
2. Allowing herself to be drawn back into the nurturing role that she has outgrown.
3. Staying in the retaliatory, or "payback," mode, in which she sets up an ongoing pattern of punishment and guilt.

* * *

For both partners, taking regular readings of their sexual barometer should be a priority. A collusive decision to deny changing sexual needs will re-create the environment for a stalemate and for more affairs. In the next chapter, I will talk about one of the major challenges for marriage at mid-life: sexual renewal.

CHAPTER SEVEN

Sexual Renewal

I N HILMA WOLITZER'S NOVEL
Silver, which so accurately depicts the joys and sorrows of a
mid-life couple, the husband states, "Married sex was friendly
and familiar, even if it wasn't that thrilling or frequent. I
could sleep afterward. I could sleep *instead* if I felt like it."[1]
This character is taking the humorous view of sex in a long-
term marriage, but for couples who resist or deny the need
for mid-life change, sex *can* indeed put you to sleep. I have
found all too often that couples *assume* that by mid-life, sexual
spontaneity and passion have been irrevocably lost. But once
a couple understands the physical and emotional changes
each of them may be experiencing, sexual renewal can, and
often does, follow. In fact, it is a critical part of the overall
cycle of renewal that takes place in healthy marriages at mid-
life.

I have heard from many clients in their twenties and
thirties about the puzzling phenomenon of good sex in a bad
relationship. Early in a relationship, incompatible people *can*
make the sparks fly; novelty alone can generate heat, while
conflict and intensity can give rise to passion. But sexual
novelty doesn't last; by mid-life even the greatest of passions
can cool. As the author A. Alvarez, in a recent essay on

romance, put it: "The truth is, you can't imagine a forty-year-old Romeo at the breakfast table, peering over the *Times* at Juliet with the same old intensity." Romeo and Juliet died young, but what if they hadn't?

Chances are, they eventually would have reached the same sexual stalemate so familiar to so many mid-life couples. Now is the time for the introduction of a new tenderness that will replace the phantom of youthful passion. Alvarez goes on to speculate that the traditional idea of romance, which is almost always associated with youth, has a doomed, terribly serious quality. But, he says, "as you get older, you get less serious—or maybe less self-important. . . . You are ready for romance in the modern sense, the mature sense, which has to do with pleasure and wit and tenderness."[2]

Mid-life gives couples the chance to incorporate this new, "less serious," more pleasurable definition of romance into their *adult* sex lives. Without the "self-importance" of youth, couples can be more relaxed, more playful and more attentive to one another's needs.[3]

SEXUAL LOSSES, SEXUAL GAINS

Unfortunately, most of what we hear about mid-life sexuality focuses on the downside. According to the experts, men must deal with the new reality of diminished desire, erections that take longer to achieve, and orgasms that are less intense. Because masculinity traditionally has been equated with sexual potency, for many mid-life men, anxiety over sexual losses is the essence of what it means to get older.

According to the experts, mid-life women may experience less vaginal lubrication, a thinning and loss of elasticity in vaginal walls, and shorter orgasms. For some women, that means experiencing more pain than pleasure in their sex lives. One woman friend in her late forties told me, "No one warned me how painful sex would become. After having sex the other night, I couldn't walk for two days. I told my husband, this is the last time I'll have sex."

But some of these problems have simple solutions. I suggested to her that she see her gynecologist, who recommended a lubricant jelly. He also told her that if the jelly didn't ease the pain, he'd recommend hormone replacement therapy (which does appear to have some risks that you'll need to learn about if you seriously consider this option). For this woman, though, the lubricant alone worked wonders. Now this friend says, "I wonder how many women decide to give up on sex simply because of vaginal dryness. Why don't women have more practical information available to them about how to deal with these kinds of problems?"

Many women are asking this same question. "No one tells you anything," complained another woman in her late forties. "I've never had hot flashes, but I started having night sweats a few months ago. Even my sleeping patterns are different. I never knew that both of these were symptoms of menopause."

The experts seem either to alarm us or tell us there is nothing to worry about. Nor is the tremendous variation among individual women alluded to. Overall, the sexuality of older women has been ignored for so long that it is small wonder that most women know so little about their own bodies. So if a woman is undergoing physical changes that she doesn't understand, she may end up feeling estranged from her body. It isn't hard to see, then, why the sex lives of so many women prematurely, and unnecessarily, wither away.

Just how premature and unnecessary has never been more apparent. We now know that even while mid-life women produce less estrogen, which affects the production of vaginal lubrication, women's testosterone levels remain constant—and testosterone controls *desire*. That means that at mid-life the ratio of testosterone to the female hormones is higher than it has ever been before; and *that* means that many women experience a greater *desire* for sex than ever before.

Treatable physical changes certainly need not put sex off-limits for women. Jane Brody, writing about menopause in *The New York Times*, says: "Since 'use it or lose it' seems to be an important component of continued sexual functioning after menopause, it is important not to delay seeking help for a sexual problem that may be related to estrogen decline."[4] We are finding not only that an ongoing sex life enhances a woman's responsiveness and pleasure but that sexually active women who are approaching menopause actually suffer fewer hot flashes than women who don't have regular, frequent sex.[5] So there are two good reasons to "use it"!

SEXUAL ROLE-SWAPPING

At mid-life, just as women and men swap roles in other areas of their lives, they swap sexual roles, too. As mid-life women experience a need for *self-fulfillment*, they also experience a powerful sexual surge, or at least have the capacity to do so. Men, meanwhile, who are now becoming more oriented toward relationships, experience a heightened need for more tender, intimate sex.

A recent study found that while 61 percent of the women aged twenty-two to thirty-five named love as their primary reason for having sex, only 38 percent in the thirty-six to fifty-seven age group claimed love as motivator over physical pleasure. For men, the results were reversed. A mere 31 percent of the younger men said that love motivated them to have sex, while *half* of those over the age of thirty-six cited emotional reasons, such as a desire for love and intimacy, as sexual motivators.[6] And yet another study claims that while a fairly large number of couples of all ages participate in erotic pleasures, such things as swimming in the nude together, buying erotic underwear, and watching X-rated videos together—women over forty place an especially high priority on them.[7]

As Amelia and Gene, a couple in their forties, discovered, a woman's mid-life sexual awakening can spark much-needed changes in a marriage. The potential is there, when a relationship isn't stalemated by the physical and emotional issues of mid-life.

As Amelia began to relinquish her phantom enabler self, she unknowingly set in motion a process leading to sexual renewal in her marriage. For years, she had been immersed in trying to help her older son, Todd, who was addicted to drugs. Siphoning all her energy into getting him into treatment programs, Amelia had relied on her husband, Gene, for comfort and support.

When a friend convinced her to attend Al-Anon meetings, Amelia realized that she had become dependent on her son's addiction: When he was most sick and needy, she was resourceful; when he was better, she felt at loose ends. But then Amelia broke her own pattern: She decided that she'd done everything she could for her son and that it was time to focus on her own professional goals, which had been on hold for years.

At the same time, she became aware of—and troubled by—her lack of sexual fulfillment. She could readily recall the sexual excitement and longing she had experienced in the early years of her marriage; just the sound of Gene's voice could arouse her then. She felt now as if she had made a trade-off: passion in exchange for comfort and companionship. Comfort was fine, but she wanted passion, too.

Gene sensed Amelia's dissatisfaction; it wasn't in what she said, but more in what she didn't say—the way she quickly drifted off to sleep after their infrequent sexual encounters instead of curling up next to him and talking as she used to do. But he shied away from probing for answers because, as he put it, he felt unable to "perform" any differently.

Amelia let her silence speak for her because she felt guilty about imposing her sexual demands on Gene. She didn't want to hurt him, so she said nothing. Like Amelia, many women keep sexual secrets from their husbands, but ironically, while a woman is quietly protecting her partner's sexual sensitivities, she is putting her *marriage* at risk.

But no matter how sympathetic toward Gene she felt, Amelia couldn't deny her own desires. She bought sexy black camisoles and nightgowns, but Gene didn't get the passionate message. Lying in bed, Amelia's thoughts turned to an attractive man she'd met at a recent dinner party. Sadly, she realized she *could* have an affair, with this man or someone else, but that she wanted a sex life with Gene—only it seemed impossible.

A few months later when nothing had changed, Amelia ran into the man from the party while she was shopping. When he asked if he could call her, she said yes. Soon they were meeting twice a week during her lunch hour at his apartment; after having sex, they would linger, sharing strawberries and champagne in bed or just talking.

Since her lover was recently divorced and still hurting, she knew there was no future in their relationship; it was a passionate sexual interlude but no more than that. What she *did* want was sensuality and passion in her marriage.

Amelia's affair was *transitional;* it gave her the self-confidence and determination she needed to instigate change in her marriage. Feeling committed to making her marriage passionate again, she suggested to Gene that they try couples therapy. He hesitated, knowing their sexual problem would be brought out into the open. But then he agreed: "I wanted to do whatever would make Amelia happy," he said.

In therapy, Amelia and Gene found that they had colluded in the desexualizing of their marriage. Over time, Gene had gained weight and experienced a slow ebbing of his sense of himself as a sexual person. He realized that he had unconsciously avoided sex by convincing himself that Amelia had lost interest anyway. And in a way he was right: Sex *hadn't* been a priority for Amelia, while she had focused her energy on her son.

But when she had refocused on her personal needs and sex had become a priority for her once again, Amelia broke the pattern of the couple's collusion. Since Gene had responded positively by listening and discussing his anxieties, I felt the couple would benefit from a program of sensual exercises to help them renew and revitalize their sexual relationship.

The best program I've found for breaking sexual stalemates is called the "sensate focus" exercises, developed by Masters and Johnson, to ease sexual fears and anxieties by depressurizing sex.[8] The strength of this program is its emphasis on the sexual *interactions* between the couple, rather than on one partner's sexual problem or aversion as the root cause of a couple's problems.

Since mid-life men are more open to exploring their sensuality, while women are more ready to take the sexual initiative, these exercises are particularly useful for mid-life couples. The main *difficulty* for them lies in breaking long-standing patterns of sexual avoidance and lack of communication. While we were discussing how the sensate focus exercises helped nurture new kinds of sexual expression in a marriage, Gene suddenly grimaced. "Sex used to be so natural," he said. "It was fun. Now it's work." (This is a common complaint couples have. As one woman put it, "Sex used to solve problems; now it *is* a problem.")

I told Gene, "I see your point. At first, it will probably feel forced, but that will diminish. It's a good sign that you and Amelia enjoyed sex earlier in your marriage. As I see it, some normal mid-life events have thrown you off, and these exercises are just a tool to help you get back on track."

"Okay," he said. "But if I feel too pressured to perform, I'm afraid it won't work."

"The point is to take the pressure *off*," I told him. "And for that reason, intercourse itself is off-limits until later."

Gene and Amelia glanced at each other in surprise. Then Gene laughed and said, "I never thought I'd find myself being told not to have sex while I'm in sex therapy!"

Most people who start sex therapy are shocked the first time they hear that intercourse is temporarily off-limits. But, like Gene, they often breathe a secret sigh of relief. Once the pressure to perform is off for women and men alike, couples can relax and explore their sensuality.

I reassured Gene that as they went along, we would be discussing their feelings about the exercises. And he and Amelia would be talking at home, too. That way, we would know whether they needed to take more time or even go back a step. Individual pacing is what counts. A couple may want to do one or more of these steps two or three times, or they may feel more comfortable taking several months. No outside rules—only their own comfort level—apply.

When Gene understood that he wouldn't have to become a sexual dynamo overnight, he was ready to begin. Amelia and Gene followed this program while they continued in couples therapy, but any couple, in or out of therapy, can try these exercises whenever both partners feel receptive to changing their sexual patterns or breaking a stalemate.

SENSUAL MASSAGE

The first step is nongenital and focused on pleasure. Set the scene with candlelight, unplug the telephone and choose a time when neither of you feel rushed. Partners should take turns giving and receiving. The woman (or the man) should lie facedown, while her partner caresses her back, moving gradually down her body. While he does this, he should focus on the sensual experience of touch.

The woman, meanwhile, should *not* worry about whether her husband is bored or impatient; she *should* focus on how his touch feels on her skin. If she likes what he is doing, she should tell him; if she doesn't, she should suggest specifically what might feel better. For a woman, this is a valuable experience in telling her partner what she likes instead of protecting his feelings and making do with a caress that is, for example, too rough.

When both partners are ready, she should turn over so that he can gently massage the front of her body, skipping the sexual organs. Both partners should concentrate on the nerve endings beneath the surface of the skin, and enjoy gentle, non–goal-oriented sensuality without feeling pressured to have intercourse.

When both are ready, giver and receiver trade places. A man may find himself in the receiver position for the first time; his focus previously may have been on initiating sex and bringing about orgasms for himself and for his partner. Now all he does is lie back and experience physical sensations—a good lesson in discovering the softer side of his nature.

Keep your sense of humor. Gene was so anxious about "doing it right" and being "thorough" that Amelia ended up "feeling like dough being pounded." Gene laughed and lightened his touch. After that, they relaxed, although they had a minor skirmish one night when Gene switched on the TV just when Amelia was setting the scene with candles and wine. Gene thought about it, then realized that he'd felt anxious about his ability to please her, and the TV seemed to place a buffer between them. Once he realized why he'd suddenly had an urge to watch the ten o'clock news, he felt less anxious. Anxiety is normal, but couples need to communicate about their feelings, not put up barriers against them.

SENSUAL AND GENITAL MASSAGE

Next, massage is expanded to include the partner's sex organs. The decision to move to this step depends upon the positive feelings the couple share about sensual touching. Often, people say they feel very intimate and relaxed, as well as relieved to find that sex needn't always have a goal. (For mid-life men who are emotionally ready to find their sensual inner selves, this can be a particularly profound and gratifying discovery.)

Again, the only goal is to concentrate on the sensation of touch. At this point, like many other couples, Gene and Amelia had intercourse. In a session, we discussed the reasons for "rushing things": Amelia said she had been worried that Gene would get bored with the process, while Gene admitted being uneasy about the sensual feelings he was experiencing. If either partner becomes anxious at this point, don't plunge prematurely into intercourse. Talk it out instead; that's the key to making these exercises effective.

Even when the no-intercourse dictum backfires, it still works. One couple I treated had been dissatisfied with their sex life for years. The sensate focus exercises had had little effect as neither of them could shed their inhibitions. In the course of therapy, we'd all been disappointed so often that before they went on a much needed vacation to Italy, I forbade them to think about, talk about, or have sex. "Just forget about it and enjoy yourselves," I told them.

Of course, once I'd "forbidden" them to have sex, they went ahead and made satisfying love every night. When they returned from vacation, the husband said to me, "I can't believe it. We pay you to give us advice, but the minute we got there, we said, 'What does *she* know!'—and we went ahead and had a great time! Did you know it would happen like that?"

I told them no, I hadn't been trying to trick them. But later, I realized that unconsciously I might have known what I was doing. Forbidding people to have sex takes the pressure off, which is sometimes *exactly* what a couple needs. Remember that each partner is discovering his or her sensuality. It is a *process;* the couple is unwinding, giving themselves the time and space to uncover their buried sensual selves.

For couples in long-term marriages, these exercises often have a poignant resonance. At this point, Amelia said she felt as if she and Gene were rediscovering each other, after a long dry spell. "I was remembering him through my senses," she said. Or a couple may feel as if they are getting to know each other sexually for the first time. Men and women have what I call "his" and "hers" anxieties about sex: "His" is the sense that he must perform while "hers" is that she must please. Now women and men have permission *not* to "perform" or "please." The only goal is to learn to see each other with new, sexual eyes and become lovers again.

Often, people find that their sexual tastes have changed; for example, a way of touching that was arousing during the early years of a marriage no longer works. Or something else *does.* "When I was younger," one woman said, "my breasts weren't as sensitive as they are now. I've found that now I really love having them caressed." These are the kinds of pleasant surprises people may very likely experience as their sexuality supposedly diminishes at mid-life!

FANTASY

Since people often feel guilty or embarrassed by their sexual imaginations, this step is designed to give both partners permission to fantasize. Some people drift into memo-

ries of erotic scenes from movies or books, or imagine
themselves making love on a beach or in a luxurious hotel.
A couple might pretend they've just met and are having sex
for the first time; sometimes, people fantasize about old lovers or an attractive stranger glimpsed on the street. All of
these fantasies enhance and enrich the sex lives couples share.

In the second part of this step, partners stimulate desire
by describing their fantasies to each other. Fantasies about
old lovers or would-be lovers may be too highly charged to
admit to, but it's fine to leave out some of the details and just
share the sexual content.

Talking about fantasies is just one way in which couples
can communicate with each other about their sexual selves.
The idea is to create an atmosphere of trust, a safe, private
place in which both people feel open and accepting of the
other. One of the most effective, relatively "new" sexual ice-
breakers for couples to try is rented X-rated videos they can
watch together at home. One woman client, married for
twenty-five years, says that she is very "susceptible" to erotic
films, and that watching them in her own bedroom has made
it easier for her "to get in touch with her sexuality." In addition to using erotic videos as a way to educate their partners
about sexual likes and dislikes (it is often easier to show rather
than tell), many mid-life couples say the videos provide just
the sexual aphrodisiac they need. (The videos you watch at
home don't have to be X-rated to be a turn-on: One male
client said he and his wife watched the movie *Bull Durham*
on the VCR one night after the kids were in bed and found
themselves remembering how sex had been for them in the
early months of their relationship. They then had some of
the hottest sex they'd had for a long time, initiating an overall
sexual reawakening in the marriage.)

GENITAL INTERCOURSE

By now, the couple has discovered a great deal about
their own and their partner's sensuality. Gene said that he
felt far more relaxed, with far less pressure to "perform." A
couple who have regular intercourse may continue to use

nongenital massage just for enjoyment and the feeling of closeness it creates.

Women should take advantage of the fact that for many men mid-life is the time for intimacy; the man in his twenties or thirties who would never share his innermost feelings may now open up. And, the man who once may have complained that it took "too long to have sex the way *she* wants to" may now become more finely tuned to a woman's body and her responses. "It took me a long time to realize I can relax when I have sex," said a man who has been married for twelve years. "In fact, I love having sex when we're almost falling asleep and every bone in my body is relaxed. It's wonderful not to worry about technique and simultaneous orgasms and all that stuff. Now I want *her*, not *it*—the way I did when I was younger. That's made me a much better lover."

A man's new receptivity can infuse tenderness and ease into a couple's sex life. As one mid-life man put it, "When my wife turns in a certain way, I can feel how it was when we first slept together. I have no anxiety about her, I just want to please. If you say you are 'comfortable' together, people assume you are no longer romantic, but knowing her well, having a sense of her body as of none other than my own, all of this deepens and enhances our lovemaking like nothing else." Making love with someone you know really, really well taps into all of the visual and tactile memories of the person that you've accumulated over time, and that makes it rich.

A vital marriage is a sexual marriage, and a marriage without sex is a marriage in trouble. Among the couples I work with, men's most common complaint is women who don't take the sexual initiative, while women most often complain that men aren't sensitive and considerate lovers.

At mid-life, men who have always wooed and pursued their partners express a desire for women to woo them. "I want her to take an active interest in sex," one man said. "I want her to make the first moves." It is normal and healthy for a mid-life man to want to ease into a more passive sexual role. For women, the benefits are clear: Without having to initiate and "perform" men are freer to become the tender lovers that women have always wanted them to be.

Since men now feel more vulnerable about their sexuality, they need *reassurance* from women that they are sexually desirable. As the same man put it, "I want to know that she really wants to have sex with me. If I'm always initiating, there's no way I can really know that she does."

Some women resist taking the sexual initiative or swapping sexual roles. That resistance means they are *avoiding* change. Since mid-life is the time to express the buried side of our sexual selves—for men, the gentler, more sensitive and receptive side and for women, the more assertive, self-fulfilling side—her resistance, or avoidance of change, can lead to a sexual stalemate.

SEXUAL AVERSIONS

An aversion to sex, or an avoidance of sex, may be traced either to a lack of desire combined with one or more significant sexual inhibitions that usually originates in young adulthood, *or* to the common sexual attrition of mid-life, in which a marriage that was once sexual has worn down.

By mid-life, many couples have experienced a gradual erosion of their sex lives; very typically, when I ask a couple to describe to me their physical relationship, I'm told, "Well, we just haven't been as passionate lately. We've been so busy with the kids, with work..." While talking about his stalemated marriage, one man said that sex with his wife was "pretty good," and added quickly, "But don't think it's going to be the engine that gets *this* train moving again." Many couples who come into treatment are making love very infrequently—less than once a month, or not at all.

Even though we now know that we can be sexually active until our seventies and eighties, we have pitifully few "older" sexual role models, and we're still bombarded with negative cultural images of aging. Physical changes or illness may make either a woman or a man aversive to sex. In other cases, the seeds of an aversion were planted in a marriage long ago, only to bear fruit now that the distractions of children and careers are taking less precedence in one or both partners' lives.

When Lisa and Gary came to consult with me about Lisa's aversion to sex, I asked them to think back to the earliest part of their sexual history. Both recalled that in the first years of their marriage, Lisa had allowed Gary to take the sexual lead, with Lisa adding that she often agreed to have sex when she didn't want to. She'd never had the chance, she said, to pick up her own body's sexual signals, telling her when *she* was ready. At the same time she couldn't imagine taking the initiative in bed; having been raised in a religious Roman Catholic family, she had been given subliminal messages that sex was shameful. As a result, Lisa felt so guilty about her sexual feelings that she repressed them.

Since she was afraid of hurting Gary's feelings, she had never discussed with him her ambivalent feelings about their sexual relationship. Lisa clearly remembered that after having her first child, she had begun sleeping on a couch in the baby's room and had continued to use it as a refuge as the baby got older.

Gary, meanwhile, had always enjoyed being the sexually freewheeling partner, the one who teaches and encourages his uninitiated mate. Coaxing an occasional response from Lisa was so gratifying that he could overlook the infrequency and lack of adventurousness in their sex life.

But for the last few years, Lisa had been less and less willing to play even a passive role in sex, saying that the demands of family and work made her too tired. Gary, meanwhile, maintained that because of her attitude, he had gradually lost his life force; feeling overwhelmed by his losses, he had even given up other physical pleasures, such as playing squash and lifting weights. His fantasies, he said, all involved his wife seducing him. He believed that the impetus behind renewing and revitalizing their sex life had to come from her because, in this long sexual drought, he had lost his vitality. Clearly, the sexual terms of Gary and Lisa's old marriage contract had worn out.

Because this couple's story is typical, I've transcribed one of our conversations so that their own voices can be heard.

Lisa: When we were first married, Gary was very tender sexually. He was sensitive to the fact that he was only my second lover and I was inexperienced. He helped me to feel good about my body, and to feel loved and desirable. He was the best partner for me.

Gary: It never really bothered me that Lisa wasn't a sexual "go-getter." She was more important to me than other women had been. She had a way of touching me that was beautiful. I loved her because she was gentle and loving.

Lisa: The turning point for me came after the baby was born. I was always tired, and I started to resent it when Gary made sexual demands on me. When we did have sex, he no longer paid attention to me; it was almost as if sex was a way to reduce his physical tensions. He even admitted that at a certain point during intercourse he would "forget" all about me. That hurt me deeply, and from then on, we weren't close anymore at all.

Gary: At first, our sex life was sensual and erotic; then it became sensual and *episodic*. After that it became just episodic. After our children were born, Lisa gave up sex for motherhood. She felt more comfortable as a mother than as a wife. When our first son was born, she slept in his room because she wanted to hear him if he cried. But after a while, this just seemed like an excuse to me. Sometimes we would still have sex, but gradually it stopped. I started spending more and more time at work.

Lisa: For a long time, Gary neglected me for his career. Now I've really focused on my own career, and he expects me to focus on *him*. Sometimes he approaches me, but it's always the wrong time! For instance, the other night after I'd gotten ready for bed, Gary wanted to have sex. I was exhausted! I resented his not taking my feelings into consideration, but when I turned him down, he sulked. Gary *says* he wants a sexual relationship with me, but he doesn't act as if he does. He doesn't make me *want* to have sex, he just makes me resentful of his demands. And he puts the whole problem on me by saying that I've taken sex out of our marriage.

Gary: Whenever I try to initiate sex, she's too something—too tired, too busy, whatever. There's never a right time. I feel as if, sexually, I'm through.

Lisa: Here's a perfect example of how we don't communicate. We decided to take a long weekend at a cottage by a lake to relax and unwind. It was just the two of us. We spent the whole first day traveling, getting settled, and then grocery shopping. Then I cooked dinner. That night, without even asking me how I felt, Gary pressured me to have sex; he kept saying what a beautiful, romantic night it was. But when I said I was exhausted, he sulked around. *That* sure doesn't make it easy for me to make overtures. All it does is make me feel guilty. Is *that* going to solve our problems? Does Gary really want to resolve this?

Gary: Maybe I don't want to solve our problems. Maybe I can't. I feel as if this marriage has taken away not only my sexuality but my motivation to want to change things.

Lisa and Gary's sexual stalemate is an unmistakable sign of a relationship that has gone stale overall. Before they can even begin to work on their sex life through sensual exercises, their task is to rebuild a foundation of affection and support. At this point both partners are holding back: Lisa turns down all sexual overtures, and Gary withdraws. In order to feel more sexual, Lisa needs Gary to feel and act more hopeful and energetic, while Gary needs her to *want* to improve their sex life.

Early on, when Lisa substituted motherhood for sex, she put her marriage on the back burner, and let it get cold there. At this point, if it weren't for Gary's pressure, she'd probably settle for a nonsexual marriage. But instead of giving up her sexual self, Lisa needs to develop a new sexual identity that is more suited to her needs and the needs of the marriage.

I urge clients never to settle for a sexless marriage in place of working out their sexual problems. Sex is an essential nutrient for every marriage; without it, in fact, a couple can be sure that their marriage *will* lose its vitality. Mid-life is a major turning point on a couple's sexual lifeline: A man needs tenderness and the assurance that he isn't sexually "through" (as many men put it); a woman needs sexual fulfillment to round out and enhance a life that is becoming richer and more rewarding in other areas. And, of course, couples need a good sex life because it makes them close.

Mid-life is the time when many couples come into their own sexually. This is the time for both partners to air their feelings, desires, and anxieties, a time for them to talk to each other about their fears of aging and any self-consciousness that they feel about their bodies. They may be able to give each other the reassurances that they both need. I would urge them to read the sensual exercises together and to discuss whether such a program would be useful to them. If so, the next step is to do them, at the couple's own pace.

SEXUAL TERRORS AND TURNING POINTS

For men, career disappointments often lead to a letdown in bed, while for men and women alike, hidden identifications with parents can have a dampening effect on sex.

Sometime after her marriage to Vincent hit the fifteen-year benchmark, Sandra noticed that he was avoiding sex. She wondered if his lack of desire had anything to do with the fact that he had been recently passed over for a promotion at work. Vincent was a proud, stoic man who didn't talk about his feelings, but she imagined that he would take this disappointment to heart.

Sandra remembered Vincent's father, depressed and defeated, as he had been in his late forties and fifties. Vincent had said then that he never wanted to end up like his father. When she'd asked him to explain what he meant, he'd said that his father had made a bad business deal and had just seemed to give up after that. Sandra wondered if Vincent feared he'd end up the same way.

Vincent was a tough guy who needed to come to terms with his softer side, which in his mind was associated with his weak, defeated father. Vincent's letdown at work touched off an unconscious identification with his father, which led him to focus only on the negative side of getting older. Without quite realizing it, Vincent became depressed, and depression often brings with it sexual ennui.

One night, after he had avoided a sexual overture from Sandra, Vincent realized just how depressed he had become. Remembering that his friend and squash partner had gone through a period of quiet desperation and depression the year before, he decided to talk to him about it. Embarrassed but determined to get to the bottom of the problem, Vincent asked him whether his dark mood had affected his sex drive. His friend said it had.

Many men think that feeling depressed or vulnerable means they are "soft" or "weak," and a man may need help and support for coming to terms with this side of his nature. One night, Sandra quietly suggested that they make love without having intercourse, which gave Vincent permission to be soft and explore the sensuous side of his nature. By introducing this new approach to their sex life, she was able to reassure him that there was a middle ground between being a superman and a sexual wimp, and other ways to achieve virility than by staying hard all the time.

If men's anxieties center around "keeping it up," women's usually concern appearance, and many a lunchtime conversation among friends will end up focusing on cosmetic surgery and dieting. A woman may find that even if her fear of the loss of attractiveness is under control, it still haunts her.

One such woman is Christine, now in her early forties. In a large changing room in a department store, she suddenly became aware of the contrast between her own body and the firm, sleek twenty-year-old bodies around her. She was shocked by her confrontation with the absolute hard evidence that she had aged.

Christine became phobic about her body. She began refusing to have sex with the lights on, and she wouldn't undress in front of her husband. If Andrew happened to walk in while she was dressing, she'd immediately grab for something to cover herself with. After he'd come into the bathroom once and pulled aside the shower curtain to look at her, she began locking the door when she took a shower.

Andrew was puzzled. He thought Christine was beautiful, and he enjoyed having sex with the lights on. His reassurances fell on deaf ears; Christine felt as if he were mocking her when he said he wanted to see her while they were making love. She didn't trust him anymore; when she was young, she had seen the admiration in his eyes. Now she wondered what he was really thinking. She'd aged—how could he not see that? How could he not be turned off?

She began dressing more conservatively, as if to underscore her feelings that she was getting older and less daring. When Andrew pointed out to her that she was dressing the way her mother did, Christine denied it. She was nothing like her mother, she told him.

But Christine had an unconscious terror of "becoming" her mother as she aged. She could clearly remember her mother's body, sagging as she aged, and the way her mother had seemed to dry up emotionally as well as sexually. For the older generation Christine was familiar with, mid-life was a time when you stopped living.

Andrew suggested couples therapy for them, and with his patience and understanding, Christine was gradually able to feel sexual again. Over a period of a few months, at a pace with which Christine was comfortable, they followed a series of exercises in which Christine at first partially undressed and then completely undressed in front of Andrew. Like so many mid-life women, Christine was coming to terms with a changed body image; as she came to accept her body and find herself attractive once again, she was better able to reveal herself to Andrew.

As we enter mid-life, we begin, unconsciously, to *identify* with our parents as Christine did, sometimes nearly to the point of "becoming" them. Sexual behavior patterns run subtly through the branches of the family tree, and a woman may find that her mother's sexuality seems to have been passed down to her, along with the color of her eyes and the shape of her face.

Mid-life couples should look at who their parents were— and who they *became*—at mid-life. Was sexuality a part of their older identities? Unfortunately, many of our parents do not present us with sexual role models that we want to emulate, even while we find ourselves doing it anyway. But a man or a woman's sexual destiny is *not* the same as a parent's: A woman friend in her early fifties told me over lunch one day, "When my mother turned fifty, I know she felt neutered by menopause. But I feel like a sexual woman." Separating our sexual identities from those of our parents makes it possible for us to have the vital, ongoing sex lives that we want and are entitled to have.

SEXUAL HEALING

At mid-life, people grieve for their physical losses, the loss of themselves as a young couple, the loss of their children. To compensate for those losses, they turn toward one another; and sex plays a vital role in healing the sadness and renewing the marriage.

Jane and Bill had seen their three children launched into successful careers and marriages. In an interesting reversal, Bill suffered more empty-nest feelings than Jane, who welcomed the chance to focus on her own interests. The empty-nest syndrome is more commonly found in men than most people think. Bill had been learning to value his family relationships, just as the kids were leaving. He became depressed thinking of the lost opportunities for genuine closeness and told Jane he didn't want to take their usual summer vacation at their house on Cape Cod. He would, he said, be reminded of summers there as the kids were growing up, and he would miss them too much.

Jane felt that she'd caught the "bug" of Bill's depression. Both of them were listless, distracted, and bored with each other. She felt cynical about rejuvenating the marriage but finally decided to push for the Massachusetts vacation as usual. She wondered if their family vacation home might become a romantic retreat for the two of them, a place to make a fresh start.

But at dinner, on their first night, they felt awkward being alone together, as if they were on a first date and had to make conversation. Finally, Jane blurted out her feelings. "I miss the kids," she said. Bill looked at her with relief. "I do, too," he replied.

Jane and Bill acknowledged their sadness to themselves and each other. They had some wine and cried together. But after that, the sadness slowly began to evaporate, and as the mist cleared, they shifted gears and began the sexiest and most romantic vacation of their lives. "We made love on the beach," Jane said. "You can't do that when you have kids around."

If a couple is able to communicate their losses to each other, they can find the reassurance and understanding they need to heal the sadness. It is also important to recognize the healing power of sex. As Jane said, "Even when other things in your relationship aren't going well, sex can keep you together. Sex is the great dissolver. It blurs the borders between you, and once again all things seem possible."

Since mid-life is the time for reinventing marriage, sex should become a number one priority in a couple's lives. They need time together and privacy. They may still be immersed in family obligations or in making career moves, but valuing, nurturing, and fortifying a marriage means reordering priorities and putting the partner *first*. And sex is the key to making this primary attachment imperishable and invulnerable to internal and external pressures.

Patricia and Greg, who have been married for nearly twenty-eight years, found that, as she put it, "Familiarity meant taking our sexuality to other, deeper places." They talked frankly about how they broke their sexual stalemate.

Like so many couples, over the years they found their sex life had become routine and perfunctory. Finally, Greg snapped the spell of silence, and the pattern. "Sex became a priority again when it became a crisis," he said. "I opened the subject up because we had just never talked about it before, and it seemed like it was now or never. Your sexual threshold changes as you get older. It takes longer to become aroused, you need more foreplay, more seduction and fantasy. You need to talk about it. Fortunately, you have your relationship on your side; if it's good, you can draw on it to make your sex life better."

"When you're young," Patricia added, "sex just takes care of itself. Now we're compelled to become conscious and verbal as opposed to just horny. We've become more sensitive to each other's needs and feelings. Familiarity can cause sexual problems, but it can help, too, because at least you can be honest with each other. Also, at this point in my life, emotional distance really is not a turn-on for me. Tenderness, intimacy, humor, these are the things that I find erotic."

Patricia said that even though she and Greg are very busy with work, they go out of their way to make time to make love—and, she added, she does not hesitate, as she once would have, to take the initiative. "I know that even on weekends I'll be exhausted by eleven P.M.," she explained. "So I'll know I have to get something going in the afternoon. And we may have to start from zero; usually, we'll feel affectionate but not sexual. But when you want to have sex, and you talk about it, and you're open with each other, you can end up feeling sexual. This is so important to me that when I plan my week, I think about making sure to have the time to make sex happen."

Placing a priority on sex, planning for it, taking getaway weekends alone together, using familiarity as a way to enhance romantic and erotic feelings, all of these will help a couple redefine sex and romance in their marriage.

People who are happy at mid-life are people who are happy in bed. Those couples have a sexual glint in their eyes; you can see it. The point is that a couple whose sexual relationship has lapsed can re-create a strong erotic glow around each other and bring that glint back into each other's eyes.

Sexual stalemates are the most *dramatic* of the mid-life crises, but other kinds of crises may contribute just as much to the continued growth of a marriage, or to its decline.

CHANGING
COURSE

CHAPTER EIGHT

Impasses

U NLIKE A STALEMATE, WHICH
results from a waning of affection and increasing distance
between a couple, an *impasse* in a marriage usually stems from
an *event* that is deeply buried in the couple's history. It may
also be an unspoken hurt or resentment that resonates with
meaning for one of the partners. More dramatic than a stalemate, an impasse often is forced to the surface during mid-
life when so many aspects of a couple's lives and marriage
are in flux.

Relationship impasses prevent the healthy process of
change in a marriage. Now partners need to become more
open and vulnerable to each other and to take risks as they
reevaluate their relationship. If a couple feels blocked, the
next step is to uncover the impasse. Usually a couple will find
that *within* the impasse lie the seeds of change.

GRIPES AND GRUDGES

No couple in a long-term marriage will be without their
share of accumulated annoyances, irritations, and complaints. The important question is how large these feelings

loom and how much they interfere with a couple's ability to be open to change in their marriage. One client of mine, after spending two sessions listening to his wife describe in general terms how tense and angry he made her feel, finally blurted out in total exasperation, "So be specific. What's your gripe?" The question was so unexpected and funny that we all laughed with relief and began dealing with each complaint she'd been harboring.

Gripes are minor annoyances that are symptoms of larger issues: Reflecting a deeper feeling that his wife is too "bossy," a husband may complain about her habit of giving him directions while he is driving; meanwhile, reflecting *her* feeling that her husband doesn't care enough about their togetherness as a couple, a wife may complain that he spends too much time socializing with business acquaintances.

When Maureen, the eternal mother in disguise from the first chapter, boiled over with old rage at her husband Ian for attending a college reunion while she was still in the hospital with their sick newborn, she was bringing up a "little" thing that loomed large in her mind, eleven years after the fact. As Ian said, "The baby was fine. We knew she was getting great care. Going to the reunion meant a lot to me. But Maureen, the main point is, how can you still be holding a grudge for all this time over such a little thing?"

Maureen *was* holding a grudge, which is a secret, deepseated feeling of resentment or anger that taps into an individual's *past*. Maureen's father had been unreliable, and she had learned from her own mother to view men this way. By never acknowledging his insensitivity at that time, Ian had unknowingly contributed to Maureen's sense of what she felt was his unreliability. Once he had understood how genuinely upsetting the experience had been for her (particularly since it repeated difficult childhood experiences), the first step was taken toward dissolving the impasse. The next step was for Maureen to let go of the grudge.

The Time Line of a Marriage

Any major milestone in the life of a marriage—the birth of children, the departure of children, job changes, illnesses, financial fluctuations, deaths in the family—may result in a marital impasse. A time line, used as an exploring tool, is a guide to locating them and digging them up.

When I do a time line, I take a history of a marriage by asking the couple to tell me about their marriage's early period—how and when they met, what their courtship was like, and how they decided to get married. Often, a couple will find that the very qualities that drew them together in the first place are now driving them apart. (The clinical term for this "attraction of opposites" is *projective identification:* We are drawn to people who have qualities we have not been able to develop, or qualities we are uncomfortable with, in ourselves. When this dynamic is healthy, a couple can flourish and learn from their differences.)

Sometimes a client will question the purpose of dredging up the ancient history of a marriage. I agree that digging deep is not always necessary, but if a couple cannot break their stalemate by talking through the immediate crisis and finding ways to handle it, then the couple will have to go *back* before going forward.

I will talk about three typical impasses in marriages. In the first case, one partner had felt misunderstood for years, sitting on his feelings and allowing them to accumulate until the marriage ended up in a serious crisis.

Impasse 1: Secret Rage

Eric and Linda had been in couples therapy for three months; by that time, all of us were frustrated because treatment had come to a standstill and we didn't know why. When Eric and Linda first consulted with me, we had made a time

line of the marriage, and Linda had identified a point two
years earlier when Eric had become withdrawn, no longer
discussing his work with her as he always had before then.
She'd found this both puzzling and hurtful, she said now;
when Eric didn't reply, she responded in frustration, "This
is exactly what he always does. He just clams up!"

When a person is harboring feelings he or she finds difficult to express, it sometimes helps if the therapist offers
explicit "permission" for airing grievances. Finally, I announced to this couple that Eric needed a gripe session, although I suspected that his gripes were of a more serious
nature. I assured them that I thought this tactic would help
them get to the bottom of their block, and asked Linda to
listen without comment as Eric spoke.

At first, Eric hesitated. It wasn't his style to complain; in
his family of origin, he had been the "good child," stoic and
steady. In his adult life, he had been hardworking at the
office and compliant at home. But, as it turned out, Eric
harbored an old, unspoken resentment against Linda, which
finally had come to a head when he turned forty and began
achieving measurable success at his job.

"Linda expects me to report back to her everything that
happens at the office and consult with her about every career
move I make," he said.

"How do you feel when she expects these things from
you?" I asked him.

"I resent having to answer to her for everything I do,"
he replied.

"If Linda stopped doing this today, would you feel better
about the marriage?" I asked.

He looked uncertain. "I don't know. Probably not."

When I asked Eric to talk about how and when this practice of discussing everything with Linda had started, he explained, "She was better educated and more ambitious than
I was. When I was first starting out in business, she knew
more about it than I did because her dad was in the same
line of work. She'd actually grown up in the family business,
and she had a whole network of contacts at her fingertips.
She introduced me to key people and gave me advice—*good*

advice. Back then, this was a great help. But now, other people report to *me*. *I'm* the boss at work, but I don't feel like my own boss at home."

I glanced at Linda, who was listening carefully, a look of complete surprise on her face. She had come into therapy puzzled by her husband's alternating anger and depression. But she had never connected his behavior to anything she was doing.

"I was always there for you," she ventured now. "You wanted my support, and I gave it to you!"

"You did," I interjected. "And Eric really counted on your being there for him. But I think there's something in here that's blocking the growth of your marriage. I know it's painful for you to listen, but if you do hear him out, you may find the key to the problems you've been having."

She nodded reluctantly, sat back in her chair, and fixed her eyes on his face.

I asked Eric how he had felt in the early years of their marriage when he had been so needy of Linda's help and support.

"Grateful . . . but . . ."

"But . . ." I prompted.

"I don't know. I felt talked down to. Even her tone of voice was scolding and motherly."

"You needed her to be strong, but you resented her, too."

"Yes, but I don't think I really knew that. I think I walked around feeling resentful for years."

With my prompting, he went on with his litany of grievances: Linda had always organized their vacations without consulting him; Linda had decided which schools their children would attend, from nursery school to high school, and had planned their activities; Linda had always insisted on choosing his wardrobe; Linda had organized their finances and selected their investments; Linda had always decided whom they socialized with. . . .

The grievances stretched back twenty years and had snowballed over time. From the beginning Eric had harbored a hard kernel of resentment toward Linda for her strength, the very quality in her that he'd been attracted to in the first place. However, in the early years of their marriage, the resentment had been masked by need. Now that he had been able to create a more positive self-image and felt less needy, he had gone into a silent revolt against the woman he had depended upon.

With Eric's mid-life revolt, the couple's marriage contract had obviously expired. After tacitly agreeing to spend his married life as a compliant, devoted husband, he was now outraged by his own compliance, and was turning his anger against his wife. In fact, at the heart of the impasse was the fact that Eric's *anger* had become a source of *strength* for him. He didn't want to let it go, and the longer he held on to it, the larger and more immovable it became.

The dissolution of this impasse would require two steps: First, Eric needed to understand that he and Linda had colluded in setting up and living out the terms of their marriage contract. While he had resented her bossiness, he also had needed her as an emotional anchor and had been an active partner in the tacit deal they had made that involved his acceptance of Linda's decisions.

Second, Linda's ability to understand the source of Eric's anger would be critical to helping ease the transition toward a new phase of the marriage. Her first, natural reaction had been one of shock, hurt, and disappointment, and even of despair, as the assumptions that had been the bedrock of her marriage shattered before her eyes. She had taken pleasure in being as *useful* as possible to Eric, not only by giving him a head start in his career, but by shouldering the burden of other family responsibilities so that he was free to focus all of his energy on work. Since she'd had no inkling of Eric's true feelings, she had felt secure in his love and acceptance. Now a sense of profound alienation accompanied her feelings of betrayal.

Before she could begin to accept the new reality, Linda needed to work through these feelings. "Eric is changing," I told her. "He's becoming more confident and communicative, and that will be good for the two of you. If you can tolerate your painful feelings, keeping in mind that you, too, are in a process of change, I think you will be rewarded with a closer, more honest relationship."

Linda's native strength helped her through the crisis. She told him honestly that she wished he had talked to her sooner, so that the problem could have been defused earlier. She also spoke about her own sense of emptiness resulting from no longer being needed by Eric in the same way—a major adjustment for her. As she was learning to respect Eric's abilities and support his need for privacy, she needed *his* support as she redefined herself and gained a new perspective on their marriage. On the day that she tentatively asked him for his support—for the first time ever—I saw Eric hesitate, then reach for her hand. I felt a softening, a draining away of anger, and I had a sense that I was witnessing the renewal of a marriage.

Impasses that don't soften and dissolve by mid-life become calcified by bitterness and a sense of hopelessness. Some therapists describe what is called a person's "bitter bank," a psychic space in which grievances are deposited over the years. The more "invested" a person is in his bitter bank, the larger the fund of bitterness will grow. I urge clients to close their accounts at this bank by getting their grievances out into the open and giving and getting support from their spouses.

While they are in their twenties and thirties, couples may not be aware that they are storing bitterness toward their partners, but by mid-life, unfortunately, many women and men have outsized accounts in bitter banks, which means that any accusatory, retaliatory behavior toward their mates seems justified.

"I don't want to feel bitter, but I do," said forty-two-year-old Melanie, who has devoted her married life to supporting her husband's career and her family's emotional well-being. Now that the kids are older and her husband is successful, she feels as if she has been used up and tossed away. Having spent her life putting other people's needs first, she now feels that she has taken a permanent backseat to everyone else in her life.

If Linda and Eric's marital impasse had continued, Linda might eventually have felt tossed aside in the same way that Melanie does. But women who have been caretakers feel less bitter once they know it is normal to grieve over having given so much of themselves and that it is now *their* time for self-fulfillment. Melanie needs to express her anger and sense of loss to her husband (instead of sitting on her feelings and letting them calcify) and have him listen empathically. The self-sacrificing woman then needs her husband's help and support in thinking of her own needs and pursuing her own goals.

Impasse 2: The Buried Child

A second kind of impasse can result when one or both partners has a secret. Small lies, omissions, or deceptions can be found in *any* marriage, but a secret that creates a marital impasse is different because the partner who harbors it knows deep down that if it ever got out, the marriage would be irrevocably altered. I think of this kind of secret as a skeleton in the closet, something that makes a person feel so ashamed or guilty that he tries to conceal it from his partner.

Years before Connolly, a photographer, married Beth, he'd had a brief relationship with a woman whom he would see when he traveled on business. The woman had become pregnant and had the child, a son. Over the years, Connolly occasionally sent money for his son, but he had never gone to visit him. Basically, he had felt guilty; he hadn't been in love with the boy's mother, and he had been far too young and immature to handle the responsibilities of having a child. Soon after, he met Beth and fell deeply in love. He had so much wanted to make a good impression on her that he never mentioned his son to her, rationalizing to himself that such a confession would only detract from the freshness and excitement of their relationship.

But one day, after several years with no communication, his son's mother had contacted him, asking him for assistance in sending his son to college. The boy, Brendan, was very bright and musically talented, but his mother couldn't afford to send him to a good conservatory.

Connolly agonized in secret for months. For the first time, much to his surprise, he was truly curious about this child and felt a sense of responsibility toward him. Like many other mid-life men, Connolly was experiencing an urge to integrate the pieces of his life, to discover where they all fit and how they made sense. It shamed him that he had not done right by his one and only son. And now that a sense of his own mortality was creeping up on him, it suddenly became very important to get to know the boy who was carrying his genes.

His accountant assured him that he could finance his son's education on the sly. The problem was, Connolly didn't feel right about it. If he intended to meet his son and make a major financial commitment to him, he would have to tell Beth. It was too big a thing not to.

He knew that Beth would be shocked, but he hadn't anticipated that her shock would turn to fury. After several days of recriminations punctuated by icy silences, she insisted they consult with a therapist to reassess their marriage. In our first session together, she said accusingly, "I'd always thought we told each other everything. I thought we had a foundation of trust." Now that she'd discovered such a significant secret in Connolly's past, she had to question their entire relationship. She shot a series of questions at him: What did it mean that he had kept this from her? What *other* secrets was he keeping? How did he intend to explain this to their daughters?

A woman with a wry sense of humor who prided herself on handling crises with equanimity, Beth was floored by this one. She just couldn't get over it, she said. It wasn't the fact of the child, she insisted; it was that he hadn't told her. Connolly felt as if his past had come back to haunt him, the proverbial skeleton tucked away in the closet that suddenly springs out. I felt it was important for Beth to vent her anger; at the same time, I wanted them to move on. Finally, I suggested to Beth that she put aside her rage for one session so that she could hear Connolly out. Reluctantly, she agreed to listen to his explanation of why he hadn't shared this piece of his past with her.

"I didn't tell you at first," he said, "because I didn't want anything to come between us. I was ashamed, and I wanted to forget about it. As time went on, it just got harder to talk about because you would have asked why I didn't tell you sooner. I didn't want to disrupt our lives with any surprises. So, I sent money. I never thought it would have anything to do with us."

"You should have told me," she said. "For heaven's sake, years ago we could have integrated this into our lives. Now it's all just coming out of the blue."

"Can you see how Connolly felt embarrassed and guilty?" I interjected.

Beth nodded slowly. "Yes," she said, "and I can see how he wants to make amends now. But I want him . . . I want you"—she turned to look at him—"to understand that you could have trusted me. I'm going to be upset about this for a while."

A spouse's understanding and forgiveness in a situation like this is critical. But as Beth said, she couldn't just say, "Well, now I know. Thank you for telling me!" It is important *not* to try to rush too quickly toward a resolution; in this case, Beth needed to take time to rethink the man and the marriage, and to integrate her new perspectives with her old ones.

Sometimes the "new" perspectives are so at odds with the "old" that no integration or resolution can take place. When one woman found out that her husband of twenty years, whom she had always thought of as a model of honor and integrity, had perpetrated stock frauds on Wall Street, she walked out of the marriage. "I'd been married to a criminal," she said. "The man I thought I knew didn't exist." Another woman discovered that her husband had had a mistress, a home, and a second family in Switzerland for nearly twenty-five years. A man who is leading an elaborate double life is concealing a secret of such magnitude that no marriage can or should attempt to accommodate it.

In this case, though, I was hopeful that Beth would for-give Connolly. He had kept a secret that should have been shared, but I didn't feel that he had been duplicitous so much as he'd simply gotten caught in the web of his own fears and rationalizations. He had made a very human error by trying to ignore and take the easy way out of a profoundly uncom-fortable situation, but the secret had surfaced at last. To his credit—and boding well for the marriage—his instincts now were right on track in terms of a man's healthy mid-life de-velopment: The affiliative side of his nature was emerging. In addition to disclosing the truth to Beth, he was also now prepared to meet his son and deal with the complexities of forming a relationship with him.

I asked Beth what she thought had motivated Connolly to open up this part of his life to her at last.

She thought for a while, then said, "Maybe he's becoming more aware of relationships, of how important they are."

I suggested to Beth that a relationship between Connolly and his son might enhance, rather than undermine, the fam-ily as a whole. She looked interested. "I like the idea of testing our family's flexibility," she said thoughtfully. "As individu-als, we're strong, and as a unit we're pretty together, too. We've dealt with our share of surprises and problems before now"—she smiled a little ironically—"although I couldn't have predicted we'd have to deal with anything quite so sur-prising as *this*."

I smiled, too. "My guess is that your family *can* accom-modate something unexpected. Your openness to consider-ing it is a sign of your strength."

Beth and Connolly arranged to fly to Brendan's home-town and meet him at a restaurant; a week later, they invited him home to meet their daughters. At their final couples session, when I asked Connolly how he felt, he said that he was both thrilled and saddened—thrilled because Brendan was a smart, nice boy and saddened because he had waited so long to meet him.

For Beth, there were more surprises: There was, for one thing, Connolly's maturity in presenting the situation to their daughters, admitting his own misjudgments and encouraging them to express their feelings. She saw then how his honesty and matter-of-factness paved the way for a good first-time meeting between his daughters and their half brother. And Beth was surprised, too, at how proud she felt of her husband as he took responsibility for his family and how good she herself felt about meeting Brendan and bringing him into their lives.

This period of repair in the marriage led to renewal: Beth felt that, with its new basis of trust and honesty, their marriage had changed profoundly. Dealing positively with the crisis had shown them the strengths of their marriage; now they were communicating more openly than they ever had before, and for this reason Beth felt confident that they would be able to handle whatever surprises lay in their future.

Impasse 3: A Traumatic Loss

We all know that marriage is made of compromises, but if one partner gives up something that is really too important to give up, that is not a compromise; it is a loss. She will be angry, even if she is not conscious of it, and she will need to mourn. Her partner must try to understand and support her in the healing process.

When Edward and Georgette first came to see me, the hostile feelings between them seemed to fill the office. They spent several sessions bickering over the details of minor events, and neither ever gave in to the other. After a while, the nitpicking and arguing seemed so automatic that I wondered if it might not be a shield for something else.

We began by making a time line of their marriage and found that the early phase had been happy and passionate. I then asked them to help me pinpoint the best and worst periods of the marriage and the turning points, when their feelings began to change. One major turning point had come eight years before, when they had adopted their son, Richie. After years of trying to have a baby, they had been delighted with Richie and were thrilled to become parents in their late thirties. The tension between Georgette and Edward had developed since then. I asked her to think hard about what had happened to cause it.

"About five years ago," she said finally, "I remember that we started fighting a lot. I remember thinking things just weren't the same between us."

"What was going on then?" I asked her. "Can you reconstruct it?"

"Nothing much," she said. "That was the year we decided not to adopt a second child, I think. So really nothing happened."

I waited quietly for her to go on. The matter of the second child had not surfaced in any of our previous sessions, and that omission made me suspect that it had something, probably a great deal, to do with their impasse. If it had been a traumatic decision in any way, then it was likely that tensions between the couple had developed afterward. I asked Georgette to tell me why they had decided not to adopt.

"Edward decided it. I wanted to go ahead with it," she said. "I love being a mother and I'm good at it. I know we would have done well with another child."

"That sounds like a big turning point in your marriage. How did you feel when Edward said he didn't want another child?"

She shrugged. "I accepted it, I guess. Richie was getting old enough so that we were starting to have more freedom, and we both enjoyed that. And Edward said we couldn't afford another child, particularly when you thought about putting two children through college."

"It would have been financially unwise," Edward put in then. "Our life-style would have been compromised, and the child would have been shortchanged. I didn't want to do that. I thought Georgette agreed."

When Georgette said nothing, I asked her if she had, in fact, agreed. "I'm sure Edward was right," she said. "He's always right. But I was angry about it then. And I think I'm angry about it now."

Edward looked amazed. "I thought you were over it," he said.

"Over it?" she snapped. "Just because I went along with what you wanted?"

The matter of the "lost" child had bothered Georgette greatly at the time, but she had pushed her feelings aside in order to avoid conflict and the possibility of further pain. On a conscious level, she had in fact "forgotten" her feelings, but unconsciously she blamed Edward for cheating her of the child she so dearly wanted. Without being aware of it, Georgette carried a grudge against Edward, which was the source of their tension and endless bickering. Her anger and pain, instead of going away, had gone underground into that psychic space where all unspoken feelings feed on themselves and flourish.

The worst part, she said in a rush now that the issue was out in the open, was that Edward had not considered her needs but had made a unilateral decision. "He does that a lot," she said. When I asked her to describe other ways in which he made decisions without her, she said that, without consulting her, Edward gave her lists of things to do during the day. When they were first married, she said, she hadn't minded it; he was very orderly while she tended to be disorganized. But now she felt insulted by the lists and by his "check-up" phone calls to see what she had accomplished.

In the little-girl role Georgette had played in their marriage, she had deferred to the decisions Edward made. As a result, she had suffered a traumatic loss, and their marriage had been at an impasse ever since. Sometimes, when a couple is stuck at a major roadblock, it is useful to make genograms (as I did with Ian and Maureen earlier) so that the unconscious forces that shaped the couple's roles can be explored more fully.

By using this method, we found that in Edward's family of origin, he had felt ignored and devalued; to feel more loved and appreciated, he had become overly responsible for his younger siblings. In school, he had pushed himself to be the best student in his class, but even then he had felt valued only for his *achievements*, never just for *himself*. In his marriage, he did not want to repeat the experience of feeling unappreciated; an important reason for his *not* wanting a second child was that he *did* want more attention for himself. One way that he could prevent himself from feeling unappreciated and overburdened was to take *control* of the question of whether to have another child.

Georgette, meanwhile, the only daughter in a family of three brothers, also had a history of feeling devalued. When it came to the allotment of the family's financial resources, her brothers had always come first. Georgette had become accustomed to deferring her needs to the needs of the men in her family, and she had unknowingly continued to play that self-sacrificing role in her marriage.

It was clear from looking at their family trees that both Edward and Georgette were grappling with lifelong issues that needed careful examination. Georgette had always felt cheated of the "good stuff"; Edward's decision against having another child had catalyzed her feelings of deprivation and devaluation. Now their marriage contract had expired; as a young woman, Georgette had accepted that she would defer to her husband, just as she had deferred to her brothers. As time went on, she began to feel increasingly uncomfortable with her subservient position. Her discomfort came to a head when Edward disregarded her feelings about having a second child. At mid-life, Georgette changed: From passivity, she was moving toward self-determination. Now she believed it was time for her to make her desires known and for Edward to learn to respect them.

The couple had to learn how to empathize with each other's feelings so that they could rework their marriage contract. Edward's sense of being unappreciated became more understandable to Georgette when she saw how few rewards he'd gotten as a child. And Edward understood why Georgette had been so angry when he saw that this deprivation was informed by her earlier losses. As children, both partners had been forced to grow up too fast and had brought to their marriage a residue of sadness common to most people who spend their childhoods as pseudoadults.

But after we had discussed this, Georgette said quietly, "I can empathize with Edward's feelings, but our chance to have another child has been lost. We're too old to adopt unless we adopt privately, but there are too many problems with that."

As Edward took in what she was saying, he was visibly distressed. "I really never knew you felt that way," he said.

"Would it have made any difference?" she asked bitterly.

In order for this marriage to get past the impasse of the lost child, I suggested to Georgette that she allow herself time to mourn her loss, as well as everything she had lost as a child. Edward needed to undertake the same process, and I explained to them that their support for each other through the mourning process would be critical. Even though this couple was facing a major challenge, I sensed that the love between them hadn't altogether disappeared, but had just gone underground. At the end of the session, in fact, I felt optimistic that they could share their pain and help each other to heal.

My intuition was borne out by a note received from them a few months after their last therapy session. They had adopted a Labrador puppy and were devoted to it. Georgette said that her mourning finally had allowed her to let go of some of her pain over the lost child. As the puppy took its place in the heart of the family, Georgette felt a sense of completeness that had been eluding her ever since that difficult period five years before.

SECRET AFFAIRS: A SPECIAL CASE

Often, clients ask if a secret affair is necessarily an impasse in a marriage, and whether you must always come clean with your partner in the interests of openness and honesty. Even though my opinion about this is controversial, I say no, not always. Affairs are special cases.

There are different kinds of affairs: those that jeopardize a marriage and those that lead to changes in the marriage. For example, women such as Leslie and Amelia each had a transitional time-limited affair that helped them explore their sexual potentials. Each ended the affair and made necessary sexual changes in their marriages. Should a woman tell her husband about an affair? If she has not brought the affair "into" the marriage by hinting at it or leaving clues around, she shouldn't confess now out of a hidden desire to punish her husband or expiate her guilty feelings. Instead, she should turn her energy toward rectifying and fortifying her marriage. If her focus is on the marriage—specifically, on the deficiencies that the affair was making up for and she now wants to correct—the affair will not act as an impasse.

On the other hand, if she (or he) is having an affair and leaving clues around, she has been trying to tell her partner something indirectly. In that case, she has created a triangle through the affair, and it will drive a wedge into the marriage. Instead of leaving clues, she should "own," or acknowledge, what she is doing and discuss it with her partner. She owes it both to him and to herself to be direct.

At mid-life, couples are striving for greater intimacy and maximum independence in their marriages. It's a fine balance to strike—getting closer and giving each other space at the same time. Unnecessary confession will *never* make a couple closer, but exposing impasses will.

When impasses are resolved, marriages can be renewed. When they are not resolved, a chasm exists between the partners that will result in a joyless marriage, a partnership of profound limitations in which individuals settle for very little pleasure or else seek it beyond the confines of the marriage.

CHAPTER NINE

The
Joyless Marriage

A COUPLE MAY GIVE UP ON each other without being able to give up their marriage. One or both partners may have thought seriously about leaving, or they may even have separated for a while but ended up coming back. At the same time, they feel there is no use trying to change the marriage because they have no faith that it can improve. Their arguments are frustratingly unproductive, and the couple's life together does not include sharing many of life's pleasures. Joyless marriages are sad marriages.

Through the years when a couple is consumed by work and family responsibilities, they may place their marriages on hold for a while. But this situation can't go on indefinitely without seriously eroding the marriage. By the time a couple's responsibilities have begun to diminish, a gradual, almost imperceptible deadening has crept up on them, and before they know it, their partnership seems to have lost its vitality.

Mid-life is the natural time for sloughing off our phantom selves—the people we once were—and moving on to new interests and identities; but if the partners resist or deny the need for change, choosing to "make do" with a worn-out status quo instead, they will find that their marriage stagnates and love inevitably withers away.

Until now, we've talked about marriages that do change, catalyzed by the partner who begins to evolve new needs or a new identity that upsets the old collusion. But now we'll talk about what happens when partners resist giving up old roles, cling to phantom selves, and to marriage contracts that for all intents and purposes have expired.

At the same time, I am not saying that all joyless marriages are *hopeless* marriages. They are marriages of *limitation,* but change within the limits is possible. I'll talk about how far a limited relationship can or should be pushed, what it means to "go too far," and how to test for the "soft," flexible areas that can accommodate change.

WHERE DOES LOVE GO?

A while ago, an old, dear friend of mine, whom I had not seen in many years, was describing to me her overwhelming elation at the recent publication of her first novel. Suddenly, her eyes clouded over, and she said, sadly, "But Gerald is always involved with his own problems; now he's so preoccupied with problems at the hospital that he just can't share the happiness with me."

My heart went out to her. "Didn't that take some of the pleasure away from you?" I asked.

"I just try to hold on to my own pleasure," she said. "That's the way it always is with us."

"That sounds awfully difficult," I said.

"It isn't *always* bad," she said quickly. "I've found that I really appreciate the good moments I have with Gerald. I've learned to make the most of those moments."

My first thought was that my friend's marriage sounded as if it had far too few good moments, and was rarely, if ever, truly joyful. But I also realized that her criterion for her marriage was not so much the experience of joy as the avoidance of pain. The other aspect of this kind of marriage—and I have seen many over the years in my practice—is that pleasure, when it comes, is often experienced *more intensely* for the very reason that it is so infrequent.

This disturbing phenomenon has been borne out by some famous behavioral studies, done with laboratory animals, which are remarkably relevant to human relationships. In experiments in which the animals are trained to press a lever to get food, they will press more often when the reward is *intermittent*. When the pattern is regular—for example, if food appears every third time the lever is pressed—the animal presses the lever *less* often than when the pattern is completely random.

When a relationship provides only random and intermittent rewards, it can keep us involved, always wanting more, always eager to pursue those elusive morsels of pleasure, which may seem all the more delicious simply because they are so rare and unexpected. When we live for the "good moments," storing them up to savor in the daily drought, we are making a habit of lowering and deadening our expectations.

MARRIAGES OF LIMITATION

A marriage of limitation is one that has far less capacity for change than a marriage in which the partners have the flexibility to make full use of the cycle of conflict, repair, and renewal. In the marriage of limitation, conflict may lead to *limited* repair, in which there is *some* analysis of the couple's problems, but not enough to result in new understandings or in a genuine determination to make the necessary changes. So the problems continue to recycle, and the process of renewal seems increasingly elusive.

Realistically, some marriages will *not* be transformed at the mid-life turning point. But the man or woman who comes to understand his or her stake in a marriage may sometimes be able to take the risks that can lead to positive change within the limits. And individuals who stay in marriages of limitation *can* make positive changes in their own lives.

When Ronnie, a new client in her late forties, first came to see me, I was upset when she told me her age. She looked far too old for her years.

Her marriage contract had always been an unhealthy one: Her husband, Leon, maintained his own shaky sense of self by exaggerating her faults and limitations and by criticizing her. Even early in their marriage she had noticed it: For one thing, Leon was very insecure socially, and he'd almost always criticize her after they got home from a party; she wasn't dressed right, he'd claim, or she'd talked too much or not enough. Nothing she did ever seemed to be right. In response, Ronnie would try first to placate him, then to distract him. When he would become still more critical, she would start defending herself. The more she defended, the more Leon criticized.

Things had only gotten worse since Leon's company had named a new managing director—someone with whom Leon had never gotten along very well. Ronnie felt that this had been a very bad break; the man seemed forever to be on Leon's tail about something. She was filled with sympathy for her husband and knew that when he picked on her, he was feeling badly about himself. An insightful woman, Ronnie sensed that Leon was trying to rebuild his own self-esteem by tearing her down. But now, fearing his attacks, things had gotten to the point that she could hardly bear to be with him.

Since Leon refused to come for couples therapy, it seemed there was little likelihood of renegotiating the marriage. However, I advised Ronnie to stop defending herself when he attacked her and to put her energy into doing things that made her feel good. Ronnie found that the strategy worked: When Leon baited her, she'd refuse to bite. One night, he began criticizing a friend of Ronnie's who had just been over for dinner. "All she does is gossip," he grumbled as he and Ronnie cleaned up in the kitchen. "Where did you get such poor taste in friends?"

In the past, Ronnie might have assured Leon she wouldn't have the woman over again. Then, when he would go on to criticize other friends of hers, as he'd done so often in the past, she'd start defending her choices. Leon's criticisms would get worse; he'd tell her she had no judgment and no standards. She'd get pulled in and defend herself some more. But this time, she simply changed the subject. When Leon tried to turn the conversation back to her choices in friends, she finished the dishes and told Leon she was going to bed.

Gradually, his attacks diminished in intensity, although not in frequency. Then Ronnie noticed that he'd started playing golf again, which he'd given up a few years ago. As the club became an opportunity to reconnect with business acquaintances in the area, he began to feel better about himself—and became less likely to be critical of his wife. Even when he still did so occasionally, Ronnie would change the subject and end the criticism session. She began to feel more comfortable spending time with Leon, and they began taking the train into the city together on weekends to go to the theater and visit museums.

A few weeks after Ronnie's therapy ended, she called me and scheduled a session as a footnote to her treatment. She needed just one more layer of confirmation that Leon's criticisms of her had been truly unjustified; insightful as she had been about their root causes, over the years her own self-esteem had been badly undermined.

A few months later, I heard through mutual acquaintances that Ronnie had found a more rewarding job, a step she had been unable to take before because, unconsciously, she had known it would make Leon, who felt somewhat trapped in his job, feel even worse. According to all reports, Ronnie was looking and feeling much better.

Ronnie's story is a good example of how one partner perpetuates a negative pattern in a marriage by playing what at first glance appears to be a minor role. But minor as the part seemed, once Ronnie stopped playing it, the overall pattern began to occupy a far less important place in the marriage.

Like many people who choose to stay in marriages of limitation, Ronnie had a strong need to be married, and never considered leaving the marriage, even though it bore little resemblance to the loving, supportive kind of partnership that was her ideal. Instead, she eventually found a way to make the marriage less conflictual, freeing both herself and Leon to focus on interests outside the marriage and allowing them to become better companions.

MID-LIFE TERRORS
AND THE JOYLESS MARRIAGE

At mid-life women and men alike become more vulnerable to the fear that should they leave their marriages, they would face rejection and loneliness. A man married to a woman whom he felt he had "outgrown" said, "I'm afraid to be alone. I'm afraid that if I try to meet someone else, I'll be rejected because I'm too old."

I was astonished to hear an attractive man in his forties expressing the same fear that mid-life women know all too well, that they are no longer desirable. But the fear of rejection knows no gender, and for men who may not have felt vulnerable when they were younger, it may hit hard at mid-life. For women and men alike, a marriage can become a place to hide from their fears.

Some people have an overwhelming need for security or stability that traps them in joyless marriages. One woman I treated named Nina, a cosmetics executive, suffered from a panicky reaction to the idea of being abandoned; deep down, she feared she would literally die without her partner, and that fear was intense enough to make her cling to a stale marriage. Like Ronnie, however, Nina was able to make the kinds of healthy, productive changes in her own life that improved the overall quality of her marriage.

At forty-nine, Nina had been married to Mitch, fifty-nine, for over twenty years. "He has a closet full of identical, charcoal-gray suits," she said about him, when I asked her to describe him to me. "He buys only one kind of button-down shirt. We always go to the same restaurant where he orders the same thing for dinner. If I had to sum up Mitch, it would be easy. I'd call him 'rigid.' "

She asked me to call her only at the office if I needed to reschedule an appointment. She didn't want Mitch to know she was seeing a therapist, because he was sure to be disapproving and defensive. Mitch disliked introducing anything new into their lives, she said, and he would perceive her therapy as a threat to the status quo.

Wondering if Mitch could really be as bad as she made him out to be, I asked her what the marriage gave her. She replied, with no hesitation, "Security." And, like my friend, she quickly added, "There are good things, of course. I got him to go with me on a vacation to Greece last year. Of course, he brought work along with him and when we got back, he spent every weekend at the office for the next month, but still . . . " She smiled at the memory of that brief, pleasurable event in her marriage.

When I then asked her if the good times had always been so few and far between, she shook her head. "Things were good at first. After divorcing my first husband when I was in my twenties, I had to support myself and my daughter with low-paying jobs. I dated for several years but never met anyone I liked until I met Mitch."

Nina liked the fact that Mitch was ten years older than she and on a steady career trajectory. With relief, she had soon settled into marriage with a man who colluded with her little-girl role by playing a father. On the positive side, he provided her with financial support and helped her feel confident enough to enroll in college and go on to business school and begin her own successful career. On the negative side, he expected her always to take his advice and to follow certain habits and routines, such as going to the same restaurant on the rare occasions when they went out and spending most of their time at home together.

By her early forties, when she became successful in her own right, Nina began to outgrow her little-girl self and, with it, her marriage contract with Mitch. Now she wanted an active companion, one with whom she could travel and share other interests and activities, such as sailing and dancing, theater and concerts.

When Nina came to consult with me, she spoke very directly, saying that she had no illusions about changing her marriage, it would not change, and there was really no point in discussing it. At the same time, she was dead set against allowing herself to dry up the way the marriage had. She had, she told me, many fantasies that she felt she didn't have the gumption to fulfill: She wanted to travel in the Far East; she loved animals and wanted to work with groups that helped protect endangered species. She craved, she said, *stimulation*. The problem was that she'd been unable to act on any of her ideas. She felt blocked, and she didn't know why.

Before discussing her block, I asked Nina if she would be willing at least to try some couples counseling. She shook her head emphatically. "Mitch would never come," she said. "It's really a waste of time even to consider it."

Although I made this suggestion several more times, Nina stood firm, insisting that Mitch was an "untouchable." Usually, I'm skeptical when clients describe their partners in this way, but Nina was so adamant that it seemed pointless to pursue it. Instead I shifted the focus to Nina herself. My sense was that she was seeking permission from me to explore her deepest desires and fantasies. At the same time, she did not want to destabilize her marriage. "I don't want the bottom to drop out of everything," she said. "My marriage is the foundation of my life."

It became more obvious to me why Nina was with Mitch: He had become her excuse for leading a life—not only a marriage—of many limitations. She needed to understand that she had *chosen* a life of scaled-down expectations, and that she could choose to change it, if she wanted. I felt strongly that she should pursue the adventurous, independent life she dreamed about; Nina was in a joyless marriage, but she was not a joyless woman. If she was to avoid drying up the way her marriage had, she would need outside activities to fuel her passion for life.

On the other hand, if she chose to act on her craving for variety and adventure, she *might* end up destabilizing her marriage and needed to be aware of the risk. "Expanding your own life may rock the boat in your marriage," I told her. "You need to be clear about that."

Nina nodded thoughtfully. "I think that's what has kept me from acting on the things I'd like to do," she said. "I'm afraid that Mitch might end up divorcing me. I don't know what I'd do if Mitch left me."

Competent as she was, Nina felt, deep down, that she'd fall apart without Mitch. Even though she had done a great deal of growing up over the years, she had not relinquished her phantom self: the little girl who needed the comfort of knowing she was taken care of and would not be abandoned, and who needed her husband's support in order to believe in her own abilities.

Since Nina perceived her marriage as the bulwark of her life, her desire to stay in it was understandable. She had an instinctive grasp of the marriage's limitations, and felt strongly that a divorce *could* result if those limits were not respected. Her goal, as I saw it, was not to let herself dry up or let her marriage stand in the way of the fulfillment of her dreams and fantasies.

It is important for a woman to trust her instincts about her marriage: When she wants to make changes *but* she doesn't want to lose her more inflexible partner, assessing the risks is critical. She must ask herself; What *are* the limits of this marriage? How far is too far to push? What are the flexible areas? Nina felt that her marriage was flexible enough to accommodate her traveling, as long as she was not away for too long. When I asked her what she thought might happen, she said she could easily imagine Mitch responding to a woman who said, "Your wife's away for two months.... Why should you sit around waiting for her?"

This is a legitimate fear for anyone who is trying to create personal space within a marriage, and it was realistic for Nina to be wary of dangerously destabilizing the relationship. Being away for six weeks might be too long; maybe three weeks was the safe limit. When Nina felt that she'd found the right balance between striking out on her own and safe-guarding her marriage, she told Mitch she wanted to travel in Japan for a few weeks over the summer. He had looked surprised, she told me, but hadn't tried to dissuade her.

After I saw Nina for the last time, she called me and told me that Mitch wanted to consult with me, and that I had her permission to see him. Apparently, once Nina had terminated therapy, she had felt safe enough to tell Mitch about it, and he now felt concerned about their marriage. When he called to make the appointment, I wondered if I would find him to be the buttoned-up man in the button-down shirt Nina had described to me, or someone more open to change.

Mitch was handsome and well-spoken, and he *was* genuinely concerned; but seeing him reinforced my sense that Nina's path of personal fulfillment was the right one for her. Pleasant as Mitch was, he was clearly unlikely to change in the ways that would have satisfied Nina. Citing the trip to Greece the year before, he said he felt that he had tried hard to accommodate her wish for him to become more fun-loving and adventurous by spending money on travel and other luxuries. But, he added, "Nina wants me to change more and more, and I have to say that I've changed as much as I'm going to."

It is very common for one partner—either one of them— to be more satisfied with a marriage than the other is. In this case, the burden of change falls on the partner whose needs are not being met. For Nina, the path was clear: She had to keep growing, even if Mitch didn't. However, her decision to make changes at least opened the *possibility* for positive change to take place within the marriage.

Sometimes therapists, as well as well-meaning friends and relatives, try to push couples to leave joyless marriages. From the vantage point of standing *outside* a marriage, it is easy to say that it should end. But it is never the place of friends, relatives, *or* professionals to say this to a couple. People have their own complicated reasons for staying in marriages that appear to outsiders *not* to be satisfying their needs. (Nina's best friend had suggested several times that she leave Mitch and could not understand why Nina wouldn't take that step. Nina's decision to stay in the marriage and emphasize self-development was her attempt to satisfy her need for security *and* her new need for change and growth. Whether the marriage will change if *she* changes is impossible to predict; but it might.)

When I supervise couples therapists, I emphasize the importance of exploring the possibilities for change in a marriage. In one supervisory session, a young therapist asked me about a couple he was working with. He was discouraged; the husband was excessively dependent, while the wife was excessively controlling. It seemed hopeless. How far should you or can you push a couple? he asked. And what could he hope to achieve with them? He added that he thought he should be helping them break up, not stay together.

But breaking up is a personal decision, and again, no therapist has the right to influence a couple in that way. I told him that most people come to couples therapy not to split up but for help in making their marriages as good as they can be.

"But is that good enough?" he asked.

Often, it is. In the case we were discussing, my feeling was that the couple could achieve a better balance. My student was rightly concerned about the unhealthy rigidity of their roles, but it was possible that the edges of the roles could be softened, and the couple could renegotiate the terms of their marriage contract. Even though the couple most likely would not make *fundamental* changes, it was possible that they could *modify* their behavior, playing up the positive aspects in ways that would benefit both of them. A husband who is overly dependent can learn to be vulnerable *without* being childlike, while a wife who is controlling can learn to be caring *without* being suffocating.

During that session, I also talked about the seemingly "hopeless" marriage of Irv and Judy. But it *did* change, or at least was modified, within its limits.

THE CHILD IN THE MIDDLE

Like Amelia and Gene, whose focus on a troubled child allowed them to avoid facing difficult issues in their marriage,

Irv and Judy centered their lives around their twenty-year-old daughter, Lizzie, who was unemployed, living at home, and seriously anorexic. When a couple does this, the dysfunctional child's problems serve as the glue that maintains the family in an unhappy limbo. The parents communicate with each other through the child, but often, when the child gets better, the husband and wife, face-to-face with each other, find their marriage to be hollow. While Amelia and Gene were able to renew their marriage, Irv and Judy repaired and moved on, within limits.

When Irv and Judy came to consult with me, it was ostensibly because of Lizzie. She stayed home most of the day, often missing her therapy appointments, and not even talking on the phone to her friends. She said she intended to find a job, but never made any attempts to do so. Judy, a soft-spoken woman in her mid-forties, felt enraged and helpless. Every night, she cooked dinner and begged Lizzie to come to the table. Every night, Lizzie refused.

Typically, there would be an argument. Lizzie would finally come to the table after Irv demanded that she do so, but then she would refuse to eat. Judy would burst into tears, and Lizzie would run to her room and lock the door. Then Irv and Judy would spend a sad evening together in front of the television set, barely speaking, all too aware of the silence from upstairs. Other times, Irv would storm out of the house, "fed up," he said, with the craziness. "You two work this out," he'd say to Judy. "It's your problem." But, out of a sense of a responsibility, he'd always come back.

I suggested that Lizzie come with them to their second session and, when they agreed, braced myself for the shocking sight I was sure she would present. Sure enough, Lizzie was a sallow, emaciated girl, with dark circles beneath her eyes and fine, dark hair that was thin enough to show her scalp. Tellingly, she immediately sat down between her parents. When I asked her if she would trade places with me, she looked at me mistrustfully but complied. My unspoken purpose was to symbolically remove her from the center of her parents' marriage.

Immediately, Judy turned to her daughter. "We are so upset," she said. "We just want to help you, to do what's right for you, Lizzie. You know that, don't you?"

Lizzie nodded. Then Judy turned to me. "But she won't even try. I'm so frustrated. I love my daughter more than my own life. But she is ruining our family."

As tears began trickling down Judy's face, I thought of the eternal mother, submerged in her children long after they've stopped needing her—that tenacious phantom self so damaging to mid-life women and their marriages.

"Mom, stop it. Why won't you leave me alone?"

"Stop talking to your mother that way," Irv said. And then to me, "This is the way it always is, conflict between them all the time. I can't take it. I just can't."

Suddenly Judy turned on him. "So why don't you move out then? That's what you want, isn't it?"

"Maybe I will!"

"And then they'll blame me," Lizzie told me, her dull eyes suddenly flashing, "because I'm the crazy one. Everyone knows that."

It was clear from this session that Lizzie was the "problem" that was keeping her parents in the grip of an unhealthy relationship. In the next session—minus Lizzie—I asked Irv and Judy to think back on their marriage and its turning points. When had things become so sad and distant between them?

We traced it back five years, when Lizzie had started to become rebellious. Until then, she and Judy had been especially close, shopping and going to the movies together, confiding in each other as if they were best friends. But then suddenly, Lizzie stopped confiding in her mother and spending time with her. One night, Judy found birth control pills in plain sight on Lizzie's bathroom vanity table and, soon after, caught her sneaking out of the house at night to see a neighborhood boy whom Judy knew and disliked.

"I was very interfering," she admitted. "I love my daughter and I was worried about her, maybe overly so. I was after her all the time to break up with this boy. But after they finally did break up, she made friends with a girl who was bulimic. Lizzie became bulimic, too, and then she stopped eating almost entirely. She refused everything I gave her. When she wouldn't eat, I felt as if she was refusing *me*."

At that point Judy had lost interest in everything. She and Irv had no sex life; they rarely went out. The marriage became increasingly shadowy, a true phantom marriage. Below the surface, mutual rage seethed. Judy felt that Irv didn't care about their "fragile" daughter and that he didn't help her in her desperate search for the right treatment programs. Irv, feeling lonely, left out, and rejected by his wife in favor of his daughter, said nothing, instead filling his bitter bank with anger and sorrow.

I spoke with Irv and Judy about the importance of their reuniting in a concerted effort to help Lizzie help herself. "The best way to begin the work of renegotiating your marriage," I told them, "is to start by making Lizzie healthy and self-sufficient. Eventually, you will evolve away from your parental roles back into husband and wife roles. At this point, the bond between Judy and Lizzie is overpowering the marriage, and I want to reduce that bond and re-create strong, positive ties between the two of you."

I told them I wanted them to begin with an experiment. For one week, Irv was to take Judy's role as the involved parent, which meant coping on a day-to-day basis with Lizzie, making sure that she ate and went to her therapy sessions. Judy, meanwhile, was to assume the role of the more distant parent: If she had a question or suggestion to communicate to Lizzie, she would ask Irv to handle it. Under no circumstances would Judy deal directly with Lizzie's problems.

In spite of Judy's protests that Irv couldn't and wouldn't be able to understand or manage Lizzie's problems, the technique showed positive results almost immediately. As her intense relationship with her mother eased, Lizzie took steps toward independence. She attended her therapy sessions regularly, began seeing a nutritionist, and even sought out a self-help group on her own. She discussed with Irv some ideas about getting a job and, at dinner one night, said she was thinking of moving out of her parents' home once she found work.

Judy went into a panic. She told Lizzie she was still far too unsteady to go out on her own. Lizzie collapsed in tears and left the table. In a family session later that week, Lizzie sobbed out her fear that if she left home, her mother would become seriously depressed. "I know Mom and Dad aren't getting along," she said. "And Dad might leave. Mom doesn't have any friends because she's made me her whole life. What will happen to her if I move out?"

I could see how torn Lizzie was: The only way she could be the good daughter her mother wanted was to be a very bad daughter. If she got healthy enough to leave her mother, she might be the cause of her mother's emotional collapse.

To reassure her and ease the pain of separation, I said, "Lizzie, your concern for your mother is admirable, but you have to trust that she is getting help in therapy. Both of your parents will be learning how to help each other. I believe that both you and your mother are stronger now than you were three months ago. This might be a good time to start thinking about going out on your own."

As Lizzie turned to look at me, her eyes huge in her thin face, I felt a pang of concern for her. Like Judy, I thought Lizzie did look fragile and vulnerable; unlike Judy, I was convinced that separating from her mother was the only way for Lizzie to get stronger. My job now was to convince Judy that this was the right path *and* to build a foundation of mutual support between her and Irv.

In our next couples session, Judy began by saying, "I would worry about her all the time. What if she doesn't eat? Who will make sure she has regular meals and goes to her therapy sessions?"

Impatiently, Irv said, "She has friends. She has her therapist and her therapy group."

Enraged, Judy responded, "No one can take care of my daughter like I can! I'm the one who's gotten her into all the programs and talked to her therapists. I'm the one who really cares."

As gently as possible, I said, "But Judy, with all the love that you feel for your daughter, you haven't been able to cure her. You've told me that you feel rejected when she won't eat your food. But I also think that was Lizzie's way of declaring her independence from you. And because she felt guilty and insecure about separating, she did it in a way that was harmful to her and painful for you. Irv is right when he says Lizzie has other people in her life who care about her. This should free you to find personal happiness and happiness in your marriage. It's been a long time since you've thought about that, but now you and Irv will be able to reassess your marriage, see where you are and where you want to go."

"He wants to go out the door," she said bitterly. "He's put most of the burden on me all along. Now he just wants to leave."

They looked at each other uncertainly. I had the impression that for the first time in years they were really seeing each other. At this point, I said, "Parenthood has been a long, complicated detour for your marriage. I believe that you can pick up where you left off and become husband and wife again."

They looked at each other again, this time even more uncertainly. There was a long pause, then the session ended. I was glad they would have a week to let these new ideas sink in.

In their next session, Judy began by saying, "Irv and I have nothing in common except for Lizzie. And now that she's getting better, I don't know anymore."

"Perhaps," I suggested, "now that Lizzie is making progress, the two of you can begin to enjoy yourselves again."

"Only if Lizzie is okay."

"Of course, you want to feel confident of that. But I think she is in good hands now."

"Do you see what I've been talking about? All she thinks about is Lizzie," Irv put in. "If you think she's going to stop, you're wrong!"

"How do you think we might begin to change that?"

"It won't change," he said stubbornly. "She has no idea how *I* feel."

I glanced at Judy. Was she up to hearing how Irv felt? I was sure it wouldn't be easy for her. To my surprise, she drew herself up and looked at him directly. "So tell me," she said. "Go on. How *do* you feel?"

At this turning point in the therapy, Judy was amazed to hear how much Irv had resented the siphoning of her energy into their daughter. "I assumed he understood I had no choice," she said.

But Irv insisted that she *had* had a choice all along.

"What was I supposed to do, *ignore* her?" Judy argued. "You certainly weren't doing anything to help."

Irv admitted that he *had* distanced himself, then added that he'd often felt that Judy hadn't needed his help with Lizzie. Judy thought about it for a moment, then nodded reluctantly.

"So," I said, "the two of you tacitly agreed to play parental roles in which Judy was overinvolved and Irv was overly detached. No wonder you've been feeling so distant from each other and so angry."

A week later, Lizzie found a job and an apartment. The question that loomed for Irv and Judy was whether or not they would stay together.

We discussed the fact that they'd reached a plateau in their lives. By separating from Lizzie and launching her into her life, they had pulled together and accomplished a major parental objective of which they should feel proud. What lay ahead now in terms of their marriage was uncharted territory.

After a short silence, Judy said, "I don't know where we go from here. Irv's been wanting to leave, but maybe I should. I want to start thinking about me for a change. Not that there's anyone else," she added. "I don't think I'd ever get involved with a man again if I left Irv."

I was surprised and saddened to hear what Irv said next. "I wish there *was* somebody else, Judy." Turning to me, he said earnestly, "She deserves it. She deserves the best there is because she is a wonderful woman."

It was a genuine expression of love and concern. But as much as Irv wanted Judy to be happy, he honestly felt that he was incapable of giving her the love and satisfaction she deserved.

"I'm not interested in finding someone else," Judy said tiredly. "That isn't the answer for me. I just know I don't want to suffer, and I don't want Irv to suffer, either. We've both been through a lot, and both of us really deserve to be happier."

What did happen was that Judy's elderly, widowed mother became ill, and caring for her filled the vacuum in Judy's life that Lizzie had left behind. Even though this was a convenient way for Judy to avoid facing personal and marital issues, it was healthier than focusing on her daughter because now Judy could be genuinely helpful. This time around, Irv was supportive, doing his best to help out, and Judy let him. Sharing some of the burden allowed them to feel closer; tentatively, they began exploring the possibilities for giving love and attention to one another, as well as to a third person.

Some of the strongest bonds of attachment between couples are born from a mutual wellspring of sadness over such losses as their own loving relationship and their relationship with their children. But for Irv and Judy, the sadness was leavened with an unspoken sensitivity to each other's neediness. Both sensed the other's sadness and truly wanted the other to feel less pain and more pleasure.

Perhaps because of their deep bond, Irv and Judy were able to find the strength to acknowledge their frustrations and disappointments, bring their crisis to a head, and let go of their daughter. Many couples don't get even that far, staying locked instead in an eternal triangle with a child. But loving and letting go is what healthy couples do. For any couple, it is an achievement, but for a troubled couple, like Irv and Judy, it is a major accomplishment.

THE DIFFICULT MATE

For some people, the emotional distance of a joyless marriage is preferable because intimacy sets off fears of being controlled or "swallowed up." But these couples, too, can take steps toward change.

In his first session, Howard, a lean, tanned man in his early fifties, said that he'd come to me for advice on how to deal with his difficult wife, Rhoda. Over the course of their seventeen-year marriage, whenever Rhoda had felt insecure, Howard told me, she had become demanding, but over the last few years, her behavior had become more extreme. For example, if he were no more than a few minutes late getting home at night, she would become hysterical. She set all the rules and insisted that he abide by them. If he forgot to pick up something at the store, she would insist he go back for it even if it wasn't essential. He didn't understand her moods, but he wanted me to believe him when he said that she was a decent, worthwhile person who was trying her best to be a good wife.

Nonetheless, Howard was frustrated by the fact that she also wouldn't sit down and *talk* to him about any of these issues, and she had refused to come into therapy with Howard. She was so insecure, he told me, that she was even opposed to his coming by himself, convinced that I would lure him into leaving her. Howard was at his wits' end, ready to try anything.

In the next session, Howard continued talking about Rhoda: He was terribly concerned because she hated her job and was depressed, too, because the kids were about to leave home. Early in their marriage, he'd thought Rhoda's moods made her "deeper" and more interesting, but he had to admit he was becoming impatient with her depression and anxiety attacks. On the rare occasions when he convinced her to go to a party, she'd retreat to a corner and make disparaging remarks about the people, the food, and the decor, expecting Howard to join in with criticisms of his own. In fact, she refused anything pleasurable: lovemaking, a Sunday stroll in the park, catching an early movie, dinner with friends. She wouldn't even shop for new clothes because she got panicky in department stores.

Howard went on to describe what sounded like a classic mid-life softening: He had worked hard; now he was shifting gears, slowing down at the office. He wanted to socialize more with friends and travel. "I want to *enjoy* life," he said, giving me an almost pleading look. "Can you help me help Rhoda to become happier?"

I had been listening intently, taking note of Howard's loving, compassionate qualities, but trying to understand why he stayed in a marriage in which he and his wife seemed to want such different things. Finally I said, "I'm impressed by your dedication to your marriage. It is important for us to understand the strong bond between the two of you, and perhaps even bring Rhoda into therapy someday."

A typical joyless marriage is one in which the difficult partner's problems become the marriage's atmosphere, coloring every interaction and decision the couple makes. Usually, the difficult mate's partner colludes by becoming an expert on the troubled one's problems, playing the part of therapist, spending inordinate amounts of time and energy analyzing, sympathizing, and "helping." (In happy marriages, people spend far *less* time thinking and worrying about each other than do people in unhappy marriages.) Not all partners of difficult people want to walk out—nor should they. Once again, the goal is to discover the possibilities within the marriage by softening the rigid edges of the roles the couple play with each other.

I began to suggest to Howard ways of modifying his behavior. When he described a recent incident in which Rhoda had first agreed to go to a Christmas party with him but had then panicked at the last moment and insisted that he stay at home with her, I advised him not to comply the next time it happened.

Whenever Rhoda became hysterical or overly demanding, it was important that Howard *not* placate her, because that was an integral part of the cycle of their fighting. To break the cycle, Howard had to learn to say, "I'll talk with you when you're calmer," and walk out.

He also had to take steps *not* to concede to all of her demands. If for example, she refused to socialize, I advised him to say, "I love you, Rhoda, but I want to see our friends tonight," and then go to meet them himself. Howard told me that Rhoda's response would be "You don't love me. I've made you unhappy," and then she would cry until he soothed

her and apologized. I urged him *not* to soothe her but to take
her on: "If you stand your ground five, ten, fifteen times,
she'll stop. I can almost guarantee it!"

But Howard shook his head. "I hate to fight," he said.
"I've never been a fighter."

When I asked Howard to describe his parents' relationship, I wasn't surprised to learn that his mother was emotionally demanding and controlling, and that his father had
been absent most of the time. To make up for his father's
absence, Howard had catered to his mother and placated
her, just as he did now with Rhoda. With both his mother
and his wife, Howard feared conflict and had found ways to
avoid it, even though the price he was paying now was a lack
of intimacy and joy in his marriage.

Week after week, I suggested to him that if he only took
the chance of destabilizing the marriage—rocking the boat—
so that the problems could be exposed and addressed, a
better relationship would eventually emerge. If one partner
stops playing his or her part in the collusion, it falls apart. I
felt strongly that if Howard stepped out of his role, Rhoda
would intensify her demands for a while but finally give them
up. Howard would listen to me, shaking his head, insisting
that he only wanted peace and stability.

Just when I thought therapy was running out of steam,
I began noticing a subtle change in Howard. Instead of re-
signing himself to Rhoda's antipleasure orientation, he attended two parties without her, telling her that although his
first choice was to attend with her, he would go alone if
necessary.

But Howard had been right about one thing: The more
pressure he put on her, the more Rhoda panicked. He feared
she would have a breakdown without his constant, reassuring
presence. Then, in what ended up as the turning point in
his therapy, he reluctantly revealed a secret. Three years ago,
Rhoda had suffered from an anxiety disorder called hysterical conversion. Literally crippled by anxiety, she had been
unable to walk for months. At the time Howard would not
allow himself to believe that Rhoda's illness had emotional,
not physical, roots, and he had been in despair, thinking that

she had a terminal disease. Instead, she had recovered; but the experience had been so traumatic for him that he was terrified to risk bringing about another frightening episode.

"This was such a significant incident in your lives," I said. "Why didn't you mention it until now?"

He shrugged helplessly, then said that because he considered himself responsible for Rhoda's welfare, he felt as if he had let her down. In our next several sessions, we discussed how, with Rhoda, Howard could always play the role of the sane, rational partner; in counterpoint to her, he was a model of mental health. When I suggested this to Howard, and pointed out that he may have been enabling her hysterical behavior, something clicked and he began to wonder how he had been contributing.

Just once before he left therapy, Rhoda accompanied him to a session. She was an attractive woman with large, vulnerable eyes, and I found that I felt more compassion for her than I had thought I would. We talked about the ways in which their collusion had led to an impasse in their marriage, and I told her about the suggestions I had made to Howard. She listened quietly and said, finally, that she had been thinking about therapy for herself, although she hadn't yet made up her mind. When I looked at Howard, he was beaming at her, his arm draped protectively around her shoulders.

A few weeks later, after Howard had terminated therapy, I was left with a sense of incompletion; at the end of our work together, we had achieved less than I would have wished for. Ideally, I would have wanted to see Howard become less dependent on his own enabling behavior and continue to take strong stands with his wife, with Rhoda, in response, beginning to take steps toward feeling stronger and more secure. I enjoy seeing couples change, and I will encourage, cajole, and tempt them to make the most of themselves and their marriages. But working with people in joyless marriages means learning to accept limitations.

Typically, a joyless marriage is so settled in its routine of unhappiness that only a major crisis can shake it loose. One partner may very much want to change the marriage but stops short of taking the necessary steps because the risk seems too great. Still, each couple moves at their own pace, and with Howard and Rhoda there *had* been some movement: Howard had become aware of the dynamics at work in the marriage, and Rhoda was considering therapy for herself. Testing the limits may be slow, and the process of change may be less dramatic than we expect, but that may be how it begins.

When my old friend, who was so happy about her new status as a novelist and so sad and resigned about her marriage, later asked me to refer her to a good couples therapist, I was surprised and delighted. She said she knew that her husband was unlikely to change in fundamental ways, but she wanted to explore the limits of the marriage anyway. Laughingly, she added that she'd certainly need a therapist who would not expect miracles or judge her harshly for accepting an imperfect marriage.

I recommended a very wise woman therapist I know who, as I told my friend, understands that life—and marriage—are *never* perfect. Not for anybody.

CHAPTER TEN

Surviving
Mid-life Divorce

Even though this is a book about renewing marriage, it is important to say that some marriages cannot be revitalized. These are marriages with a long history of crises, impasses, and joylessness, marriages that are now running on empty. Sometimes one partner will find that as she (or he) renews herself, she does not want to work on renewing her marriage. In those cases, divorce can be a *positive* solution, giving both partners other chances to build satisfying relationships.

We all know how commonplace divorce has become, but the latest statistics have actually begun to show a small but steady decline in the overall rate of divorce.[1] There is some question about whether the rate among younger people has gone down at all, but most sociologists agree that as the baby boom generation moves into their forties, they are generally less inclined to want to start looking for new lifetime partners, especially in an era of economic recession. These factors, as well as the continued, frightening presence of AIDS and rising rates of gonorrhea and syphilis, are reinforcing a quiet return to the values of the long-term marriage.

Even with all this, it isn't realistic to think that the divorce rate will shrink to a pre–1960s rate. Nonetheless, in my practice over the last few years, I have noted that more and more couples are coming to therapy to repair and heal their marriages. By now, people know, from books, from hearsay, and from personal experience, that no matter how commonplace divorce has become, it hurts like hell, having a *lasting* impact on one's life.

For mid-life couples, this is particularly relevant because it is so difficult to rebuild lives after a long-term marriage has ended. "Going back to square one" is the way one man somberly put it after his twenty-two-year-old marriage had ended. "I can't believe I'm out on the meat market again" is another way that many people express the same feeling about divorce now, at this stage of life.

Since the stakes are so much higher, I strongly recommend that couples think seriously before deciding to dissolve a twenty-year partnership. A marriage may look hopeless, and may not be. Other couples who shouldn't hang in there, do. But when so much precious time and energy has been invested in a marriage, it makes the best sense to set aside one more year, see a therapist, if necessary, and find out for sure whether all is lost. It's encouraging to know that the statistics are on the side of mid-life marriages: Reconciliation is likelier to occur in relationships in which the couples have been married for more than twenty-five years, as well as among those without children at home.[2] Couples with a long shared history have more motivation to stay in their marriages. Once children are out of the equation a couple *has* to deal more directly with one another.

THE TIME-LIMITED MARRIAGE

At mid-life, many marriages can be *renewed;* others may be *repaired* to the extent that they can accommodate the partners' needs more fully than before. Still others never had the vital juice necessary for growth and change and now lack the adrenaline necessary to face the challenges of mid-life.

I have been asked why I am including a chapter about divorce in a book that focuses on *reviving* marriages. The reason is that mid-life divorce is a reality for some people, and I don't want to give the impression that all marriages can overcome the mid-life stalemate. The difference between marriages that last and marriages that end lies in whether or not the couple can proceed through the cycle of conflict, repair, and renewal. Because some marriages *cannot,* in this chapter I will discuss the time-limited marriage—the kind of marriage that survives for years, then ends at the mid-life turning point.

The primary characteristic of the time-limited marriage is profound, chronic, long-term dissatisfaction. A woman may be embittered by her husband's long-standing inattention to her needs, for example, or a man may have felt for years that he has outgrown his wife. These dissatisfactions are intractable enough to rule out any possibility of renegotiating a marriage contract. Renewing a marriage takes energy, desire, and dedication, which a couple is unlikely to have on tap when their energy has been used to fuel their unhappiness.

The marriages that don't survive the turning points of mid-life generally share at least one of these four themes: (1) a lack of a strong sense of commitment in either partner toward the other or toward making the marriage work; (2) an ongoing absence of sexual or emotional chemistry; (3) a lack of conflict-free areas that the partners share and enjoy together; (4) a dissipation through conflict of mutual liking and respect.

Sometimes couples don't understand what I mean by "conflict," and in fact, the word does have more than one meaning. On the positive side, a certain amount of conflict is actually necessary for the continuing growth and energizing of a marriage, and many passionately conflictual marriages have a great potential for renewal. But those marriages in which conflict is so destructive that the couple cannot communicate about most topics and issues probably will not survive mid-life.

This is the time when the hidden limitations of individuals, and marriages, are brought to light. A couple may now confront the fact that their marriage lacks elasticity and the capacity for change, that its center doesn't hold. As negotiations stall and fall apart, a marriage of fifteen or twenty years' duration may come to an end.

Why Men Leave

Men and women have different motivations for divorce at mid-life. As we have seen with the man who has a mid-life affair, the man who divorces his wife does so at least partly to ward off his sense of decline, as well as to avoid confronting mid-life issues. At this point, a man also may crave *more* from life—intimacy, as well as excitement and adventure—but find that his marriage cannot accommodate his need for personal renewal. Sometimes, a man meets another, younger woman, falls in love with her, then impulsively rejects the old in favor of the new.

When Bob, a fifty-one-year-old financial adviser, initiated couples therapy, he knew already that he wanted a divorce from his wife, Tamar. After a few sessions, he told me, privately, that he was having an affair with his secretary, and we designated the next couples session as the one in which he would tell Tamar. As that session wound down, and Bob still had said nothing about the affair, I tried to catch his eye, but he avoided looking at me. In the next few sessions, instead of detailing his grievances and dissatisfactions and bringing the affair into the open, he would say only that he was unhappy sexually. At that point, the couple's unconscious collusion would kick in: Instead of confronting the problem, Tamar would cry, and Bob, feeling guilty, would back off.

A therapist who knows about a secret affair is in collusion with the partner who is keeping it secret. My dilemma was that while I had to allow Bob the latitude to divulge his secret in his own time and way, I also had to keep pushing him to do it so that my neutrality would not be tainted. Once that happens, the therapeutic process breaks down.

Throughout this uneasy period in the therapy, Tamar had been urging Bob to take her on a romantic trip to Paris. At forty-eight, she was a little girl, living in a wishful fantasy of marriage. Bob, consumed with guilt that he could not make her fantasy come true, finally reluctantly agreed to the vacation. With growing frustration, I watched as Tamar's eyes shone softly at the thought of this special interlude with her husband. I was, in fact, frustrated with both of them, with Bob for his procrastination and with Tamar for her blind fantasizing. I knew that on their return, I would tell Bob that he either must put his cards on the table or end the therapy at once.

In their first session upon returning, Tamar talked at length about how lovely and perfect the trip had been—about their walks along the Seine; long, relaxed afternoons at sidewalk cafés; an entire day together in the Louvre. When I glanced at Bob, I saw him take a deep breath and knew the moment of truth had come.

He had something to tell her, he said. For him, the trip had not been a romantic interlude, an opportunity for "renewal," as she had so naïvely put it. It had been torture for him because, in fact, he was in love with another woman. Even when Tamar began to cry, he didn't back off but waited quietly until she stopped and calmly told her he wanted to separate.

In the weeks that followed, both husband and wife suffered. In individual sessions, Tamar wept and said repeatedly that she wanted Bob back at all costs, while Bob, miserable with guilt, said he felt like a monster for leaving but that he'd had no choice.

After a while, though, Tamar began pulling herself together. Gathering her strength, she demanded that Bob tell her how long the affair had been going on; upon learning that it had lasted for a year, she saw clearly that the marriage was indeed over.

Tamar now could look at Bob with eyes unclouded by her idealization of him and their marriage. As she thought back on their years together, raising their family, building his career, shaping a *life*, she began to see his limitations, too—the fact that he was unable to be close with anyone, including their children, and that he had no real friends. She saw, too, that he had begun drinking heavily. In a session she told me, "Bob is not in touch with any of his feelings. He hides behind his suits and ties, and that's what he's always done." She saw that he had fallen in love with an "inappropriate" woman, years younger and less educated than he was, with whom true intimacy could not be possible. She saw, too, that she had poured her energy into playing the role of the undemanding, selfless superwife in order to meet Bob's needs, all the while neglecting her own. Also, she came to see that his stated sexual dissatisfaction with her had been a smoke screen for his own sexual guilt, which had placed as much of a restraint on their sex life as any problems she had brought to the marriage bed.

Demythologizing, de-idealizing, and reexamining an ended marriage are necessary steps toward processing its loss. As she faced reality squarely, Tamar was able to take action on various issues: To ensure that their children spent time with Bob, she put into effect a realistic visitation schedule, and she also demanded the alimony he owed her.

By the time I had finished treating this couple, I had had some self-realizations, too. I had felt uncertain about the success of the treatment, because I tend to define success as the resolution of a couple's problems. But, as was the case with Bob, whenever one partner has already made up his mind to leave and is simply going through the motions of couples therapy so that he feels he has "done everything" he can, the therapy will not be able to save the marriage. The difference between Jason, the museum curator, who believed himself to be in love with his young assistant, and Bob was that even though Jason *seemed* to have made up his mind to leave the marriage, in truth he had more invested in his family than he had thought. Bob, on the other hand, did not feel committed to his family; nor had he experienced any revival of interest in his wife, as Jason had about his wife, Valerie.

Even though the therapy had not saved the marriage, the treatment had worked on other levels. As a couple, Tamar and Bob had been classic conflict-avoiders—she'd deny there was anything wrong; he'd back off—whenever any difficult issues were raised. *All* topics ended up off-limits; nothing could be discussed. Only Tamar's illusions had held the marriage together, and they were a very unreliable glue.

Finally, though, they had moved off the dime. Tamar's fantasies might have died, but she had come to life. No longer breaking down in tears whenever reality came too close, she mourned her losses and moved on. Within a year, a friend had introduced her to another man, and she wrote to tell me that she was sure she wouldn't make the same mistakes this time around: "I feel as though I've become so much stronger through everything that happened with Bob. Now I deal with problems instead of running away."

I felt proud of her for accepting the loss of her fantasy marriage, bearing the pain of its loss, and moving on with her life.

THE ABANDONED WOMAN

As we've seen, a husband's other woman is not always young and "inappropriate." Like Will, in an earlier chapter, who had an affair with a woman colleague in her late thirties, a man may fall in love with a professional woman who is his equal in the working world. He leaves his wife because he finds her old-fashioned and feels he has outgrown her. As increasing numbers of women move into highly responsible jobs, this situation has become almost routine. Far from routine, however, are the emotional consequences for the wife and children who have been left behind.

I first became acquainted with Alison through her daughter, twenty-seven-year-old Nancy. Nancy had come to see me because she was going to be married in a few months, but found herself increasingly panicked as the day drew nearer.

She said she'd heard about my work with commitment-phobic men—did I think she was a commitment-phobe? Was it even possible for *women* to be that way? Why was she so afraid to marry the man she loved?

It turned out that Nancy's parents had split up several years before. Her father had left her mother for another woman, a cable television executive, and her mother, Alison, had not recovered. At a superficial glance, Nancy said, her mother seemed fine, and in many ways, she *was* fine: At fifty-two, she was attractive, cheerful, and busy. She worked hard and had made many friends as a volunteer fund-raiser for the local hospital.

But Nancy, who was close to her mother, knew the whole truth: Every year since the divorce, when Alison's birthday rolled around, she waited for a surprise gift, a card in the mail, or a phone call from her ex-husband. Of course, she was always disappointed. On *his* birthdays, she sent cards to him; receiving no reply did not deter her from trying again the following year. And her mother still wore her wedding ring and kept her married name.

Alison's badge of identity, her self-definition, was "di-vorcée," and she had been living in the shadow of rejection for years, blaming herself for the failure of her marriage. Nancy had tried to argue and cajole her mother out of the quagmire of sadness and self-blame she was caught in, but it seemed hopeless. Her mother, like so many wives with low self-esteem, believed that if she'd only been a better wife, her husband would not have fallen in love with someone else.

No wonder Nancy was fearful of committing herself to marriage! She was traumatized not only by the divorce itself, but by her mother's inability to move on, thaw out of the deep freeze she'd put herself in, and start a new life. Nancy also feared that by getting married, she would be abandoning her mother, just the way her father had.

Nancy postponed her wedding once, then twice. But as she began to understand the reasons behind her fear of mar-riage, she decided, with my encouragement, to discuss the situation with her mother. Unfortunately, when Nancy next walked into my office, she was clearly depressed.

The talk had gone badly. Her mother had been offended, saying she felt as though Nancy was blaming her for Nancy's own fears about getting married. Feeling as if her mother had turned on her, Nancy had lashed out at her, asking, "Who took care of you after Dad left? Who have you leaned on all this time?"

Nancy was guilt-stricken and remorseful about having said more than she had meant to, and I was worried that I had pushed her too hard to confront her mother. But the outcome convinced me differently.

Nancy decided she would not postpone her wedding date again. And as the weeks went by, she began noticing changes in her mother. Alison joined a local organization for divorced women, and then she and a friend organized a reading club for women who, like themselves, wanted the stimulation and good discussion a book group might bring. Next, Alison officially took back her maiden name, and finally put away her wedding ring for good.

As Nancy watched her mother's recovery process, her own anxieties about love and loss, as well as her fears of abandoning her mother, began to diminish. We discussed the fact that as Alison saw Nancy's life evolving, she had gathered the courage she needed to move ahead with her own life. It seemed that Nancy's wedding would actually be a positive event for both mother and daughter, and in fact, to Nancy's delight, her mother came to her wedding escorted by a male friend, a widower she'd known and liked for years.

Nancy told me that in a frank talk with her mother after the wedding, Alison said she had decided that Nancy was right: She hadn't moved on with her life, and it had hurt both of them. Also, she told Nancy, she hated the idea that she had become pitiful. She'd had an insight that people were starting to feel sorry for her—"Poor Alison, she never got over her divorce"—and she hated to provide such grist for the gossip mill. After the divorce, she had honestly felt that her life was over; but now, she said, she was enjoying the company of another man, and of the many new friends she'd made as she expanded her activities. In the excitement of her life in the present moment, she could see at last that her marriage had been just one part of her life, and that another part was beginning.

When a woman who has always seen herself as one half of a couple suddenly finds herself single, she may very well feel like just half a person, or even as if part of herself has died. The other common postdivorce reaction is to *downplay* the marriage in an attempt to deny the trauma of its loss: "It wasn't any good anyway, I don't see why I should be upset" is a typical statement. But both of these reactions are distortions of the situation. Women who survive well learn to be more realistic. They acknowledge their losses and undergo a mourning process. Then they rediscover the pieces of themselves—with Alison, those pieces were the wide variety of interests she had—that they had put aside while they were part of a couple.

Her daughter's marriage had been the impetus she needed to take control of her life once again. Ultimately, "losing" Nancy meant that Alison could take the necessary steps toward finding herself.

As for Nancy's father, in a situation common to many mid-life men, he had walked out of his marriage just as he was at the pinnacle of his career, with all the intense pressures and power that accompany professional success. At that point, a man will often say of the woman to whom he has been married for twelve to fifteen years or more, "She doesn't understand me. She doesn't appreciate who I am or what I do."

Sadly, this is often true, especially in those instances when a woman does not work outside the home and has no way of understanding a man the way a working woman does. This woman can grasp the excitement, the tension, the sense of accomplishment, as well as the fear of "not making it," that accompany the wins and losses at work. She is riding the same roller coaster he is.

What often happens at just this time is that a couple's children hit adolescence, as Alison's had. *Unlike* Nancy, they may become rebellious, do poorly in school, or develop drug or alcohol problems. Often, a husband will blame the wife who has stayed home, whose job it was to raise the kids. In a marriage in which the partners play gender-defined roles, the husband, who has been relatively uninvolved with the children, is likelier to want out at this point. In a situation in which both partners have had a hand in child rearing, they are more likely to stick it out and problem-solve together.

WHY WOMEN LEAVE

A woman taking the divorce initiative is usually not acting impulsively—as many men do—but has probably considered all of her options. Most women are aware they must be realistic about their chances for remarriage: According to one study, a woman divorced in her twenties has a 76 percent chance of remarriage; a woman in her thirties has a 56 percent chance, while a woman in her forties has a 32 percent chance. The woman in her fifties has less than a 12 percent chance.[3]

But even though men may initiate divorce more often than women do, and have more options in terms of new relationships, women usually end up—in spite of the sobering statistics on remarriage—stronger, more self-confident and more autonomous than they ever imagined they could be.

Often, like Julie, forty-one, the woman who opts for divorce at mid-life has experienced a profound inner transformation. Julie knew that she was supposed to be a happily married wife: Her forty-two-year-old husband, Dean, was a successful psychiatrist, and they had two well-adjusted teenagers. But for as long as she could remember, Julie had felt frustrated by Dean's remoteness. Even when he was at home, he was emotionally absent from the family. Their sexual relationship, which had been satisfying in the early years of marriage, had become mechanical, and Julie felt sexually anesthetized. All that they shared now was a love for tennis; on the court they connected, but at home and in bed, they missed every shot.

Julie wanted to walk out of the marriage, but she was afraid. Beneath her lively, energetic exterior, she was frightened and dependent. She had worked part-time for years but had a sneaking suspicion that she couldn't *really* make it in the workplace. Like so many other mid-life women who didn't have careers when they were young, Julie was her own worst enemy; crippled by her fears and lack of self-confidence, she took cover within an unsatisfactory marriage.

One day she noticed that her period was late, then learned she was pregnant. She waited until she got home from the doctor's office before dissolving into tears. Having another child would mean that she was trapped, once and for all, in the marriage. She realized she could not deny herself one last chance for self-fulfillment, and even though it was a bitter choice to make, Julie finally decided to have an abortion.

When she told Dean, he was deeply affronted, accusing her of caring only about herself, not about him or the marriage. But Julie didn't waver; she had decided to break her pattern of submerging her own needs in those of other people. Having the abortion was a powerful symbol of her lack of faith in the marriage, as well as of her determination to take independent action in her own best interests.

After the abortion, Dean was cold and unforgiving, and a few months later, Julie fell into a steamy affair with a divorced neighbor. (This is one of the ways in which women use temporary, *transitional* affairs: to help them shore up their self-confidence so that they can *leave* a marriage.) Emotionally reinforced, Julie then found a good lawyer and an apartment for herself and her kids and moved out.

Julie was flying high—liberated and jubilant. For the first time in years, she knew she was doing something that was right for *her*. But what many women don't know is that the transitional affair is *dangerous;* a woman may have an inflated, almost euphoric sense of well-being once she is out of her marriage and into a relationship in which she feels appreciated. At the same time she may have unrealistic expectations of her lover, and she may be trying to avoid the process of mourning and healing that must follow the loss of her marriage and family life.

Julie learned this in a particularly painful way. The first time her husband took the kids for the entire weekend, she suggested to her lover that they spend the time together. He agreed, then at the last moment canceled, matter-of-factly telling her that he had decided to go back to a former girlfriend. Julie felt as if the breath had been knocked out of her; and in the following weeks, she was hit by a sense of loss and a devastating depression. All the worse because it was so belated and unexpected, her panic over leaving her marriage finally had been triggered by her lover's abandonment. The weeks that followed saw all of her newfound self-confidence crushed. Worst of all, feeling that she must "make do" because she deserved nothing better, Julie continued to see her lover.

Five years later and fully recovered, Julie looks back at herself as she was then with great compassion. She said, "I just didn't have a strong enough sense of self to deal with what life had in store for me. I relied on the affair for sustenance, without understanding how much I had invested in this man. When I saw that I was truly alone, I fell apart."

Now in her late forties, Julie is happily remarried to a man who is warm and caring, and says she "feels like a different person." Her one regret is her parents' poor reaction to her divorce; they had raised her to be taken care of by a successful, financially secure man, and it proved to be beyond their ability to grasp her reasons for leaving her husband. No longer the good little girl her parents and her husband had expected her to be, Julie feels she is on her own, saddened in some ways, strengthened in others. "This is the second half of my life," she says. "I could never have predicted it would turn out like this."

Julie's marriage was time-limited because she changed and it didn't. (Looking back, we can see the same dynamic in Charlotte and Will's marriage: Charlotte, a Resister, didn't change; she only focused on making herself a "better" wife, and her marriage thus became time-limited; however, Emily, a "woman who waited" for the affair to end, changed *herself*, and her marriage ended up changing, too.)

In Julie's case, after a point her marriage became a masquerade, with Julie acting the role of the happy wife while she was dying inside. When a marriage speaks only to a false self, a person is living a false life. It may *look* like a life, but there is no real connection, no authenticity. Leaving the marriage allowed Julie the opportunity for growth and change, for rebirth.

Women must pay careful attention to any deep, ongoing sense of suffocation and entrapment. One of my clients came into therapy for the first time at the age of fifty-five. Fifteen years before, she had remarried after the sudden death of her first husband. Her new husband helpfully took over many of the details of her life until she was ready to get back on her feet. What she discovered later was that he needed to be in control at all times, not only when she needed him to be. Now, he is demanding and difficult, and the emotional effect the marriage has had on her is disturbingly apparent: She said that her hair is quickly going gray and she sees lines in her face she has never noticed before. Ironically, this prematurely aging woman is a little girl who never grew up, circumventing the process of healing and growth by marrying a man who, in the guise of taking care of her, actually took control of her life. If a woman's husband is abusive or excessively demanding, controlling or distant, leaving him may be the only way that she can save her own life. This particular woman is just beginning to explore that option.

At mid-life, many women are more willing than ever before to take important risks. When a woman is younger, she may be looking for a man she can take care of or she may tend to idealize men. Or she may be compromised by her own neediness and not place enough trust in her own instincts, even when they are on red alert.

Learning self-trust was, for my friend Olivia, a matter of hard-won experience. A sweet, soft-spoken woman, Olivia had always wanted to trust her husband, Ted, so she accepted his assurances that he was not having an affair with their mutual acquaintance, Evelyn. Before they were married, he had told her that in his first marriage he had had affairs, but that he'd seen the light and learned his lesson. He swore he'd never do it again.

Much as she wanted to believe him, Olivia was uneasy. She is a cellist in a small symphony orchestra, and she works in the evenings. Often, she would return home to find that Ted and Evelyn had spent those evenings out together; but always Ted would make light of Olivia's fears that there was more than friendship between the two of them. After a while, he swore he would stop seeing her completely, simply because he didn't want to upset Olivia.

"But my inner voice was telling me he was still seeing her," Olivia said. "At the same time, I began doubting my own perceptions. Pretty soon it came down to, either I was crazy for thinking he was seeing her or he was lying. In order to stay in the marriage, I had to go along with *his* idea that *I* was crazy." And so began Olivia's nightmare. As Ted continued to deny he was having an affair, treating Olivia as if she were paranoid any time she brought it up, she began "feeling crazier and crazier."

Olivia said, "Each person has a breaking point, and once it happens you can't go back. In that moment, everything shifts and changes, and it's never the same again." Her own personal breaking point, the moment when she "couldn't live that way any longer," came when she returned after a performance one evening. Ted was nowhere to be found, and did not return home that night.

When she confronted him the next day, he said that he'd been out with friends and had fallen asleep on someone's couch. The details of his story were so farfetched that Olivia knew absolutely that he was lying. "Something snapped," she said. "I told him, 'I can't do this anymore.' At that point, my life depended on leaving. I packed my clothes and moved in with my sister."

That weekend, Ted finally admitted to her that he'd been sleeping with Evelyn for years. "I felt so many things," Olivia said. "Rage over the way he'd systematically lied to me and tried to convince me I was crazy; relief at knowing I *wasn't* crazy; and then fear over how this had happened. How had

I let him have so much power over my mind?"

When he realized that Olivia hadn't just moved out for a few days, Ted began calling her every day. "I'm turning fifty," he told her. "I don't need this. Why are you doing this to me? Why don't you come home?" He moved from this position to saying, "I've learned my lesson; I swear I'll never do it again." Olivia listened, in sorrow and in anger, to the promises she'd heard so many times in the past. This time she knew she'd never believe him again. "He wanted things back the way they had been," she said. "And I didn't. I realized we wanted completely different things."

Olivia went into group therapy, and found that many of the women in the group were in the process of recovering from ended relationships. "I felt inadequate as a woman and as a wife," she said. "I'd thought that if I could only *be* enough, *love* enough, that it would work out. But nothing was enough. When I left Ted, I didn't have a shred of self-esteem left. It had been totally destroyed." She also found a therapist she could see individually so that she could examine "unfinished childhood business. The last thing I want to do is repeat destructive patterns in relationships."

Paradoxically, Olivia now feels as if her experience with Ted was a gift of sorts, which, after the initial anguish, opened her to a wealth of new insights about herself. "What happened with Ted will affect every relationship I have in the future," she said. "What I've learned will help me create the tools I need to understand myself and the way that I relate to other people."

Olivia is unusual in her determination to use the painful experience of divorce as a vehicle for self-discovery. And even if viewing divorce as a gift may at first seem impossible, it is eventually possible, as Olivia found, for people to use it as a unique opportunity to take a deep, enriching look at themselves and their relationships. Divorce, in this case, becomes a *transforming* experience, a reconstruction of a person's life during which she discards that which is self-destructive. And on this, Olivia said something that intrigued me: "I want to understand the difference between *trust* and *denial*. Did I deny what I knew all along was the truth because it was so important to me to trust Ted? I can't answer this yet, but I do need to learn never to override my own instincts and to respect and treasure the signals I send myself. I spent seven years denying those signals. In the future, I will always listen to those first."

As they age, many women become more vulnerable in some ways but stronger in others, better equipped with the tools they need either to make their marriages work or to leave the ones that don't.

DEATH OF A 1980S MARRIAGE

In my practice and among friends, I have seen some marriages that have not survived the changing social and economic milieu of the 1980s. Those were marriages based on an *appearance* of financial and emotional stability that in the end were unable to withstand unexpected hardships and disappointments.

For some people, the 1980s were a time of seemingly limitless personal ambition, self-gratification, and grandiose dreams of money and prestige. A sense of immortality, the feeling that we as a society were on an endless roll, went hand in hand with the belief that all things material were possible to achieve. People didn't think about the long-term consequences of big earnings and big spendings: Having it all and living it up were the mottoes of the age. Some marriages that flowered in this atmosphere have not been resilient enough to flourish in harder times.

When Anthea, fifty-two, said that her twenty-year-old marriage to Alex, fifty-five, had died with the decade, she remarked that Alex had been the "the best possible husband for good times." During the 1980s, the couple had colluded in living beyond their means, extending their credit, buying state-of-the-art computers for their antiques business, and purchasing a Park Avenue apartment and a Porsche. Even when it began to become clear that their finances were flimsy, they continued to maintain their life-style and take extravagant vacations.

The only change they made, in fact, was that the flimsier their financial base became, the more immoderately Alex spent their money. When Anthea finally began demanding that he take charge of their business in a more responsible way, Alex, a classic Denier, responded by buying more office equipment, and a sable coat for her.

Alex was one of the most charming men Anthea had ever known, but the charm was wearing off fast. "Life with Alex began to seem like one big prop," she said. "When the creditors were hounding him, and we were obviously teetering on the edge of financial ruin, he booked tickets for a vacation to Indonesia. That was when I knew I couldn't live with him any longer."

Their business failed, and the couple's only remaining asset was the Park Avenue co-op, which Anthea managed to sell. Now she is living with friends and working. Six months after their split, Alex still denies the marriage is over. "She'll be back," he states confidently.

Nor has he accepted that an entire era of his life is over. He is living on money left over from the sale of the apartment, traveling, trying to make deals. Meanwhile, Anthea is facing the music. "Our marriage was as precarious as our finances," she said. "So much was based on image. As long as things *looked* great, they had to be great." At this point, Anthea doesn't know what the future holds for her; she only knows she will be leading a far more scaled-down and realistic life-style.

None of us is on an endless roll. Facing our limits and looking reality squarely in the eye are an inevitable part of life. In the 1980s, it seemed for a while as if there was no end to youth and good times. Denial was built into the way we lived. But both societies and individuals reach turning points, and as we could not avoid the inevitable "crash" at the end of the 1980s, we cannot avoid the issues and turning points of mid-life.

The Dilemma of the Mid-life Baby

Another sign of the times that I'm seeing among clients is a whole new category of stress that affects mid-life marriages as childless women in their late thirties and early forties bring their growing desire to have children into partnerships that have a long history of being "just us." A woman approaching forty may realize that it is now or never if she wants to have children, and some marriages are not holding.

Forty-year-old Lorie recognized that her marriage would have to undergo considerable change if she and her husband, Evan, decided to have a child. Evan was used to scheduling his time for his own convenience, and she, too, had become accustomed to leading a life focused on her own pleasures and goals. But now she felt ready to refocus on family, and she assumed that Evan would make the shift, too.

Evan and Lorie had been together for a number of years, and although Evan had been commitment-shy at the beginning, eventually he had come around and agreed to get married. With most major decisions involving the two of them—from deciding to see one another exclusively soon after they'd first met, to living together, to getting married— Lorie had been the one to push, with Evan passively complying.

In their marriage, each had pursued their independent lives and careers, with Evan traveling on business several months of every year. But they had enjoyed their time together so much that the absences hardly seemed to matter: Together they'd go off to country inns on weekends and sometimes meet for late afternoon movies on weekdays. They took ballroom dancing lessons together and went club-hopping all over the city with a circle of friends who shared their new passion.

After nearly a year of discussion, forty-two-year-old Evan finally agreed to go along with Lorie's desire to have a child.

Relieved and happy, Lorie went on to become pregnant and give birth to a son. She was not prepared, however, for Evan's reaction. Throughout the first few months of the baby's life, he acted resentful any time she asked him to help out with caring for the baby, cooking, or cleaning up. He continued to go out with friends several nights a week and worked longer hours than ever. Lorie told herself that Evan needed time to adjust, and she went through agonies of self-doubt: Had she been unfair to Evan by having the baby? Had she been selfish? Had she ruined the marriage? Was this whole situation her own fault? When she tried to discuss these questions with Evan, he'd turn away.

When she insisted that he come for a couples session, he said that he felt that he'd only agreed to having the baby because Lorie had insisted. He'd felt as if he'd given in to her once more. With much bitterness, he said, "Lorie's always been in the driver's seat. Now she's gotten her way again."

He did not attend more sessions, and Lorie continued on her own. When several months had gone by, and Evan's absences continued, Lorie finally decided that his withdrawal from their life together left her with no choice. Hard as it was to leave the marriage with a ten-month-old infant in tow, Lorie packed up and left.

After the split, she puzzled over what had gone wrong in the marriage, telling me that she couldn't stop wondering if it had been something *she* had done. She also could not comprehend how Evan's former love for her had seemed to evaporate, and how he could seem to have so little feeling for his son.

Lorie and I discussed the sad reality that even though Evan probably had loved her in his own way, sometimes love turns out not to be enough. As long as his own needs had come first, the relationship had worked. (Tensions had only developed when Lorie had "pushed" him into making more serious commitments to their relationship and, finally, into agreeing to start a family.) But Evan had not been willing to make *real* accommodations to family life, and he had not allowed himself to develop feelings for his child.

Narcissistic love places the self first and foremost, while mature love involves the ability to place equal importance on the needs of others. Evan had not been able to make the transition from love of self to love of others; his love had not been able to expand, to become greater and more inclusive.

After she had spent some time processing her loss, Lorie related her own situation to a tragic turn of events in Evan's family of origin. While his mother had been dying of cancer two years before, his father, a prominent corporate lawyer, had continued his demanding schedule of litigation and business travel, leaving his wife to grapple with her physical and emotional suffering alone. "The thought of my mother-in-law haunts me," Lorie said, "because I knew very well that that could have been me and Evan twenty years from now. Evan's father was simply unable to change his own routine and accommodate to a new reality, and his mother died alone. I wouldn't want that to happen to me. It just isn't the kind of marriage I want or the kind of model of marriage I want to show to my child."

I agreed with Lorie that if Evan had been unable to come through for her and for their marriage after the birth of their child, he most likely would have been unable to come through during other important crises of mid-life or old age. Evan had shown no sign that he was open to change, and his behavior had been too hurtful to Lorie for her to tolerate in the hope that he would someday change.

Evan had been another good partner for good times, who had not been able to make difficult but necessary accommodations. When Lorie understood that he would not change his life-style, and that she would have no real partner in child raising, she knew this would be intolerable for her.

Their marriage, until the birth of the baby, had been untested, a partnership of two independent people who made few demands on each other. "Evan and I spent an extended adolescence together," Lorie said ruefully. "In our early forties, we had to grow up fast, sink or swim. Our marriage sank, but I'm still swimming."

Lorie lost her marriage when she gained a child—a difficult loss, a valuable gain, an unfortunate trade-off for a woman to have to make. But the higher a woman's income, the likelier she is to divorce. Lorie, who was not economically dependent on Evan, knew she could make it on her own. Ultimately, she and I both felt that she had chosen what was best for her and her child.

I often tell women, such as Lorie, who choose to divorce that they will find within themselves survival skills they never dreamed they had. A woman who has been married for most of her adult life may feel especially terrified at the thought of being on her own after she has been married, although unhappily so. But she should understand that her fears may be temporary. In fact, one startling study has shown that married mid-life women are no more content than their un-married counterparts, while mid-life men without a spouse were twice as likely to die within ten years as men living with a spouse.[4] In other words, a lot of women are a lot tougher than they think they are. (As we discussed in the Introduc-tion, by mid-life, women have more experience than men do in handling difficult life transitions, so it makes sense that women have the resources they need to grow and change after a divorce.)

At the age of forty-seven, Irene, a client whom I had been seeing for some time, decided to leave her alcoholic husband. For years, she had colluded with Barry in denying his prob-lem, but when his drinking started affecting his health and he wouldn't even consider stopping, Irene became depressed. Finally, she took stock of her marriage by asking herself, "Does this work for me?" and realized that it would only work if she were willing to forgo her joy in living. Through talking with friends in Al-Anon, she began to see that the familiar, enabling role she had always played with her husband was hurting both of them. Sadly, the realization came too late to save the marriage.

Her decision to leave upset her grown daughters. "How can you leave Dad now?" the younger one asked. "And how will you make out on your own?" It is common for a woman's grown children to feel loyal to the parent who is being left behind, as well as feeling personally betrayed. But Irene, now fifty, is flourishing: She has a city apartment near her job, a wide network of friends, and she travels as often as she can. Being fifty and alone may make her seem vulnerable, but she *feels* far less vulnerable now in the happy, productive life she has created for herself than she did in a marriage that was injurious to her emotional well-being. The danger lies in looking for salvation through a transitional affair or in not facing the fact that rebuilding your life takes time and work.

A divorce can make you terribly, but temporarily, vulnerable. If you have a realistic handle on recovery and rebuilding, you can end up in a position of new strength.

After an affair—or any other kind of major crisis—has severely disrupted a marriage, a client often will ask me whether or not I think the marriage will survive. A number of women have put it this way: "Can you tell which marriages will end and which won't?" This is, of course, impossible to foresee, but in evaluating the effect of the crisis on the marriage, I do look at such things as the quality of the marriage *before* the crisis, as well as the amount of bitterness on the part of one or both partners. (With a high degree of bitterness, there is a great likelihood that the marriage will not survive.)

The key question for couples after the crisis is: How did we get to this point? *Both* must then be willing to seek out the answer; *both* must be willing to reinvest and rebuild.

CHAPTER ELEVEN

The
Mortal Heart

T HE RICHER AND MORE COM-
plex the tapestry of a marriage becomes, the harder and more
painful the eventual adjustment to sickness and death. Of all
the mid-life terrors, this may be the hardest one to live with.

While men more often express the fear of death itself
(often earmarking a father's age of death as the life-or-death
year for themselves), women are likelier to speak of their
fears of loving a man and losing him. One woman friend
spoke of how, after her husband's illness, "death had cast its
shadow on him." She found that a new wariness had invaded
her feelings toward him, which she could only explain as a
premonition of future loss.

In *Love and Other Infectious Diseases,* a personal memoir
about her husband Andrew Sarris's devastating illness, film
critic Molly Haskell focuses on the ways in which the illness
affected their long-term marriage. She describes the moment
when she realizes that her husband will never understand
what she, the well spouse, has suffered as a result of his illness.
This realization allows her to experience a "crack of light"
between them—not so much an end to their "oneness," but
the first inkling of separateness in an extraordinarily close

union. Later, she says, "I was praying for my life when I prayed for him. I could no more imagine eating, breathing, walking the face of the earth without him than I could imagine hanging upside down from a tree branch, or living underwater."[1]

Marriage is supposed to be our safe harbor in an uncertain world. It is the closest we can get to a "guarantee" that we are not alone; that someone else is pulling along beside us. Our sense of self is defined and shored up within the marriage. Illness can seem to be a betrayal of the promise of security that marriage offers. When a spouse becomes ill, we feel alone, which we are not supposed to feel when we are happily married. Suddenly, we are confronted not only with a partner's new frailty but the frailty of marriage itself.

There is no way to avoid the grief that accompanies the realization that neither our spouses, nor ourselves, nor our marriages are safe from mortal harm. After an illness, a couple must also face the fact that the two of them—and their marriage—will never be the same. It is important to remember that just as an individual must gradually recover from a traumatic experience, so must a marriage. And, as other mid-life crises ultimately can renew a marriage, so can the trauma of an illness, as long as we guard against denying the issues and resisting necessary change. In this chapter, I will describe the healing process, step by step, in several marriages in recovery from the devastating physical and emotional effects of serious illness.

THE AILING MARRIAGE

After any crisis (and an illness is the most dramatic crisis of all), a couple will try to resume their old roles as well as their familiar "dance"—that is, their old pattern of relating. But since the "dance" and the roles no longer correspond to the couple's reality, the behavior will seem *exaggerated.* For women and men alike, phantom selves are likely to resurface in an extreme or distorted way; for a woman, reassuming her little girl or enabler identity is a major hazard of the postillness recovery period. A man who has been ill may exaggerate his old tough guy identity, overcompensating for his sense of personal frailty by driving himself to achieve. In every instance, couples must confront past selves in order to manage and move on from the crises in their marriages.

When her husband, Charles, got prostate cancer at the age of fifty-two, Lucy was angry. She'd always relied on Charles's strength and competence in handling their finances and felt as if she'd been deserted just at the critical moment when all of the financial arrangements for sending their son to college had come due.

After surgery, Charles pulled himself together enough to handle these matters and quickly tried to resume his usual work schedule, even the extra freelance consulting he'd taken on a few years before, reassuring Lucy all the while that there would be no changes in their life-style. For a while, he struggled not only to handle his usual work load but to take on more consulting in an effort to make up for the time and money he'd lost recovering from his operation. A few months later, finding himself overwhelmed with exhaustion, he cut out his consulting and then pared down his regular work schedule, too.

Two years later, he had made a full physical recovery. However, Lucy's anger and depression lingered. After a few sessions of therapy, she began to speak about her feelings of abandonment, as if Charles had let her down by becoming ill.

Illness will produce a *regression* in both partners; in Lucy's case, her little girl self was panicked at the thought that her husband would no longer be able to take care of her. In an unconscious attempt to punish him, she usually avoided sex, and she also became obsessed with money and security.

A crisis erupted one day when the couple was window-shopping. Lucy's birthday was coming soon, and she had pointed out an exquisite ruby ring she'd noticed a few days before that she loved. When Charles gave her a bracelet instead—nice, but obviously not as expensive and strikingly beautiful as the ring—she was crushed.

As Lucy and I talked about this in session, Charles sat and listened. Finally, he said quietly, "Lucy, I just don't want to keep up our old life-style anymore. I don't want to put in the extra time and energy that I used to. I'm doing the best I can, and that will have to be good enough." I strongly supported Charles in sticking by the choice he had made and in presenting it clearly and directly, but not hurtfully, to Lucy.

Traumatized by the evidence of Charles's mortality, she had demanded that he be stronger than ever in his old role of financial provider. Charles, too, had needed to reassert the tough guy role as a bulwark against his new sense of weakness and vulnerability. At the same time, Charles was in a bind: He couldn't play the role with the same energy as before, so he had been forced to start saying no to Lucy's impossible demands. Once he did, the marriage began turning slowly toward health.

Within a marriage, illness traumatizes *both* partners, sometimes affecting the well partner even more profoundly than the one who is sick. In addition to the fact that the course of the partner's illness is unpredictable and recovery often uncertain, the disruption of familiar roles may be unexpectedly upsetting. In a situation in which both partners are relatively independent, an ill partner's sudden, disruptive dependency may cause a crisis.

A few years ago, my husband was briefly incapacitated by knee surgery, and I would never have suspected that such a relatively minor crisis would affect us as much as it did. Since we lead very independent lives, neither of us was accustomed to having to take care of the other. I hated seeing him helpless and needy, and I was disconcerted by having to accommodate my life to his needs—as he would have felt if our positions been reversed.

Illness disrupts both the major and minor terms of a marriage contract, and both spouses have enormous adjustments to make. Just one small example: Maintenance of the family car has always been my husband's domain, and when the car wouldn't start one day (when I was in a particular hurry to get to an appointment), I was furious at him for not being recovered enough from his surgery to handle this emergency!

Because of my recent personal experience with these issues, I felt particularly empathetic toward the following client who came for treatment in the aftermath of her husband's heart attack.

How Will I Go On?

Shelley had sparkling eyes and shoulder-length brown hair. At fifty-one, she seemed to vibrate with energy. In our first session, she told me that her husband, Harry, fifty-eight, had had the forcefulness and stamina of a much younger man until his illness a little over a year before.

Married when they were in their early twenties and the parents of two grown daughters, the couple had owned and managed a flourishing gourmet food shop for more than ten years. Accustomed to working hard together every day and sometimes into the evening hours, Shelley said that when Harry's heart attack had sent him into the hospital, she'd felt as if she'd lost her ballast. "Before then, Harry was this big, bossy guy," she said. "He was a pain in the neck, and we yelled at each other a lot, but we had fun. Now he's so subdued I barely know him." She looked somber. "I feel guilty about saying this, but I want him back the way he was, not the way he is now!"

Throughout her first six or seven therapy sessions, Shelley wept through several boxes of tissues while speaking eloquently about her sense of loss. "Harry feels *physically* different to me," she said. "When I put my arms around him in bed, he isn't the same man. He's changed." To Shelley, Harry's changes went deeper than the physical; she sensed that he was profoundly altered, that he had become a stranger and was not the man she'd known and loved for most of her life.

In her first session, Shelley recalled that terrible night when she woke up and found her husband sitting on the side of the bed, doubled over in pain. "I don't know what woke me," she said, her eyes wide and frightened with the memory. "Maybe it was his breathing, which was labored. He managed to tell me there was awful pain in his left shoulder and along his arm. I said, it must be heartburn, and he said, yeah, right, but I knew it wasn't and so did he. I got up and called the doctor, and he met us at the emergency room."

For the first few months after Harry's heart attack, Shelley had wrapped herself in denial, which was useful for handling all the many details of their altered lives. A few months later, she began feeling disoriented and chronically fearful, as if she had lost control of her life. She found it impossible to imagine that she would ever have a normal life and marriage again. She began feeling deeply estranged from Harry and had serious questions about whether the marriage would survive.

Shelley told me that Harry is the kind of man who "prefers talking himself out of a depression to spending money on a shrink," and so after a few months, he had begun to take charge of his life again. As he overhauled his eating habits and conscientiously took his daily medications, she cheered him on. But much as she supported his doing this, she hated the new routine. In the past, Harry had never been sick, could keep going on five hours of sleep a night and could eat and drink prodigiously with no ill effects. For her part, Shelley had delighted in his enormous appetite for life and had seen him as nearly omnipotent. With that cherished myth destroyed, she had begun fantasizing about walking away from the marriage, which, fortunately, she was too responsible to do.

A year after the heart attack, their sexual relationship, always satisfying before Harry's illness, still had not regained its old vigor. Even though he'd been repeatedly assured by his doctor that it was safe to have sex, Harry told Shelley that he felt as if his sexual spark has gone out. To reassure both himself and Shelley he said, "I just need to feel a bit stronger, and then I'll be ready to make love again."

It is very common for a newfound sense of physical vulnerability to lead to a *temporary* aversion to sex. A man who
has had a heart attack might tell his wife, as Harry did, that
he can hear his heart when he has sex. For a man in this
situation, sex and death may suddenly feel too close for comfort. In the midst of a sexual encounter—one of life's most
intense experiences—he may feel as if he is teetering on the
threshold of death. His aversion to sex is directly related to
his aversion to death.

A man may make an unconscious deal: He'll give up sex
if it means he can live. In the case of Harry and Shelley, her
ambivalent feelings about Harry contributed to her own desire to avoid sex, and neither partner felt prepared to talk
about it.

The worst part for Shelley—and for anyone with an ill
spouse—was how guilty she felt about her own ambivalence.
"I'm just not loving enough," she said miserably. But Shelley's
courage and honesty made it possible for her to express her
painfully mixed emotions about her husband, which all well
spouses must be encouraged to do. Guilt almost invariably
dissipates once you talk about your feelings and understand
there is nothing "wrong" with them, or with you.

"You are having a delayed reaction to the trauma," I told
Shelley. "And you need to give yourself time to heal. You
need to accept all of your reactions as normal." Again and
again, I reminded Shelley not to be too hard on herself for
feeling ambivalent and for her fantasies of escape. At the
same time, I encouraged her to "escape" as much as possible.
When she was with Harry, her anxiety sometimes seemed to
have no ceiling, while when she was out with friends, she
enjoyed herself, feeling almost normal. The next step was to
set at least two dinner, movie, or museum dates a week.

Her worst time was usually at night, when she was assailed
by the fear that something terrible would happen to Harry
if she didn't watch him constantly. (This is a common reaction
to severe trauma, which is called "hypervigilance.") Since she
was able to sleep more soundly on the living room couch,
she decided to spend occasional nights there. She found the

couch to be a refuge, an alternative to tossing and turning all night.

Illness and its vast and various effects on the emotions and on relationships is still largely a taboo topic. In our culture, we are taught to expect quick comebacks: "Don't be morbid," we are told. "Don't dwell on things. Try to get over it."

During a crisis, friends and relatives may be extremely supportive, but many people find that in the aftermath of the crisis, just when the most intense feelings hit, their support networks disappear. If the well spouse prides herself on her strength and independence, as Shelley did, she won't want to burden other people with her fears and anxieties. And, if her husband has been her closest confidant, she will feel as if she has no outlet at all for her feelings. In desperation, she may finally turn to an adult child but find that she is *overrelying* on this child. Shelley leaned too heavily on her daughter until her daughter eventually set limits on visits and phone calls. Shelley had felt rejected while recognizing that her daughter was right. It is unfair and unrealistic for a woman or man in this situation to look to their children for the kind of support they once got from their partner.

Both the ill spouse and the well spouse have difficult recovery work to do. The ill spouse must recuperate from the physical trauma and begin to absorb a new sense of loss and frailty into his or her self-definition. The well spouse's task is to help the partner accomplish this, as well as to reorganize his or her own self-definition. To manage all of this, the well spouse needs to turn to family for support, while at the same time taking care not to overrely on them and end up alienating them.

"I should be over this by now," was one of the first things Shelley told me, in a voice trembling with anxiety. "I feel like a burden to my friends and my family. The reason I'm here is to find out what's wrong with me."

As we saw earlier with Bart, the man who was finally able to mourn the loss of his child ten years after the child's death, there is no right or wrong timetable for recovering from a major life trauma, no right or wrong way to mourn. At mid-life, people often find themselves dealing with a *cluster* of losses: At the same time that a spouse becomes ill, a son or daughter may be getting married or graduating from college, or perhaps a grandchild is born. All of these are happy events but also unmistakable signs of aging. An illness can be the last straw, the event that disrupts the entire marital system, sometimes sending a marriage right off the stress scale.

When Shelley was reassured that her sense of helplessness and panic in the face of her spouse's life-threatening illness were altogether normal, she was able to start putting the pieces of her life back together. But even after anxiety becomes defused, it may still return, seemingly as strong as ever.

One day, Shelley articulated what she called "her worst fear," which was not that Harry would die but that someday he would be incapacitated by illness. "I can't bear thinking of this vital man becoming dependent," she said, then took a deep breath. "And I hate myself for saying this, but I don't want to have to take care of him." It is an entirely *normal* reaction to dread the idea of taking care of a sick spouse, but for Shelley (and for many people) there is more to it than that. Even emotionally healthy people in healthy marriages can expect to encounter phantom selves that have been hidden until now. Independent and feisty, or so she had always thought, Shelley now had to come to grips with a little girl self she'd never known she had. For Shelley, "taking care of" Harry meant not being able to rely on him. It meant that someday she might have to take care of *herself* more than she had ever wanted to.

But Shelley found that she *could* take care of herself. Without Harry, there was no one to manage the financial end of the business unless Shelley took charge of it herself and hired sales help. At first, she panicked at the thought; many women who are little girls at heart have an unrealistic wish not to know how to handle finances. With my encouragement, however, she slowly brought herself around to handling the books, even taking an accounting course to help her learn to become more self-reliant.

Harry is reinvolving himself in the store, but because he feels less in control of his life—a normal aftereffect of a life-threatening illness—his old bossiness has become exaggerated. Now he tries to manage the smallest details of Shelley's life, right down to advising her on what kind of tea to drink!

"That makes me feel as if things are getting back to normal," Shelley laughed. But even as she welcomes the return of Harry's basic vitality, Shelley is finding his bossiness more irritating than she did in their pre-heart attack days. This is a natural outcome of a shift in a marital system: As Shelley "grows up," she has less need for a "father" who will tell her how to live.

Several months later she confessed, "It's still hard to stop worrying that something will happen. Now he's looking forward to playing tennis again this summer, and that's great. But I'm dreading it! I keep picturing him collapsing."

Since my husband and I often play tennis together, I had a graphic picture in my mind of just how that would look and feel. I said, "When you watch him play tennis now, you may *always* hear a voice saying, 'Oh, my God, what if . . .' This illness has become part of your perception of him, and you're now adjusting to a different husband. He isn't the same in your eyes. But understanding and accepting this will eventually mean being able to enjoy life with him again, in spite of that little voice."

THE MID-LIFE MARTYR

When a husband gets sick or when he is recovering from an illness, a woman who has been an enabler most of her married life may "exaggerate" that role by becoming her husband's full-time caretaker. For her, that is a way of staving off her fear of losing him, as well as an attempt to reinstate the closeness that was disrupted when the illness struck. Devoting her life to caretaking means that the illness will take center stage in the marriage, and the mental health of the individuals, as well as the ability of the marriage to recover and heal, will be compromised. In healthy marriages, the well spouse maintains his or her independent life while being supportive of the partner who is ill.

When Sam had a stroke at the age of fifty-four, it was all too easy for his wife, Rose, who was the same age, to fall back into her familiar motherly role. After their two children were grown, she had returned to full-time teaching. But when Sam got sick, Rose decided that she must quit and stay home with him, even though the doctors told her that visiting nurses would be checking up on him at home for as long as necessary. "I want to be as supportive as possible," she said. "If I leave him by himself, he may get depressed. And his doctor has been warning him for years to follow a diet to keep down his high blood pressure and cholesterol levels. But Sam didn't pay attention, and he had the stroke. I'm afraid if I leave him alone, he won't stick to his diet. And what happens if he has another stroke while he's alone?"

Rose's desire to take care of Sam came naturally: She was a warm, nurturing woman, an old-fashioned wife, whose focus had always been the well-being of her husband and children. In their original marriage contract, the couple had tacitly agreed that Rose would be the stay-at-home partner while Sam would pursue a career in physics. Throughout their marriage, Rose had worried and watched over Sam's weight—he ate compulsively whenever he was anxious or depressed. Before the stroke, pressures at work had led to a weight gain, a rise in both his blood pressure and cholesterol level, and the doctor's warnings.

But she had not been able to prevent Sam's overeating, and may have contributed to it by unknowingly allowing his compulsion to function as a bond between them. As a co-dependent, Rose had worried constantly, counted every calorie and kept the butter hidden in the back of the refrigerator. But the more she "watched" his diet, the more Sam had silently opposed her sensible suggestions that were supposed to be "for his own good." Undermining all of her special, lovingly assembled, no-cholesterol, fat-free meals, he snacked freely on cheese, dips, and ice cream. She had been hurt and outraged and had redoubled her efforts to convince him to stick to his diet. Unfortunately, she had managed only to egg him on to achieve greater cholesterol levels than before.

The best advice I can offer for women like Rose is to stop trying to control a spouse's behavior. If you give up the fight, he will lose the impetus to resist. In almost every case I have seen in which a woman breaks the pattern of collusion, a man will put the butter away by himself within two or three months.

In exactly the way that Rose had not been able to prevent Sam from overeating in the past, she would not be able to force him to stick to his diet now or prevent him from having another stroke. Her anxiety was natural, but it blocked her from being genuinely supportive. I advised her that the best possible way that she could help Sam to maintain his health and prevent a second stroke would be to resist her exaggerated reaction to the crisis and continue working. She needed the outlet of work, and they needed her income. It is also very reassuring to both partners to maintain routines and structures during a time of extraordinary stress and upheaval. Fortunately, Rose kept her job, deriving fresh strength from her sense of herself as competent and functioning in the world, and was able, as she said, to "give much more to Sam than if I'd been shut up with him all day, worrying and nagging him."

The martyr who gives up everything to wait on her husband is not doing him or herself a favor by resurrecting an old role. Many women are taught to be caretakers, and there is much societal support for the woman who devotes her life to a sick spouse. But that is a decision that is bound to foster mutual dependency on the illness as the tie that binds the marriage rather than focusing on a constructive healing process.

Being loving and supportive does not mean that the well spouse gives up her own productive, independent existence. On the contrary, she will derive a flow of positive energy from the life she has built for herself. And a marriage needs that now more than ever.

THE RETURN OF THE
OLD-FASHIONED MARRIAGE

There are many women, such as Rose, who see themselves as "old-fashioned" wives wanting to take loving care of their husbands and provide for their needs. And in spite of the inherent dangers of falling into the martyr trap, Rose also showed the "good" side of an old role—the life-giving strengths of the traditional caretaker.

Interestingly, men who "come through" for their wives and their marriages in this kind of crisis make use of some admirable old-fashioned *male* virtues we often assume are gone for good.

When I first saw Seth and Adrienne, several years ago, I would never have expected Seth to "come through" in a crisis. Their marriage had serious, all too modern kinds of troubles. Adrienne, who herself juggled a demanding career with family life, described Seth as a workaholic. It was clear that her dissatisfaction ran deep: Seth was insensitive to and neglectful of his family's needs. He rarely attended events at his children's school, and he usually spent most of his weekends playing tennis or squash, while Adrienne did chores or planned activities with the children. As she talked, Seth sat impassively, finally saying only that he felt her demands were excessive.

To try to break the stalemate, I used a technique that therapists call sculpting, an exercise in which a couple or a family try to express the essential nature of a marriage by creating a living sculpture. Adrienne's sculpture had been hauntingly evocative: She had placed Seth's briefcase on the floor of my office, with herself on one side and Seth on the other. Then she had leaned yearningly over the briefcase, toward Seth, but without being able to reach him.

Graphic as this living image was, nothing changed in their pattern of relating—or nonrelating. In frustration, the couple left therapy shortly afterward, with no idea of how to break their stalemate, only to return a few years later after finding that Adrienne had Parkinson's disease.

Sometimes, when a crisis is thrust upon them, a couple make major changes, practically overnight. In amazement, I watched Seth rise to confront a marriage's greatest challenge. Life-threatening illness, he said emphatically, was a test of what a person was made of. He accompanied Adrienne when she went for tests, and when she was in the hospital he visited her for hours every day.

Seth's own mother had had cancer, but her sickness had been shrouded in shame and secrecy. He said that his parents almost never mentioned it, but that his mother had seemed depressed for the rest of her life. "I don't want us to follow in my parents' footsteps," he assured Adrienne. And he added, "We can't afford to be bitter with each other anymore—not after this. I don't want to lose you, or our marriage." He was right to assume that from then on, their pattern of relating would be different.

In a sad way, Adrienne's illness gave Seth the chance to show her how he had changed, to make up to her for the years of neglect and emotional detachment. The specter of mortality is the most shattering crisis a couple can face, but Seth rose to the occasion, successfully juggling responsibility, loyalty, and self-survival. He did not submerge himself in Adrienne or in the illness; instead, he figured out how to maintain a healthy work routine *and* be there for the family by conducting some of his business from a home office. He found a support group they could attend together and made himself available as a source of medical information and emotional support for their teenagers, who needed to understand and cope with their own devastating fears. The crisis allowed Seth to achieve a balance between work and personal relationships for the first time in his life.

The major drawback of the old-fashioned marriage was its reliance on rigid gender roles: Men were supposed to be tough and aggressive; women were supposed to be soft and nurturing. But as Seth showed, there is another side to the tough guy, a *good* side. In the face of the crisis, Seth lived up to the traditional ideal of the husband as the protector and guardian of his family's well-being. Crisis strengthened his resolve; Seth would have scorned any man who had shirked either his personal or professional responsibilities.

This male model of behavior is such a healthy approach to a spouse's illness that I often present it to *women* clients who tend to treat the caretaking of an ill husband as an all-consuming occupation. Old-fashioned men often are able to be strong, loving, and supportive when their wives fall ill, without falling into the martyr trap.

It is time to pull the time-honored strengths and virtues from the marriages of yesterday and apply them to our marriages today. I don't advocate trying to replicate a form of marriage that is no longer relevant for most of us: As we've seen, couples who adhere rigidly to outmoded marital roles and resist change often find their marriages failing at mid-life. But there is a very important place in modern marriages for the good side of the macho guy, as well as for the loving strength of the woman who nurtures.

THE SUPPORTIVE COUPLE

A few days after interviewing an acquaintance of mine named Isabelle about the effect of illness on her marriage, I decided to call her and thank her for sharing her tremendously moving story with me. "Your marriage has such a solid base," I told her. "You and Raymond come through for each other in ways that many couples don't."

There was relief in Isabelle's voice as she thanked me for my assurances that she and Raymond had handled their series of crises well. "But you know," she added, "it's hard for me to take when people idealize us. People are inspired by us, but what happens if I feel like falling apart?"

Isabelle's question is typical of the straightforward, realistic attitude she has maintained throughout the course of her own and her husband's illnesses; this, and the mutual support system that exists between her and Raymond, have been the solid ground beneath the frightening, shifting sands of their lives over the past five years.

At the age of fifty-two, Isabelle found during a routine mammogram that she had breast cancer. Terrified and devastated, she turned to Raymond for support.

"After the diagnois," Isabelle said, "Raymond was a rock. If I needed to cry or scream, he was there. I stayed home for a year because I was so debilitated from chemotherapy, and he took over most of the caretaking and housekeeping responsibilities, in addition to going to his job every day.

"I worried about how he would see me physically, after the mastectomy," Isabelle continued. "He had to help me bathe, so he saw what I looked like. I really believed him when he said it didn't matter to him. When my hair fell out, it was, in a way, even more traumatic. Raymond said, 'Look, I know it's disturbing to you, but it doesn't bother me.' When I'd gained weight from the chemo, I had to buy new clothes. Raymond said, 'I forbid you to buy unbecoming clothes. Get something that will make you feel good.' And he was right, if he hadn't said something about it, I would have bought junk because I felt so awful about myself."

Seemingly fully recovered, Isabelle eventually began making plans to take up her life where it had been left off. Then, Raymond was diagnosed with chronic leukemia and was placed on alpha-interferon, an experimental drug for treating cancer. The couple was taught how to administer the injections, but for the first year, Raymond would not allow Isabelle to do it. By the second year, he was letting her help him.

One day, as she was walking along the street, Isabelle noticed an "old man" walking toward her. She wondered who it was, then realized, with a shock, that it was Raymond. "He had lost forty pounds, it was painful for him to walk, and it was painful to look at him." Shortly afterward, Raymond told her that he wanted to stop taking medication because he felt like giving up.

"It's your life," she told him, "but first, give me a chance to fatten you up." At this point, the healing properties of their relationship took full effect. Isabelle became a "real Jewish mama," as she put it, making sure Raymond ate lots of nutritious food, and he also cut back on the medication. Soon, Raymond began gaining weight. Deriving physical and emotional strength from each other, the couple began to feel in control of their lives again.

But another blow was yet to come. During a checkup two years later, it was discovered that Isabelle's breast cancer had metastasized to the bone. "Raymond has been wonderful," she said. "We can be there for each other; our marriage has strengthened throughout all of this. We've been fortunate in that there's no resentment on either of our parts."

As a couple Raymond and Isabelle had always maintained a healthy balance of closeness and autonomy; their differences in background, temperament, and overall outlook kept their marriage alive and well over the years. In this time of severe crisis, Raymond, who is from a Protestant background in which stoicism was a virtue, helped strengthen Isabelle's resolve, while Isabelle, who is from a Jewish background, taught Raymond how to "kvetch," get his feelings out into the open and avoid debilitating depression.

Also, both partners had childhood histories riddled with losses; Raymond's mother had died when he was young, and Isabelle had lost many members of her family during the Holocaust in World War II. This legacy of loss contributed to their ability to support each other; having learned empathy early in their lives, they could now give each other solace and reassurance.

The mutually supportive couple can help each other find the "balance between hope and reality," as Isabelle put it. A prevailing myth in our culture is that physical fitness and good nutrition will stave off illness and even death. When this belief is carried to an extreme, the result is an unhealthy *denial* of reality. But in dealing with serious illness, *constructive* denial plays an important role. I advise people in Isabelle and Raymond's situation not to bury their heads in the sand, but I also advise them not to dwell on the damages.

"We don't talk about death too much," Isabelle said emphatically. "In our individual therapies, we can talk about

the fears we have for each other. It's helpful to have a place
to do that. The only thing I made Raymond promise me was
that if I die first, he won't withdraw and become a burden
on the kids. He said, 'You're right, I really don't want to do
that.' "

Instead of focusing on the daily presence of terminal
illness in their lives, Raymond and Isabelle concentrate on
their work and their family. The recent birth of their first
grandchild "has lifted us up," Isabelle said. "Raymond can't
get over the fact that he has survived long enough to see this
wonderful baby."

And she showed me a snapshot of her husband, smiling
joyously as he bent over the tiny newborn cradled in his arms.
Raymond may be seriously ill, but the beaming, youthful-
looking grandfather I saw in this picture was brimming over
with life.

FAMILY HEALING

Sometimes, in a period of tremendous stress, a couple
learns to tap into the healing power of the family. It is not
at all inappropriate to bring adult children into the healing
process (while taking care not to overrely on them). This may
be a difficult personal transition for an enabling woman, but
relying on sons and daughters in this way strengthens them
and protects her from becoming overwhelmed by her husband's needs. When fifty-five-year-old Bill suffered an almost
fatal heart attack, his wife, Diana, eventually learned that she
could rely on other people, in this case an adult child, to share
some of the burden.

When they first came to consult with me, Diana was so
panicked by Bill's illness that she was unable to sleep at night.
Meanwhile, Bill's doctor had ordered him to cut down his
working hours, and his visible weakness made it clear that
he needed to set new priorities. But Bill adamantly refused
to cut back, while Diana unknowingly colluded with him in
his work addiction by frantically "helping out" at the office.

To offset her own fear of loss, she was unconsciously trying to bolster Bill's self-image as "invulnerable." Even when her friends pointed out to her that her "help" was only facilitating the work addict's ability to take on more work, Diana's "exaggerated" enabler self drowned out their sensible advice.

But one night she admitted to her son, Thomas, over the phone that his father was working harder than ever, then broke down in tears as she confided her fear that it wouldn't be long before Bill had another heart attack.

Soon afterward, I received a long-distance phone call from Thomas, who, in deep distress, asked me what he could do to help his parents. I had an idea that at first I rejected as too risky, but then, on a hunch, decided to try. "Are you prepared to try something unorthodox?" I asked Thomas. When he said he was, I asked him to fly into town to attend his parents' next therapy session. "I want you to imagine that you are coming to attend your father's funeral," I told him. "And to think about what you would say if you had to prepare a eulogy for the service. In the therapy session, read this mock eulogy to your father, and let's see what happens. My suggestion is to focus on your feelings of love and admiration for him, and your pain at his untimely death."

Thomas's "eulogy," which he read aloud in the session in a voice breaking with emotion, expressed deep love, and anger. "My father was a wonderful man," he said. "He always worked hard to provide for us, and he always let us know through his words and actions that he loved us." Thomas then went on to describe how supportive his father had been when he'd been through a period of crisis in college, and how much he thought his own kids would lose by not having Bill in their lives. "I want him to take care of himself for *all* of us," he said. "We all want him with us for as much time as we can get." Thomas stopped and looked at his father, whose eyes were filled with tears. In the next few weeks, I saw Bill hesitantly begin to take his son's words to heart, cutting back on his work schedule, arranging to visit Thomas and his family for several weeks and agreeing to look for a weekend house in the country with Diana when he returned, something he'd never had time for until now.

When his vulnerable heart gave him literal evidence of his own frailty and mortality, Bill's exaggerated tough guy response had been to attempt to deny the evidence by becoming the hero of his own life, moving mountains of work and outproducing younger achievers. Fortunately, Bill was able to articulate what many men feel but don't express: "My self-esteem took a terrific beating when I got sick," he admitted. "I was afraid of becoming helpless."

As healthy people age, they become more aware of their physical vulnerabilities; "Oh, my aching knees!" a man may groan as he gets up from a kneeling position, or he may notice that he feels the effects of a late night out as he never did when he was younger. These small physical changes are accompanied by a subtle sense of loss—the loss of our youth—to which we adjust over time. And indeed, Bill felt that initially he had been coping well with the gradual effects of aging, but even so he had been completely unprepared for the physical *and* emotional effects of a sudden, life-threatening illness. The fact is, illness superimposed on the aging process creates a *double* loss, as suddenly, sometimes even overnight, our lives are irrevocably altered.

Bill's son's "eulogy" had helped him face this new reality. When he cut back on his schedule, shifting away from work as the cornerstone of his identity, he felt frightened and vulnerable. I encouraged the couple to acknowledge this change in Bill's self-definition and to openly confront the changes they'd have to make in their marriage now that he could no longer see himself as invulnerable. The healthy couple can relinquish phantom selves, confront their vulnerabilities together and draw on each other's strengths.

Bill and Diana not only decided to invest in a vacation home—previously Bill had insisted he didn't need vacations—they planned on spending at least three months of the year there. "I'm just grateful I have the chance to do this now," he said. "I don't want to be on my deathbed wondering why I hadn't spent more time with my family. I want to do it now before it's too late."

* * *

Like Diana and Bill, many couples assume that after the critical stage of the illness has passed, life should simply get back to "normal" as soon as possible. However, now is when the hardest work has to be done: The couple must evaluate the impact that the crisis has had on their lives.

Shelley and Harry eventually began couples counseling to help them adjust to their new, postillness self-images. Harry's necessary adjustment meant learning to accommodate his new sense of mortality. As he put it, "Making my business bigger and more successful used to be the main event of my life; then the biggest event in my life became my sickness." Harry felt diminished by this change in status in the business world, and his "work" now was to rebuild his sense of self.

Shelley came out of the crisis feeling more vulnerable in terms of her husband's mortality but *stronger* in her belief in her own ability to make her own way. As a survivor, she felt more frightened *and* more self-reliant. Her work was to negotiate within the marriage for greater autonomy, with her husband paying attention to the changes that have taken place within *her* through the course of *his* illness.

For a marriage to proceed on a new basis, both partners must be able to leave the old routines and assumptions behind and work together to accommodate a new reality. For individuals and couples alike, reinvesting and reinventing marriage are the best antidotes to illness.

Portraits
of Mid-life Marriages
HIGH POINTS, LOW POINTS,
TURNING POINTS

SINCE CRISIS IS INDIGENOUS
to mid-life, all mid-life couples now can expect their marriages to be disrupted to a greater or lesser degree. I have found, though, that most couples assume that their marriages are in *more* serious trouble than they really are. In this chapter, I will describe, through portraits of some typical marriages, the three levels of marital stress, so that couples can learn to evaluate their own level of crisis and follow steps toward repair and, ultimately, renewal.[1]

The couple sitting in my office one warm April morning were new in treatment. The wife was explaining why they had decided to come for a consultation.

"I'm desperate about the course this marriage is on now," she said. "And if that's the way I feel today, where will we be five years from now?"

For several moments, her question seemed to reverberate in the air. Then her husband said that while he was reasonably content with how things were between them, he had agreed to couples therapy because his wife had urged him to. "I'm here because if she's unhappy, I'm concerned," he said now.

When one or both partners pose the question of where a marriage will be five, ten, or fifteen years down the road, it is often a signal that a period of questioning and reassessment of the marriage may be about to begin. To help get this particular couple started, I first suggested that they divide their marriage into an early and middle period and plot events along the continuum, marking the major turning points—times when important choices were made.

Turning points in a marriage occur when children are born, when they leave home, when elderly parents die, when either partner makes a career change—or whenever there is any major loss, shift in expectation or even a new insight that one partner has into her own life or into the marriage. (In the case above, an *internal* shift in one partner set off *external* changes in the marriage.)

Turning points may be either positive or negative junctures in the life cycle of a marriage. The crucial question is how the couple responds to a new demand or to a challenge. Most marriages in trouble at mid-life have so far survived the *crises*, while avoiding the *issues*. In these cases, impasses may result, which freeze the process of change; when the couple rises to the challenge, instead of freezing, the marriage is freed up.

The majority of couples find, when they look at the time line of their marriage and locate the turning points, that there were times when both partners rose to the occasion and other times when one or both did not. Each time a couple "rises to the occasion" they bring about a period of renewal in their marriage. These times, as well as the times when they didn't, are tremendously important in a marriage's history. The more often the couple *didn't* renew in the past, the harder it becomes to make positive changes now and in the future. Harder, but not impossible.

The couple who came for a consultation that spring day turned out to have a strong history of renewal to bolster them during their current crisis. In short-term counseling, they were able to hear out each other's grievances: The wife had begun to resent her husband for his "stuffiness," while he finally admitted to being concerned about her "irresponsibility."

As so often happens with mid-life couples, this couple had forgotten the reasons for their original attraction to and for each other. At one time, his "stability" and "consistency" had appealed to her, while her "spontaneity" had been the very quality that had drawn him. I asked the husband to think about how his wife could help him become a freer, looser person, and then asked the wife to consider how her husband could help her appreciate stability and consistency.

Sometimes just seeing that a partner is the same person she or he was back then (and *more*, now that years have passed) can infuse a couple with renewed interest in each other and form a basis for rebuilding.

THE THREE LEVELS OF MARITAL STRESS

The question that I am most often asked both by mid-life couples in treatment, as well as by professionals in the field who attend my lectures on mid-life, is "How can a couple keep a long-term marriage alive?"

As recently as fifteen years ago, serial monogamy—sexually exclusive relationships commonly lasting about six to eight years—was thought to be the best way, maybe the only way, to satisfy our powerful needs for passion as well as stability. But now we're reassessing the long-term marriage and recognizing its obvious benefits both for ourselves and our children. Repeatedly, though, I find people assuming that it is impossible for a couple to stay together over a lifetime *and* retain their sexual and emotional chemistry. "It's a trade-off," more than one person has said to me. "Passion for consistency. We can't have it all."

It is true that some couples can't. But many—sometimes to their own surprise—*can*. I have found that different marriages operate at different *levels*, or *degrees*, of stress, and that the cycle of conflict, repair, and renewal can have a surprisingly positive impact at each level, even the third, when a marriage is most resistant to change and difficult to renew.

Often, when a couple comes into therapy, it appears as if the marriage is hanging by a thread. The couple will convey a sense of urgency, even panic, and frequently a therapist is affected by the atmosphere of crisis. In fact, to the relatively inexperienced therapist, *almost every couple* that comes into therapy may appear to be in similarly serious trouble; the couples are fighting a great deal, feel deeply disappointed in each other, and are often convinced their marriage is failing. Far, far too many therapists may tend to agree, too quickly, erring on the side of seeing a marriage as more fragile and hopeless than it really is.

For the mid-life couple whose marital crisis may be amplified by one or both partners' personal crises, the situation may seem particularly precarious. In those cases, both the couple and the therapist may fear that the therapy will expose so many negative feelings that the marriage will collapse right in front of everybody's eyes.

Learning how to use the three levels of marital stress as a way to *evaluate* relationships can be extremely effective both for treating couples in crisis and for teaching inexperienced therapists *how* to treat them. Also, couples who are not in therapy can use them to evaluate their own marriages and to see how to make necessary changes.

We will now take a close look at five marriages, each at a different level of stress, in order to see exactly how couples break stalemates, re-creating partnerships that are both more stable *and* more vital.

The Level-One Marriage

Often, couples assume that a Level One marriage is a new marriage in which problems have not had a chance to accumulate; however, the levels of stress are related *not* to longevity but rather to the capacity of the couple to repair and renew. When a Level One marriage is affected by conflict (whether it be at two, ten, twenty, or thirty years), the couple can, with relative ease, prevent the new problems from building into a stalemate.

Typically, in the Level One marriage, a couple may be colluding in denying a problem that is becoming harder to ignore or stalling in taking action in *one* area of the marriage. A common crisis is the one that arises when a couple goes on vacation alone, without the kids, for the first time in twenty years. Instead of the romantic escape that they expected, they find themselves groping for things to talk about. Each secretly fears that the chemistry between them is a thing of the past.

The *worst* thing to do is to pretend nothing is wrong, or to become resigned to the idea that loss of chemistry in a long-term marriage is inevitable. At this level, a marriage is not in trouble; it is in normal transition. Awkwardness is natural and predictable for *any* couple in this situation. When my husband recently suggested taking a vacation in Australia, I agreed enthusiastically, assuming that we would take our two teenage children. When he let me know he had in mind a vacation for just the two of us, my heart sank. Just the *two of us?* How could we go without the kids? The underlying question was, Who *were* we without the kids?

If a couple goes on vacation together and they *do* miss their children, they should acknowledge it and discuss any sense of letdown or lack of ease in being alone together. It helps to discuss the fact that as a normal, healthy part of the life cycle, a couple must get to know each other as people, not just as the parents of their children, once the children get older and prepare to leave home.

If such major events as the departure of children, retirement, a new job, or a demotion are ignored, they can snowball into a full-fledged crisis. People should *expect* these events at mid-life, and learn to confront them together. At this level (and at Level Two), the issues surrounding these events have not intensified and a couple may not necessarily need therapy; they can articulate their feelings and know how to listen actively to the partner's feelings.

Couples are often unaware that the *longer* they have been married, the more reparable the marriage may be. A couple like my clients, Art and Phyllis, married for thirty years, lost sight of this simple, reassuring fact when they were hit by a crisis that looked more dire than it really was.

Art, fifty-five, had been a dedicated Navy man whose career had taken him all over the world, and who had often been absent from the family. In the first several years of marriage, before he had begun traveling, he and Phyllis had been a close, loving couple, but inevitably, physical distance had resulted in emotional distance. Still, over the years in which their son and daughter were growing up, the couple had managed to share good moments with each other and, a decade earlier, had pulled together through their daughter's serious illness. Even though their marriage lacked day-to-day intimacy, it had always seemed strong enough to weather any crisis that might come along.

But that was before Art announced his intention of taking an early retirement in order to help Phyllis with the mail-order business she had started in an office in their converted garage. At the time, even though she was pleased by her husband's desire to spend more time with her, something about Art's plans made her uneasy, and it didn't take long before she'd figured out what it was.

The fact was that being together all day meant they were fighting much of the time. It seemed to Phyllis that Art didn't take her seriously as a businesswoman and was always giving her advice she didn't need; it seemed to Art that Phyllis didn't appreciate the organizational skills he had to offer. Phyllis became increasingly upset and wondered whether physical distance had been the key to their marriage's longevity. She worried that, at this late date, they were about to discover that they had become completely incompatible.

Art was distressed because his dream of early retirement was turning into a nightmare. He loved Phyllis but was saddened by the years of distance. He felt that he'd withdrawn from her after the children were born, and even though he'd built fairly good relationships with his son and daughter over time, he felt now that he had missed out on his chance to become truly close to them. At the same time, he believed that he now *did* have a chance to make up for lost time with his wife.

But he was also experiencing the urgency of time limitations; if he and Phyllis didn't rediscover each other and become closer now, they never would. He had a poignant sense that this was their last chance to build a life together, only it wasn't working out.

By the time Art and Phyllis came into therapy, they were both convinced that their fighting meant they didn't love each other, and that, in fact, their marriage might fail. But each had made two overly simple assumptions: first, that they *should* be happy working together, and second, that, since they weren't, they were unsuited to each other as partners in business and in marriage. The fact is that, even when a transition seems as if it should be a happy and positive event, it will still destabilize a marriage. Art and Phyllis needed to understand that they were in the midst of a highly stressful life transition, and that their unrealistic expectations of a smooth passage were intensifying the conflict.

Before matters improved, they worsened. Art continued to insist on supervising and advising Phyllis on every decision. In the past, she said, she would have given in and let him take over. But now she dug in her heels; this was *her* business. Finally, she rented office space in town and moved out of the garage.

Art was shocked and hurt. "Why are you being so stubborn?" he asked. Phyllis felt belittled by that question and decided that her husband would never understand her needs. She said nothing and spent as much time as she could in her office. Art, meanwhile, was at home alone and at loose ends. Finally, with my encouragement, he faced his dilemma. He hadn't really been ready to retire, but he had been ready for a job change and a change in his marriage. Soon, he was back with the Navy in an administrative position, a job that didn't involve traveling and was far less stressful.

The key was for Art and Phyllis to find a way to maintain a level of togetherness and distance that suited both of them. Phyllis had not been able to deal with her husband's sudden dependence on her. Their customary ratio of closeness and togetherness had been overturned, and its new proportion actually had suited neither of them. Each had felt vulnerable to the other: Phyllis had sensed a threat to her hard-won independence, and Art had felt the terror of having to depend totally on Phyllis for a purpose in life.

For this couple, a period of renewal began when Art went back to work, and they were able to negotiate and accommodate their differing needs for intimacy and independence. Now Art is more relaxed and can spend more time at home. Phyllis enjoys him more and doesn't feel as if she has to fight him to have a life of her own. The challenge for Art is to see Phyllis as a successful businesswoman in her own right, with her own goals and ambitions; the challenge for Phyllis is to see and accept the vulnerable, dependent side of her tough guy husband.

Art responded with a sense of immediate recognition to an image that I often use to describe the way that many men feel at this stage of their lives. Three large water glasses represent the three most important aspects of a man's life: one full to the top (his work glass), one half-full (his family glass), and one nearly empty (his marriage glass). Like so many men, such as Bart, who discovered the hidden pain that had created so much distance between himself and his wife, and Jason, who decided to reinvest in his marriage after an affair, Art had wanted to fill the empty glass of marriage; his premature retirement had been a precipitous, last-ditch effort that had ended up flooding the marriage with *too much* closeness. Now, at last, Art can experience the satisfaction of knowing that the three glasses representing his life are in far more equal proportion.

The Level-Two Marriage

On the second level, problems that have been denied or avoided in the past are beginning to escalate, and conflict may become increasingly frequent and unconstructive. A major unresolved issue may be "contaminating" other areas of the relationship, and a couple may find themselves in a cycle of accusation and blame instead of repair and renewal. For example, a man may be angry or depressed or overly critical of his wife in response to career setbacks or to an overall sense of ennui. His wife may be trying to deny the problem or else trying to solve it for him. In either case, the couple is not confronting the issues.

While the longevity of a mid-life marriage should be working *for* the couple, it becomes overshadowed by personal and marital crises. Instead of recognizing their shared history as a source of strength, they see it negatively, as a burden. Remembering only the bad things about the past, they feel bogged down. One major earmark of the Level Two marriage is that the couple does not recognize how resourceful they really are.

But a Level Two marriage is not bankrupt; the partners haven't given up on each other and have an overall commitment to the marriage. Since there are still uncontaminated areas in the relationship—sexual chemistry, for example, although the frequency of sex has probably fallen off, or they may enjoy socializing together—this is a productive time to repair and renew.

Offsetting their substantial resistance to change, the couple's past experiences with renewal now provide them with a solid foundation for further growth. Conflict and withdrawal are more manageable and easier to overcome than at Level Three, and often, recovery is quickly achieved.

With some couples, a major change in one partner's self-definition may destabilize even a marriage that has been relatively crisis-free until now. The level of stress may soar, as a relationship's negatives suddenly seem to overwhelm the positives. The couple's task, as we shall now see, then becomes to renegotiate and create a new middle ground to accommodate their new needs.

By the time he was forty, Russell was a hugely successful foreign exchange trader. He also was a heavy smoker, who, at his wife Sandy's urging, finally began attending Smokenders meetings. For the first time, Russell made close friendships with other people. He identified with the group and eventually was made co-leader. He felt proud of the contribution he was making to other people's health and well-being.

"At about this same time, I realized that the pressure at my job was what had driven me to smoke in the first place," Russell said. "I started to hate feeling so driven all the time. I had to psych myself up every day just to get to the office, and then I worked till ten or eleven every night." When Russell first came to consult with me, he said he felt trapped, driven, and depressed. "I want to start doing more for other people," he said, and after a while, began having a growing conviction that he wanted to become a psychotherapist.

I told Russell that his new interests corresponded with some of the things we now know about mid-life: that new studies have found that at this stage of the life cycle, altruism often replaces the intense self-preoccupation of youth. I also told him that it often happens that people who threw themselves most energetically into their careers earlier were those who became the most giving at mid-life.

"That does sound like what I'm going through," he admitted, "but what did those people in the studies do when their wives didn't understand?"

Russell's big problem in making a major life change was Sandy. She was dead set against disrupting their lives and felt that Russell had no right to change the family's life-style by quitting his lucrative job and becoming a student.

When Russell brought Sandy in for a couples session, she said emphatically that she had always relied on Russell as the main breadwinner in the family, while she had worked part-time at an art gallery and focused on raising their children who were now teenagers. If Russell quit his job, they would have to make radical changes in the way they lived. The other alternative was to go in as a partner in the gallery as the owner had been urging her to do, but which Sandy had until now considered to be more of a commitment than she wanted to make.

Russell and Sandy's marriage time line showed a positive early phase, up to and including the births of their children, followed by a negative series of turning points as Russell became more job-obsessed. He was smoking three packs of cigarettes a day, and Sandy was deeply distressed; Russell's father had been a heavy smoker, too, and he had died of a heart attack in his late forties. Sandy had envisioned the same thing happening to Russell and had told him again and again that by not safeguarding his health, he was hurting not only himself but, potentially, the entire family.

A major positive turning point was Russell's decision to quit smoking. For two years after that, the couple had been closer. But now, Sandy said, they fought a lot and felt very distant from each other, and for the first time in their marriage, sex could not break down the barriers between them.

We discussed whether or not the couple could envision this period of conflict as leading toward a renegotiation of their marriage contract, and a renewal of their partnership. Shaking her head, Sandy said, "I just don't understand why Russell wants to shake up our lives. I thought we were doing fine."

When I asked Russell to explain to Sandy why he now felt such a strong urge to make a fundamental change in his life, he said, "Some of the things I've been thinking about lately have taken me by surprise, too. Things like my father. Since he died so young, I feel that my own time is limited, that if I want to make something useful out of my life, I need to do it *now*."

Sandy broke in. "Well, you're taking much better care of yourself now. Just because your father died at forty-eight doesn't mean . . . "

"I know, I know," Russell said. "Rationally, you're probably right. But I can't really get it out of my mind."

"All right," Sandy said slowly. "I can see what you're saying. But you're going to have to explain this to the kids, you know, because they'll have to make a lot of changes in their habits, too."

I could see how tempting it was for Sandy to try to make Russell feel guilty for depriving his sons of their life-style, but fortunately, she held back. When Russell told his sons about his plans, and why he wanted to make such a big change in his life, they just listened. Later, Sandy reported to Russell that she'd overheard the younger one saying to the older, "Well, I guess you can forget about going to college!"

This provoked another big argument between Russell and Sandy. To help Sandy and their sons begin to process the new reality, I suggested a compromise: Russell would keep his job for at least a year, cut down on his hours, and take courses at night.

Sandy's response at this point was critical. If making this accommodation had been unacceptable to her, their marriage might prove to be time-limited. However, she said, finally, "I can't really fault Russell for what he's trying to do. He's being responsible and serious." She sighed. "But now I need to decide what *I'm* going to do."

She and I discussed how for men in particular, mid-life is a time for a reorientation toward relationships and the development of compassion and empathy. So Russell was developing in a way that was healthy and appropriate for this period of his life. I then pointed out to Sandy that for women, mid-life tends to be a time for self-actualization, and she began to open up questions for herself about whether she wanted to push ahead in her career.

For both Russell and Sandy, the middle period of their marriage became a time for reexamination and reflection and a fundamental change in life-style. It also became a time for looking toward the future to see where they wanted their lives to go.

Many couples have been helped by making individual life plans and sharing them with each other. In their life plans, each partner takes some time alone to project into the next five years, writing down specific goals in the areas of finances, work, personal development, sex, and marriage. A life plan can also include reflections on how a person thinks his or her values will change over time.

Russell and Sandy sat down separately to think through their life plans. Sandy was surprised to find how much she had changed: In the area of finance, she projected first a scaling down and then expansion if she decided to become a partner in the gallery, which she was increasingly tempted to do. To develop her knowledge and expertise, she saw herself taking courses both in art history and in business administration. Looking at her marriage, she projected that their new career commitments might actually infuse new excitement into it. Another major goal for Sandy was to be sure to find the time and space to develop a deeper sexual and emotional intimacy.

Russell's goals were to develop his new career *and* maintain his obligations to his family; he particularly did not want his sons to feel as if they would be shortchanged. At the same time, he wanted them to understand how he had come to his decision and that the overall quality of their lives was not dependent on a big income. He saw himself involved in other altruistic projects on a volunteer basis but also said that he did not want his shift in values and interests to interfere with his marriage. On the contrary, he saw his new focus as a sign that he was *more prepared* for genuine intimacy in his marriage.

The next step was for Russell and Sandy to share their life plans with each other. Russell was excited by what Sandy projected for herself, and both partners ended up feeling that they could give one another help and support in following up on their individual plans. The couple agreed that it might be useful to do life plans periodically to keep in touch with all of the many changes that were happening in each of their lives.

I have worked with a number of couples whose generally low level of conflict rose at mid-life when a woman accustomed to placing other family members' needs ahead of her own decides that she must focus on self-development. In an early chapter of this book, we saw what happened when Marsha discovered that the only graduate program that suited her needs was in a city 150 miles away from her home. Since she had always defined herself in terms of her relationships to others, she had balked at leaving her family, barely able to imagine herself leading an autonomous existence. At the same time, she sensed that she had to take the risk and make the change, both for her own sake and for that of her marriage. In that case, a major life change caused a minimum of marital conflict; but more often, when a woman refocuses on personal autonomy, the level of conflict will intensify, even in a strong marriage.

When Mary was a young wife, she had her two children within the first four years of her marriage to Al. She stayed at home with them, eventually joining the local garden and bridge clubs and the PTA.

But by the age of thirty, Mary had become restless and knew she needed more of an outlet for her energy and creativity. Her father, who had been an architect, suggested that she study architecture, and Mary was thrilled by the idea. "I was so happy, I felt as if I were flying!" she said, recalling those jubilant early years of self-fulfillment. With Al's support, this first major change went smoothly. Mary said, "I'll never forget when Al's best friend said to him, 'How can you allow her to do that?' and Al said, 'I don't *allow* her. She makes her own decisions.' If it hadn't been for Al's ability to understand me, we wouldn't be together today."

When Mary had been working the same job for ten years, she decided to take further classes toward a master's degree in city planning. This time a positive turning point led to some difficult times; and indeed, it isn't uncommon for a positive event to at first disrupt and destabilize a marriage. It turned out that one of Mary's classes met on Tuesday and Thursday evenings, so she needed Al to be home early on those days to prepare dinner for their daughters. But Al, who initially had been so supportive, came up with one excuse after another for why he couldn't leave the office early. Mary was furious, convinced that Al simply didn't care about her career or was perhaps even trying to sabotage it. She was so upset that she actually started thinking about leaving the marriage.

Writing down and sharing their life plans broke the stalemate. When Mary explained to Al that her major, long-term goals were to develop herself and her career, he listened. When she explained that she needed his wholehearted support in order to do so, he kept listening. For him, having the larger picture in his mind's eye helped him to understand that his help was absolutely *essential* in order for Mary to achieve the goals that meant so much to her.

He pitched in on those weeknights, but when Mary's job responsibilities continued to increase and she found that she sometimes would have to attend meetings early on Saturday mornings, Al's response was "That's ridiculous! It's too early, and it makes things rushed for everybody. Besides, there's my squash game. Who will be here with the girls? Turn them down." She reminded him of her goals, pointing out that attending meetings would continue to be an important part of her job, and asked him to put himself in her shoes for a moment. Al then had to admit that if his career were at stake, he'd attend the meetings and expect the family to accommodate his needs. He rescheduled his squash games for the afternoons.

When Mary was offered a dream job, working with a well-known architect designing a new medical complex, she was elated. The only catch was that the two-year position meant moving to a city fifteen hundred miles away. She hesitated; Al balked, pointing out that since he couldn't leave his job, she'd have to go by herself and leave her family for a year. How would he take care of the kids by himself? Mary was torn: A career opportunity like this one was rare; on the other hand, she feared tearing apart the fabric of the family.

The marriage then entered a period of serious destabilization. Al told Mary to go ahead with her plans, but deep down, he was furious. Mary sensed his anger but, hoping that he would adjust to the idea, decided to take the job anyway. Over the next several weeks, they fought about everything. Al was bored with his own job and resentful of Mary's success; he also felt that she was abandoning him, and this time, he agreed with friends who asked him why he should allow Mary to go.

Meanwhile, Mary lay awake nights, fearing that her self-interests were in such grave conflict with the interests of her family that ultimately she would be forced to choose between them. And, she was convinced, making either choice to the exclusion of the other would mean amputating an essential part of herself.

At some point Al began to notice Mary's insomnia and depression. Remembering her restlessness from years ago, before she had decided to go back to school, he also recalled that it had not been dispelled until she had begun working toward her goals. He began to ease out of his rigidified position when he had a flash of insight about Mary: For her, self-fulfillment through work was critical, and his support for her school and career back then had ended up *strengthening,* not undermining, their marriage. Perhaps the same solution was called for now. . . .

When Mary and Al sat down together and discussed family vacations and visiting schedules, it began to seem more realistic, and less cataclysmic. A period of repair followed the conflict, as each partner was able to talk *and* to be heard. They then spoke together with their teenage daughters. "Go for it, Mom," her older daughter said. Mary and Al smiled at each other spontaneously, and Mary suggested, to her daughters' excitement, that they help her find and furnish an apartment.

"After that, I felt that both my marriage and my relationship with my daughters were strong enough to stand the separation," Mary said. "And in fact, it was the most romantic thing that ever happened to Al and me! Figuring out together how to make our lives work made me feel more loving toward him."

Mary and Al achieved several other important goals after Mary's sabbatical from the family. They both recognized and acknowledged to each other the vital importance of having separate lives, in addition to family life. They also realized that while their daughters were growing up, they had defined themselves as parents and that they now needed to rework their relationship. When they projected five, ten, and fifteen years into the future, they saw themselves supporting each other's goals while becoming closer as a couple.

An important part of making life plans is for couples to share them with each other and make a habit of revising and updating them. Their new understandings and resolutions will then become incorporated into the marriage, ensuring that it continues to grow.

The Level-Three Marriage

Usually, a mid-life marriage at this level of stress is an unhappy marriage—a joyless marriage or a marriage at an impasse—that has gotten worse. Now one or both partners may be having an affair, or one or both may be ready to walk out. As a couple resists change, they take rigidified positions, becoming ever more distant and conflictual. These couples come into mid-life at a disadvantage because over the years they have made little use of the cycle of renewal. If at one time they had a repair mechanism, it has broken down. Without the tools to repair or a history of renewal, they have fewer resources, and more bitterness, to draw on.

While marriages at lesser levels of stress have a good chance of recovering without therapy, a Level Three marriage, which has deteriorated into chronic fighting or withdrawal, lacks the resources necessary for resolving and rebuilding without help. And while couples in Level One and Two marriages *should* share their life plans with each other and practice active listening exercises at home, the Level Three couple need a therapist who functions as a *conduit* through which they learn to communicate until they are ready to negotiate on their own.

Now couples therapy is the best tool a couple can have, but it will take *longer* to break the stalemate than it would for couples at lesser levels, and they will have to dig deeper. If a Level Three marriage is renewed, it will need active vigilance: The partners must work out a new marriage contract in which they agree not to create triangles through affairs with other people, to discuss issues openly in regular active-listening sessions, and to be especially aware of patterns of denial and conflict-avoidance.

In the two very different Level Three marriages I'll talk about, one was repaired but not renewed, while the other was dramatically repaired *and* renewed.

Karen and Jed's marriage is a case of a partnership in which, as Karen put it, the couple "drew away from one another in increments." In looking closely at their marital history, it quickly becomes clear that at every important turning point, conflict had led not to repair and renewal, but to more conflict and greater distance.

Karen told me in an interview that it would have been impossible to predict these developments from the marriage's early phase, which had been a time filled with high spirits and adventure. Jed had been a musician, while she had studied music history at New York University. They had lived in Greenwich Village on Jed's erratic earnings from playing dates at clubs. Karen had believed strongly that Jed's talents were unusual and that he would eventually become successful. She had also believed that her role was to support and encourage him, and she thought nothing of staying up all night with him while he composed songs on his guitar and cooking breakfast for them the next day before running off to class. They were extraordinarily close; as Karen put it, their lives were completely intertwined, and at first she had assumed this was exactly what she wanted.

But the closeness and fusion that Karen had craved at the beginning of the marriage soon became overwhelming and threatening to her, as she discovered within herself just as strong a desire to be autonomous. The first turning point, which marked the introduction of conflict into their lives, was a few years later, when Karen earned her bachelor's degree from NYU and decided to take education courses. "Before then," she said, "I had so little confidence in myself. But then I realized that I *could* do things on my own. I saw myself seriously developing a life independent from my life with Jed." When she eventually landed a teaching position in one of the best private schools in the city, much to her surprise Jed became deeply depressed and said he could no longer compose music.

Jed, whose own career had not developed beyond occasional local playing engagements, finally decided to get a "real" job, as a sound mixer for a recording studio, but nothing was ever the same again. Looking back now, Karen said, "I relate Jed's depression to being unable to move on from the first years of our marriage when the focus was on him.

But I didn't understand that then, and we couldn't talk about the gap that existed between us."

She went on to describe the marriage's second turning point, which occurred when she decided to go back to school to get her master's degree in music therapy. Jed's reaction was lukewarm, and Karen understood that he resented the time and energy she put into her work, and that he would be unable to give her emotional support. "Since that time," she said, "I have turned to friends for the emotional support I've needed to pursue my career. I've known that my work, which is a source of so much pride for me, is an ongoing nightmare for my husband because he needs me to be in a supporting role to him. Also, he is so insecure that without complete togetherness, he feels abandoned."

Now the couple's conflict worsened. Karen continued her graduate education, but had trouble finding the time and energy to write her dissertation. As she confided in friends about how hard it was to study and do all the housework, in her own mind she was blaming Jed. She asked him for more physical and emotional support during this time, but Jed distanced himself, spending little or no time at home. Finally, Karen took matters into her own hands, announcing one day to Jed that she would no longer cook and clean. She stuck to her guns and hired a housekeeper. With some of that pressure off, conflict between the couple smoothed out temporarily. They began working more effectively together in managing the household, and Karen felt progress was being made.

Around this time, Karen's mother died of cancer. After arriving home from the hospital in the middle of the night, Karen, in desperate need of comfort, woke up Jed. He held her and comforted her, and she remembered how intimate they had been years before. But when Jed fell back to sleep, Karen said, "I realized how hard it had been never having his support for so much of what I've done in my life. I also realized that Jed was probably doing the best he could, and that things were unlikely to change very much."

Until then, Karen had believed that at some point she and Jed would become closer again, and in fact he continued to be supportive in helping her deal with her mother's death, although he would not discuss with her the lack of closeness in their marriage. Karen finally decided to withdraw her demands for more intimacy and more support. Their unspoken agreement then was that Karen would have to rely on her social network for her emotional needs. "This was a sad realization," she said. "For a while, I was very bitter. Jed's emotional makeup consists of a lot of distancing and denial, while I need to vent my feelings and work them through. We're very different in this way, and we weren't able to bridge the chasm during that important time."

Karen marked the fourth turning point six months later, shortly after their fourteenth wedding anniversary, when she went into individual therapy to decide whether or not to divorce Jed. She realized that she *could* leave—she didn't mind the idea of living alone—but she preferred being married. "I realized that I *like* having a husband," she said. And over the next year, it seemed to her as if Jed had become happier. He had become head of production at the recording studio, and had even started composing music again. He spent time building new bookshelves for her study and refinishing an antique desk for her, then helped her buy and learn to use a personal computer. Karen felt, then, that this was Jed's way of making up to her for their problems in the past.

After two years of therapy, Karen felt more able to be open with Jed. She told him frankly what had been lacking for her in the marriage but that she still wanted to be married. Relieved, Jed said that when she went into therapy, he had feared that she would end up leaving him. He told her he wanted her to stay, and that he would try to be as supportive of her as he could. Karen felt sad acknowledging what was missing between them, but more able to accept the terms and limitations of the marriage. "I think that up until this point, I'd always believed that someday, something would happen that would change Jed into the warm, involved person I wanted him to be. I saw then that this would never happen, but I felt much less bitter."

Shortly after she and Jed talked, Jed threw a surprise birthday party for Karen, which touched her deeply. "It was lovely," she said. "He invited everyone who was or ever had been important to me." But that night, after the guests went home, she was more aware than ever that occasional loving gestures could not offset the distance between them.

Even though this was a period of repair—as new understandings and empathy were acquired by both partners—it was not followed by a period of renewal. Instead, Jed went through another period of turning inward, becoming self-involved and bitter, more than ever resenting Karen's career and independent social life. During this withdrawal, Karen turned to friends and family whom she saw for dinner and movies several times a week. "I have so many interests," she said. "There are more work goals that I want to achieve. My life is full and rich, even though I know there are many important things that I can't share with Jed."

Karen ended the story of her marriage by saying thoughtfully that in spite of everything, she felt personally fulfilled. "We started so close, and we've ended up so far apart. But I *had* to pull back and make my own life." One of Karen's most important insights was into her own *need for distance*. The early closeness—the fusion—that had existed between herself and Jed had made it impossible for her to develop independently. Understanding her own role in the dissolution of their early "oneness" made it possible for her to take some of the blame off Jed for the lack of closeness that followed.

She would not call her marriage "joyless," she told me. "Bittersweet" would be more accurate. The strong memory of their early passion for each other made her feel now that she and Jed had been "meant for each other." Later, they had taken different paths, and had been unable to find a truly satisfying middle ground, but she had never imagined herself with anyone else, and neither had Jed.

At mid-life, many people have a stronger sense of *time* limitations and, along with that, an urgency in their desire to make the most of their marriages and their lives. These years are a natural time for reflection: Couples now have the advantage of being able to see where they have been, where they are, and where they are likely to go if they follow the course they are on now. A forty-six-year-old woman in a stalemated marriage came to consult with me for the first time. "This might be my last chance to make things better," she said. "I don't want last chances to become lost chances."

Therapists and couples alike often give up on a Level Three marriage, but I have been amazed by the power and endurance that sometimes come to light, usually when the couple and the therapist are least expecting it. With Les and Elaine, who had a very different kind of Level Three marriage, a dramatic turning point led directly to a period of profound renewal.

Les and Elaine were married in 1964, on the air force base where Les was stationed. Les remembered an idyllic honeymoon stage in which he and Elaine were "buddies." Both very athletic, they played on the base's softball and volleyball teams. But off the playing fields, they sparred. In their early twenties, neither Les nor Elaine had a mature understanding of what love and commitment really meant, and both carried on flirtations with other people that inevitably led to tears and recriminations. Conflicts were smoothed over temporarily, but always left unresolved. Then Elaine got pregnant and gave birth to a son. Four months later, Les was sent to fight in the war in Vietnam.

In this case, a major external event beyond the couple's control led to an earth-shattering turning point in their relationship. Without this interruption in the normal course of their lives, Les and Elaine would have had to address their conflicts sooner and more fully, but that became impossible. Looking back, Elaine saw that neither she nor Les had been able to risk feeling vulnerable to the other, and their flirtations with other people, and the arguments that followed, had served to create and maintain a safe distance between them.

But back then, she'd understood none of this. Like many women whose husbands went to war, she was angry at being left alone. To make matters worse, she felt anxious and burdened at having to take care of an infant by herself. She wondered if Les would ever come back, or if she would end up having to make a life without him. Alone, she agonized over this question, and felt as if her life were in suspended animation.

By the time Les returned, three years later, they both had been so traumatized by the separation and the events of those grueling years that neither was able to provide any of the love or support that *both* needed so desperately. Les's homecoming only led to increasing distance between them, while they worked hard at presenting the facade of a happy marriage to the world.

In the following years, Les and Elaine had a second child and moved off the base to the suburbs. If the marriage outwardly functioned well, internal tensions were mounting. Elaine said, "The minute any kind of problem came up between Les and me, we'd drop it. We never talked about anything. I did stuff with the kids, and Les would go out with his friends." As their two sons grew up, Elaine felt at loose ends. Soon she became involved in a long-term affair, and then found out that Les was having an affair, too. Stung, Elaine confessed to hers in order to hurt Les. Soon afterward, her affair burned out, and she delivered an ultimatum to Les. "Maybe we really shouldn't belabor this marriage anymore," she said. "Maybe it's really all over." But she left an opening: She would agree to talk things over, if Les ended his affair.

At Les's suggestion, they began couples therapy. In the first session, both said they felt hopeless about the marriage and that they were sure nothing would change to make them feel closer. They each admitted not being able to risk making the marriage better, and that over the years they'd colluded in maintaining emotional distance.

Together, we discussed conflict avoidance, and the possibility that in therapy they might feel safe enough to open up some of their hidden issues. In the following session, Les confessed that the weekend before, he'd had a one-night stand. When Elaine reacted furiously, Les was chagrined; he had told her about it in the new spirit of openness they were trying to establish in their relationship! "If we don't become more open with each other *now*," he argued, "*when* will we do it?"

Les's confession marked an important turning point. They began to speak about the early days of their marriage. Having come from families in which there had been little love to go around, they each had brought to the marriage a sense that they'd missed out, and a desire to find a closeness with each other. But they had felt too needy and vulnerable to express their feelings to one another. Then, with the coming of the war, the marriage had been interrupted before they'd had time to deepen their relationship, and they had returned to each other as strangers. For the first time, Les and Elaine understood that each of them had been through a personal war. At first hesitantly, then openly, they began empathizing and supporting each other. Until now, they had been unable to give *or* to take from each other. At the same time, Elaine said, "There was always a bond between us. Maybe deep down, we sensed the other's pain."

At mid-life, we have the chance to change the course of our lives. Les and Elaine, a couple torn apart early on, whose marriage had been stunted by absence and trauma, were able to return at mid-life to the feelings of love they'd had for each other so long before.

But this time around, they had a far greater understanding of themselves and each other: Exploring the motives behind their affairs, they discovered they had used them to distance, and to wound. Unconsciously, they had been testing each other's love. The unspoken question, for both of them, was "Do I really matter to you?" But due to their early histories, they were too mistrustful, too fearful of rejection and abandonment. For Les and Elaine, mid-life was a time for *reclaiming* one another and rebuilding their relationship on the deep and enduring love they had been too afraid to share until now.

Second Honeymoon

FOR BOTH WOMEN AND MEN at mid-life, relationships have a new weight, authority, and stability. For a marriage to stay strong over time, two essential ingredients—independence and intimacy—must be present in equal measure. Women who were always relationship-oriented now need their marriages to strongly support a focus on self-development. Men, meanwhile, need their marriages to fill deep cravings for tenderness and intimacy. Even when differing needs and periods of personal upheaval make a marriage break down in nearly total disrepair, it is possible to use that flux to rebuild on a new, stronger basis.

Two recent encounters confirmed that view for me. At lunch with my friend Cecilia one day, our general conversation finally led to the difficult subject of the crisis she and her husband, Nate, had survived six months before. Nate had had to begin phasing out his small advertising business at the same time that Cecilia had been promoted to editor in chief of a major magazine. Feeling diminished and defeated, Nate at first had resented her success and become depressed and bitter. Eventually, though, he had begun the work of rebuilding his self-image by rediscovering the paintings he'd done twenty years before and setting up an art studio for himself in the garage. Now he could focus on his creative side, the aspect of himself he'd neglected while managing his business. As Cecilia described this process, I was struck by how, instead of recounting all the negative, traumatic details of the experience, she could only marvel at the transformation in her husband—and in their marriage. In their renewed love and appreciation for each other, this couple truly were experiencing their second honeymoon.

"As you know," she told me, "we were never an *un*happy couple. We were always basically happy together. When there were problems, they were usually at times when I felt that Nate took me for granted. But now something has changed. It seems that when Nate's work life was turned upside down, he began seeing everything more clearly. He says he really appreciates the people he loves now. And for the first time, I *feel* appreciated, and loved. He's become so much more open, so much more present.

"I'd have to say that our relationship has *deepened*. Isn't it wonderful how"—and she looked at me, smiling—"as people enter their fifties, they change. Men become so much warmer, so much more loving. And women really get happier. I certainly am."

The paradox of mid-life is that, when couples use their inevitable life crises in order to renew their marriages, traumatic events become positive turning points. But Cecilia and Nate didn't surprise me as much as Seth and Adrienne, who were discussed in the chapter about the effect of illness on mid-life marriages. When Adrienne's illness first hit, Seth rose to the occasion: When he understood that he could *lose* Adrienne, he realized how much she meant to him. At the time I was moved by his truly gallant response, but when I heard from him five years later, my original feelings about him were confirmed and deepened.

It was a call that could not have been more unexpected. One evening, Seth, on an impulse, stepped up to a pay telephone on a New York City street corner and dialed my number. He and Adrienne were on their way to dinner and the theater to celebrate their eighteenth anniversary, he told me. Then, sounding almost abashed, Seth said, "I'm sorry to bother you, but I just wanted to tell you that Adrienne and I have never been happier, and that we both appreciate all the work we did with you to get to this point. We've been through a lot, and we've made a lot of mistakes, but now we both know how much we have going for us." Another second honeymoon coming at the end of a long period of crisis and change.

All mid-life marriages have long histories, none without at least some problems of adjustment and accommodation. Most people anticipate this; what most of us don't expect is the extraordinary capacity mid-life couples have for changing their relationships. What we also don't expect is that flux, destabilization, and disruption are just the first steps in the dynamic process of repair, rebuilding, and renewal.

What we must learn, above all, is that if ever there is a time for the "marriage glass" to be filled to the brim, mid-life *is* that time.

Workbook
for Mid-life Couples

T HIS WORKBOOK IS DE-
signed to help couples begin to focus on the changes they
may need to make in their marriages. The best way to use
the workbook is to approach one topic at a time. The partners
should think about the questions *separately,* then jot down
their thoughts on each topic question and, finally, set aside
time for a full discussion of each topic.

Choosing a time when you feel sure that you will not be
interrupted is important. Also important is gauging your
moods: both of you should feel relaxed, reflective, and ready
to share your thoughts with each other.

EXERCISE 1: LIFE CYCLE EVENTS THAT AFFECT MARRIAGE

Check any or all of the life cycle events listed below that
have affected you and/or your partner over the last five years.
Make a list of how these changes have affected your life.

A. EMPLOYMENT-RELATED CHANGES:
1. Enrollment in an educational or degree program
2. Recent employment or career changes
3. Job promotion or increased responsibilities

4. Job demotion or reduced responsibilities
5. Unemployment—planned
6. Unemployment—unplanned
7. Retirement—planned
8. Retirement—forced, earlier than expected

B. ILLNESS:
1. Physical disability (knee problems, back pain, tennis elbow, fatigue, sleep problems, you name it!)
2. Medical problem involving surgery
3. Medical problem requiring nonsurgical intervention
4. Chronic illness

C. CHILDREN OR STEPCHILDREN:
1. Child leaving home for boarding school, college, job, or armed services
2. Child returning home after a substantial absence
3. Child's marriage
4. Child's divorce
5. Birth of grandchild
6. Birth or adoption of child in your own mid-life marriage

D. PARENTS AND IN-LAWS:
1. Death of a parent or in-law
2. Illness of a parent or in-law
3. Emotional or physical disability of any older person for whom you are responsible, such as a sibling, a parent, a relative, or a friend

Leaving at least an hour for discussion, with the idea that you may need more time, take turns speaking about how these changes have affected both of you. Active listening plays an important role in these discussions.

EXERCISE 2: PERSONAL CHANGES

Every couple needs to work out a satisfactory ratio between *private* time (when each individual pursues separate activities or simply spends time alone) and *shared* time (time spent with the partner).

The following statements are geared toward helping adjust or modify the amount of time you spend alone and the amount that you share with your partner. The statements will also help you think about what you do when you spend time alone and together.

1. I'd like to spend more time alone.
2. I'd like to spend more time with my partner.
3. I never have enough time to myself.
4. There are so many things I'd like to do—if only I had the time!
5. I feel that my partner hovers over me.
6. I enjoy my partner as a companion for leisure activities.
7. My partner and I don't share enough common interests.

Write down your answers to the following statements:

1. For me, the most satisfying period of our marriage was:
2. For me, the most difficult period of our marriage was:
3. I feel the biggest turning point in our marriage took place when:
4. Over the last five years, I have become more independent in the following ways:
5. Over the last five years, I have become less independent in the following ways:
6. Over the last five years, I have become more involved in my relationships with people. (Consider your partner, children, grandchildren, colleagues, siblings, and friends.)
7. Over the last five years, I have become less involved in my relationships. (Consider those relationships you have placed more limits on or that you have given up on.)

8. My greatest pleasure *used* to be:
9. My greatest pleasure *now* is:
10. One need that I used to have, which I now consider obsolete, is:

EXERCISE 3: SEX

First, answer the following questions alone. Then discuss your answers together. Leave plenty of time for discussion so that you are both ready for this tough but important task.

1. In the early period of your marriage, how important was sex? (very, moderately important, of little importance, don't know)
2. In mid-life, how has that changed? Are you satisfied with the changes?
3. In your marriage's early period, who was more likely to take the sexual initiative? Has that changed over time? Are you satisfied with the arrangement? If not, what would you like to see changed?
4. Assuming that you and your partner at least occasionally discuss sex with each other, do you talk more frequently now than you did in the early period? less frequently? the same? Are you satisfied with your present sexual dialogue?
5. Has the frequency of sex increased, decreased, or stayed fairly constant over time? Are you satisfied with the frequency?

Men's checklist: Which of the following physical and emotional mid-life changes are affecting you?

1. More time needed to achieve erections.
2. Erections lasting a shorter time.
3. More time and stimulation necessary to reach orgasm.
4. More time and stimulation necessary after orgasm before another erection can be achieved.

280 WORKBOOK FOR MID-LIFE COUPLES

5. More anxiety and self-doubt associated with sex.
6. Occasional avoidance of sex, or sexual preoccupation, in response to sexual or other anxieties.

Women's checklist: Which of the following physical and emotional mid-life changes are affecting you?

1. Less vaginal lubrication.
2. Frequent or occasional pain during sexual intercourse.
3. Either less or more time needed for arousal.
4. Changes in the number, frequency, or intensity of orgasms.
5. Slackening off or increasing of sexual desire.

Some couples find that sexual playfulness and experimentation increase the longer they are married. Others experience decreasing adventurousness in their sex lives. Check which of the below you have done with your partner. Then, use the checklist to think about which sexual activities you would like to try with your partner and share your thoughts with him/her.

1. Undressing each other.
2. Exploring each other's bodies with mouths and tongues.
3. Having your anus stimulated during sex.
4. Buying erotic underclothes.
5. Making love outside the bedroom—in the kitchen, the shower, outdoors, anywhere unusual.
6. Using a vibrator.
7. Watching erotic films together.
8. Reading erotic books and magazines together.
9. Sharing and/or acting out sexual fantasies with each other.
10. Arranging weekend getaways for the two of you.
11. Making sex more tender, more playful, more fun.
12. Genital and nongenital massage.

It takes courage to begin these discussions, but once you do, you will probably have several in-depth talks about the ways in which the two of you would like to improve your sexual relationship during this stage of your marriage. You may be surprised at what you discover about yourself, as well as what you find out about your partner. But once you've had a chance to absorb the new information, you may want to return to Chapter Seven, "Sexual Renewal," and try the sensate focus exercises, as I have outlined them. This program will be most useful to you after you've had a full discussion of these workbook items on sex.

EXERCISE 4: LIFE PLANNING

Fantasize about the life you would like to be leading by this time next year. Imagine freely, but include elements of reality, such as how you will be supporting yourself, where you will be living, and what the major focus of your life will be.

Develop this Life Plan both as a dream and as a set of goals, merging your wishes with what is possible and attainable. Consider how you would begin to initiate some of these changes now.

Go on to make Five- and Ten-Year Life Plans. Discuss your One-, Five-, and Ten-Year Plans with your partner.

NOTES
and
SOURCES

CHAPTER ONE *Introduction: Necessary Changes*

1. Carol D. Ryff and Susan Migdal, "Intimacy and Generativity: Self-Perceived Transitions," *Signs*, Vol. 9, No. 3 (Spring 1984), pp. 470–481.
2. Courtesy of the National Center for Health Statistics, Washington, D.C.
3. Helene Deutsch, *The Psychology of Women*, Vol. 2, *Motherhood* (New York: Grune and Stratton, 1945), p. 456.
4. Pauline Bart, "Depression in Middle-Aged Women," in J. M. Bardwick, ed., *Readings in the Psychology of Women* (New York: Harper and Row, 1972), pp. 72–91.
5. Quoted in Daniel Goleman, "Wide Beliefs on Depression in Women Contradicted," *New York Times*, January 9, 1990, p. C–1.
6. The concept of the "phantom self" was developed by Dr. Samuel W. Perry to refer to the "illusionary misperception of the body" (in middle age) ("The Phantom Self of Middle Age," in *The Middle Years: New Psychoanalytic Perspectives*, ed. John M. Oldham and Robert S. Liebert [New Haven, Conn.: Yale University Press, 1989]). "This younger sense of self is preconscious and is fundamentally based on an inherent difficulty in modifying one's

body perception rather than on conscious or unconscious fears about growing old" (p. 196).

7. The term "loving grief" was introduced in a seminal early article on mid-life crisis written in 1965 by Kleinian psychoanalyst Elliot Jaques. In his "Death and the Midlife Crisis," he states that fears of death, which are characteristic of mid-life, can be calmed by "loving grief." Loving grief, in the context of Jaques's terminology, refers to working through the anger and depression of early infancy associated with the internalized image of the mother. See Elliot Jaques, "Death and the Midlife Crisis," *International Journal of Psychoanalysis,* Vol. 46 (1965), pp. 502–514.

CHAPTER TWO   *The High-Risk Woman*

1. Dr. Carol Feit Lane's comments were obtained in a personal interview. Her research is reported in a dissertation entitled "The Meanings of Returning to Work for Women at Mid-life," New York University. Dr. Lane practices career counseling in New York City.

2. See Judith M. Bardwick, "The Seasons of a Woman's Life," in Dorothy G. McGuigan, ed., *Women's Lives: New Theory, Research and Policy* (University of Michigan Center for Continuing Education of Women, 1980), pp. 35–55.

3. R. Barnett and Baruch G. Barnett, "Towards Economic Independence: Women's Involvement in Multiple Roles," in McGuigan, op. cit., pp. 69–93. Janet Zollinger Giele, "Crossovers: New Themes in Adult Roles and Life Cycle," in McGuigan, op. cit., pp. 3–13.

4. Ruth A. Droege, "Psychosocial Study of the Formation of the Middle Adult Life Structure in Women," unpublished doctoral dissertation, California School of Professional Psychology, Berkeley, California, 1982. This study and three other doctoral studies are summarized in an article by Priscilla Roberts and Peter M. Newton, "Levinsonian Studies of Women's Adult Development," *Psychology and Aging,* Vol. 2, No. 2 (1987), pp. 154–163.

5. Henry Grunebaum, "Middle-Age Marriage: Affiliative Men and Aggressive Women," *American Journal of Family*

Therapy, Vol. 7, No. 3 (Fall 1979), pp. 45–50.

See also Kathryn L. Cooper and David L. Gutmann, "Gender Identity and Ego Mastery Style in Middle-Aged, Pre- and Post-Empty Nest Women," *Gerontologist,* Vol. 27, No. 3 (1987), pp. 347–352.

Dr. David Gutmann is frequently quoted in books and articles on the sex role reversals that occur in mid-life men and women.

6. Emily G. Tinsley, Sandra Sullivan-Guest, and John McGuire, "Feminine Sex Role and Depression in Middle-aged Women," *Sex Roles,* Vol. 11, Nos. 1/2 (1984), pp. 25–32.

Also, Droege, op. cit., pp. 154–163.

CHAPTER THREE   *The High-Risk Man*

1. Tom Brokaw, "Senior-Circuited," *New York Times,* January 6, 1991.
2. Lois M. Tamir, *Men in Their Forties: The Transition to Middle Age* (New York: Springer, 1982). Tamir found that the job is no longer the means toward self-fulfillment and life satisfaction for men at middle age, regardless of educational level (pp. 54–68).
3. Gina Kolata, "Study Finds Ways to Fight Career Malaise," *New York Times,* September 27, 1988, p. C–6.
4. Quoted in Daniel Goleman, "For Many, Turmoil of Aging Erupts in the 50's, Studies Find," *New York Times,* February 7, 1989. p. C–1.
5. Quoted in Ibid.
6. Since 1964, there have been many research studies documenting that middle-aged men become more affiliative, nurturing, and sensual. A few of them, listed in order of their appearance in the literature, include: Bernice Neugarten, *Personality in Middle and Late Life* (New York: Atherton Press, 1964); Bernice Neugarten and David L. Gutmann, "Age-Sex Roles and Personality in Middle Age: A Thematic Apperception Study," in *Middle Age and Aging,* ed. Bernice Neugarten (Chicago: University of Chicago Press, 1975); and David L. Gutmann, "The Cross-Cultural Perspective: Notes Toward a Compara-

tive Psychology of Aging," in *The Psychology of Aging*, ed. J.E. Birren and K. Schaie (New York: Van Nostrand, 1977).

7. Jaques, op. cit., pp. 502–514.

8. Tamar Lewin, "When or Whether to Retire: New Ways to Handle Strain," *New York Times*, April 22, 1990, p. 1.

CHAPTER FOUR   *The High-Risk Marriage*

1. John M. Gottman, "Predicting the Longitudinal Course of Marriages," *Journal of Marital and Family Therapy*, Vol. 17, No. 1 (1991), pp. 3–7.

Very recently, I came across an article that cited some new research pertaining to the subject of the high-risk marriage. A longitudinal study that asked the question "What marital interaction patterns were related to the deterioration of marital satisfaction over time?" was cited. Dr. John M. Gottman reports on research he did with Dr. Robert Levenson at the University of Washington in Seattle. In summarizing their results, Dr. Gottman says:

Put very simply, couples who are likely to separate and divorce at Time Two were already separating emotionally at Time One.... Couples who are more likely to dissolve their marriages were more defensive at Time One. I think that defensiveness is a fending off of contact....

The first stage (of divorce) begins with marital conflict in which the husband...stonewalls with his wife. Then, finally, emotionally withdraws from the conflict. Over time he becomes overwhelmed by his wife's emotions and avoids all conflict with her.

The husband's stonewalling is very aversive for the wife.... She responds by trying to re-engage her husband.

The second stage is marked by the withdrawal of the wife. She expresses criticism and disgust. Their lives become increasingly more parallel and he is fearful. In short, the husband's withdrawal from hot marital interaction is an early precursor of the wife's withdrawal. When both withdraw and are defensive, the marriage is on its way toward separation and divorce. [p. 5]

CHAPTER FIVE   *The Mid-life Affair*
1. Sue Miller, *Family Pictures* (New York: Harper and Row, 1990), p. 220.
2. This idea is suggested by Dr. Edmund Bergler in *Midlife Revolt* (New York: International Universities Press, 1954). This book is an early, comprehensive account of the male mid-life crisis and its impact on marriage.
3. Barbara Gordon, *Jennifer Fever: Older Men, Younger Women* (New York: Harper and Row, 1988), pp. 19–23. In her discussion of the motivations for affairs with younger women, Gordon draws on her reading of psychologist David Gutmann.
4. June M. Reinisch, with Ruth Beasley, *The Kinsey Institute New Report on Sex: What You Must Know to Be Sexually Literate* (New York: St. Martin's Press, 1990), p. 73.
5. From "Love and Marriage," a study done for *Psychology Today* by the Gallup Organization, 1989–1990.

CHAPTER SEVEN   *Sexual Renewal*
1. Hilma Wolitzer, *Silver* (New York: Ballantine Books, 1988), p. 160.
2. A. Alvarez, "Romance," *Lear's* magazine, November 1990, p. 98.
3. Ibid.
4. Jane Brody, "Personal Health," *New York Times*, May 10, 1990, p. B–15.
5. Stephanie Young, "Health and Fitness," *Self* magazine, June 1988, p. 75.
6. *Psychology Today*, December 1989, p. 12. Reporting on a study conducted by University of Kansas sociologist Joey Sprague, Ph.D., and Florida State biologist David Quadagno, Ph.D.
7. Andrew M. Greeley, *Faithful Attraction* (New York: A Tor Books, Tom Doherty Associates, 1991), p. 180.
8. William H. Masters and Virginia E. Johnson, *Human Sexual Response* (Boston: Little, Brown & Co., 1966), and *Human Sexual Inadequacy* (Boston: Little, Brown & Co., 1970), pp. 67–91.

CHAPTER TEN   *Surviving Mid-life Divorce*
1. The decline in the divorce rate has been documented by the National Center for Health Statistics in Washington, D.C.
2. Andrew M. Greeley, op. cit., p. 56.
3. Pepper Schwartz and Philip Blumstein, *American Couples* (New York: William Morrow & Co., 1983), p. 32.
4. Natalie Angier, "Marriage Is a Lifesaver for Men After 45," *New York Times*, April 17, 1990, p. C–3.

CHAPTER ELEVEN   *The Mortal Heart*
1. Molly Haskell, *Love and Other Infectious Diseases* (New York: William Morrow & Co., 1990), pp. 68 and 147.

CHAPTER TWELVE   *Portraits of Mid-life Marriages: High Points, Low Points, Turning Points*
1. Dr. John Gottman, the researcher who is studying variables associated with dissolution of long-term marriages, states: "What has been left out of this grim picture is the pathway by which marriages improve over time. Interestingly enough, hot marital conflict by itself is not destructive enough for a marriage if it also includes positive affects such as affection, humor, positive problem-solving, agreement, assent, empathy and active nondefensive listening" ("Predicting the Longitudinal Course of Marriages," *Journal of Marital and Family Therapy*, Vol. 17, No. 1 [January 1991], p. 6).